From Camera Lens To Critical Lens

From Camera Lens To Critical Lens
A Collection Of Best Essays On Film Adaptation

Edited by

Rebecca Housel

CAMBRIDGE SCHOLARS PRESS

From Camera Lens To Critical Lens: A Collection Of Best Essays On Film Adaptation, edited by Rebecca Housel

This book first published 2006 by

Cambridge Scholars Press

15 Angerton Gardens, Newcastle, NE5 2JA, UK

British Library Cataloguing in Publication Data
A catalogue record for this book is available from the British Library

This volume is dedicated to all individuals who support movies; movies invite imagination and encourage story-telling among all peoples. Film helps to enlighten and enliven the audience beyond the boundaries of society, and also opens sometimes closed doors on the human condition.

TABLE OF CONTENTS

ACKNOWLEDGEMENTS

Thank you to each of the wonderful contributors. Your exceptional scholarship and hard work elevated the volume to a place beyond articulation, and all your many efforts are greatly appreciated. Also, I'd like to specifically acknowledge Jean Lourette for her extraordinary assistance in formatting the book, as well as her extraordinary friendship. I must also thank multiple colleagues who helped spur many of the ideas for the volume, including Suzanne Eggins, William Irwin, Eric Bronson, Tom Morris, and Howard Wolf. Appreciation is due to my editor at Cambridge Scholars Press, Andrew Nercessian, for his patience and kindness. My utter gratitude belongs to Bob Housel, my inspiration and support, and to Gary Housel for accompanying me to a lifetime of films and beyond. Thank you to Eva Schwartz-Barson and Mary Conley-Thomas for invaluable assistance in instilling a love of all stories. Final acknowledgements go to Russell Peck, Thomas Hahn, Joanna Scott, Amanda Millar, Rich Lourette, Leslie Fife, Marguerite A. Schwartz, Anne Brewster, as well as the entire team at Cambridge Scholars Press who helped to make the volume possible.

AND SPEILBERG SAID, "LET THERE BE LIGHT!" AN INTRODUCTION BY REBECCA HOUSEL

Film adaptation is a vehicle for life experiences. From memoir, like Anthony Swofford's *Jarhead*, to adapting history in movies, like *Gladiator* with Russell Crowe, the mass-audience is along for the Hollywood-driven ride of their life. Because of the inherent uniformity with all film, the movies make for an almost automatic societal mythology. Twenty-first century gods, like Brad Pitt and Colin Farrell help guide "the people" with their tales of how to deal with the epic nature of life. Leading ladies in Hollywood, like Angelina Jolie, Nicole Kidman and Halle Berry, are goddesses with heavenly looks and talent and who continue to forge new frontiers in feminism as some of the most highly paid and respected actresses in Hollywood. But the caveat, as with any mythology, is to remember that while film is vibrant and larger-than-life, it's not a mirror.

Much of film, from even the earliest years of Hollywood, has an agenda. Nothing is an accident. Use of color, light, shadow, narration, even use of specific actors to fill a character's shoes, deliberately leads the audience to certain societal conclusions. Sure, everyone understands that movies aren't real, except, that's not exactly true.

As a professor of literature for the last decade, I can't even begin to count the number of students who truly believe that *Titanic* and *Gladiator* are historically accurate, or the seemingly endless student sexist comments (both male and female) from a subliminal embedded message on gender from some musical and brightly-colored anime film. Even Disney's in on the act with their adaptations of the Brothers Grimm fairy tales of motherless children. Think of the messages these movies are sending ....

Film adaptation is a subject deserving of serious study by academics and movie-audiences alike. How many Christians were steeled upon seeing Gibson's *Passion*? How many of us seek the escapism of a heroic film to feel empowered during a time when terrorism knows no bounds? We live by what we see in the movies. Even when we're not watching movies, we're watching movie stars on television networks like HBO and E! that highlight the lives of the rich and famous. Celebrity hot sheets, or magazines, like *Us* and *Entertainment Weekly*, are reporting skyrocketing sales. People host Oscar parties during the Oscar Awards show—I mean, we just can't seem to get enough. Though sixty percent of American women are overweight, women continue to try the latest fad diets or drugs to look more like the incredibly thin and beautiful starlets of Hollywood. Even morning news shows like Today and

CNN have caved in to the pressure, highlighting the ridiculous antics of Tom Cruise, and, will Katie Holmes become a Scientologist? Please! Though Buddhism is an ancient philosophy, the ideas are still quite pertinent today: Be mindful. Don't take the movies for granted. Audiences need to beware of moving pictures offering easy answers to difficult societal issues.

I'm no different than anyone else though—I grew up on Disney movies in the seventies and the brat-pack teen romances of the eighties. When I was offered the area chair of film adaptation for the Popular Culture Association, I jumped at the chance, having loved film of all varieties my entire life. Movies are even a mandatory part of my writing and literature classes—nothing else makes the same kind of impression. A fan of film adaptation forever, my long-time dream is to see more female hero films, like *Elektra* and *Catwoman*, only much, much better. *Everafter* with Drew Barrymore wasn't bad, but female heroes are few and far between in film. The recent slew of comic book adaptations has sometimes been disappointing, but more often quite thrilling. Videogames are a newer popular genre of film adaptation from *Resident Evil* to *Tomb Raider* to the more recent *Doom*. Film adaptation is only limited by the human experience. Illness narratives like *Wit* and *Terms of Endearment* bring messages about female health and healing. There are seemingly endless adaptations genres to explore. Film adaptation has the ability to reflect on the infinite facets that make up the human condition—let us, as audience, not sit idly by in our hubris mindlessly munching on nachos and popcorn while taking in the incredibly life-like computer generated images (CGI) and messages on the silver screen.

The fourteen essays in this book examine different areas of film adaptation from Alfred Hitchcock to Charlie Kaufman and everything in between. The scholars who authored each essay first presented their thoughts on the following film adaptations at the 2005 San Diego Popular Culture Association/American Culture Association conference. Each essay reveals exciting new theory in the area of adaptation and brings audiences, both academic and movie-goers alike, closer to more fully realizing the meanings behind the movies. So grab your popcorn and hang on tight! The ride you've so often taken visually in theatres is about to get dangerous. You will be traversing alone in your mind on an individual quest to rival any hero's journey you've seen on the silver screen.

CHAPTER ONE

FROM FILM TO LIFE: THE CONSTRUCTION OF IDENTITY IN *ETERNAL SUNSHINE OF THE SPOTLESS MIND* AND *I "HEART" HUCKABEES*

by Erin Hill-Parks

"I'm just a fu**ed up girl looking for my own peace of mind. Don't assign me yours."

Clementine, *Eternal Sunshine of the Spotless Mind*

"How am I not myself?"

Brad, *I "Heart" Huckabees*

Adaptation in terms of film is usually thought of as the process of taking a pervious work, be it a novel, play, or television show, and transforming it for the cinema. What is not as often discussed, however, is how an audience member may take cinematic lessons and adapt them to everyday life. The early Surrealist films of Luis Buñuel and Salvador Dali incited violent reactions and political furor (Decherney 86), but can films impart more subtle messages to audience members, especially in this day and age of market-driven Hollywood blockbusters? This paper will explore the construction of identity, and how we can use film via philosophy to help understand and define our personal identities and interactions with the world. By looking at philosophy through the filter and construction of film, we are afforded a comfortable distance to properly analyze and ask questions about what it ultimately means to be an individual in the world. This discussion will center on two recent American films, *Eternal Sunshine of the Spotless Mind* (Gondry 2004) and *I "Heart" Huckabees* (Russell 2004), focusing on their duel positions of being Hollywood films done in an independent vein, and both films' central concern of de-constructing identity in their characters in able to better understand individuals. Once a character finds the essential element, or core, at their center, they can effectively construct an identity and build relations with others. By showing the journey the characters must go through, the audience can take away some semblance of how to get to their own core.

In "The Social Function of Philosophy," Max Horkheimer wrote: "The opposition of philosophy to reality arises from its principles. ... Philosophy has set itself against mere tradition and resignation in the decisive problems of existence, and it has shouldered the unpleasant task of throwing the light of consciousness even upon those human relations and modes of reaction which have become so deeply rooted that they seem natural, immutable, and eternal" (257). Building from this, if we, for the moment, look at these two films as philosophically informed meditations on reality, instead of merely vehicles of mass entertainment, we can attempt to decipher what the films tell us about the deeper meaning of life, so to speak. (Max Horkheimer famously derided the cinema as not being a true art form, but rather essentially being a vehicle for financial gain, and one of the lowest forms of mass entertainment. In this article, however, I am taking the liberty of using some of Horkheimer's meditations on philosophy for a discussion of film, as it seeps apt.)

I posit that film, like philosophy, can lead to a somewhat enlightening of the soul. While each film holds a wealth of material for discussion, due to the scope of this essay, I will focus on only one aspect–what do these films tell us about how we build an identity? (Although volumes of literature are available on the issue of identity politics, this essay will rely on close readings of these individual films and how identity is constructed, so this literature will not necessarily come in to play here.)

Understanding the Films

To properly understand the argument and discussion, a brief summary of each film is necessary. These films, however, do not lend themselves easily to simple or concise descriptions, which is one reason they both beg a more thorough investigation both in this paper and beyond. *I "Heart" Huckabees* is the more obviously philosophical film of the two. Billing itself as an "existential" comedy, *Huckabees*, directed and co-written by David O. Russell, espouses theories of, among others, nihilism, zen, commercialism, environmentalism, and, yes, existentialism in a barrage of colorful visuals and wordplay. With its conflicting theories and philosophies the film has been hailed alternately as brilliant and horrible. Many see it as a didactic, unfocused rant on the meaning of existence, while others see it as a clever call to arms to question reality. Apart from the issue of the film's final merit, it is hard to deny that there are genuinely interesting questions underlying the film.

Generally the film focuses on the crises faced by Albert (Jason Schwartzman), an environmental crusader losing his coalition to Brad (Jude

Law), an executive at Huckabees, a chain of department stores. Albert enlists the help of married existential detectives Bernard (Dustin Hoffman) and Vivian (Lily Tomlin) to help him make sense of his life and discover a deeper meaning in his recent coincidences. Also helping Albert along the journey are Isabelle Huppert as a rival detective leading him down the path to nothing, Mark Wahlberg playing Tommy, Albert's so-called other–a fireman recovering from the "big September thing," and Naomi Watts as Dawn, the face, body, and voice of Huckabees in their advertising–she is literally the model for corporate commercialism. Throughout the film all of these characters, plus about a dozen others, attempt to discover the "ultimate truth about reality" through any means, or philosophic borrowing, necessary.

The more commercial and widely seen of the two films is *Eternal Sunshine of the Spotless Mind*, an untraditional romantic comedy with hints of the fantastic. Directed by Michel Gondry with a screenplay by Charlie Kaufman, *Eternal Sunshine* basically follows the relationship of Joel (Jim Carrey) and Clementine (Kate Winslet). Joel has discovered that after a fight Clementine chose to erase all of her memories of him and their relationship. Joel then enlists the team from Lacuna, Inc, the company that does such specific memory erasure, to perform the same operation on him. As the erasure occurs the audience witnesses Joel and Clementine's relationship backwards–from the final fight back through to when they first met. Midway through the procedure, as Joel re-lives the good memories along with the recent bad ones, Joel realizes that he does not actually want to erase Clementine and attempts to hide her in memories in which she did not originally appear. The audience then witnesses both the events within Joel's head–his fight to keep the memories of his relationship alive–and the technicians in the "real" world attempt to remove them while dealing with their own relationships and issues.

Upon first glance there may not seem to be an obvious reason to address this particular issue of identity construction using these two films together besides the more obvious similarities; they were both released in the same year, made by young directors, star a mixed cast of established Hollywood stars and those on the rise, and feature quirky visuals and a non-typical narrative structure. (In an odd coincidence–perhaps–the two films also both feature original scores composed by Jon Brion and poster art featuring a similar motif of scenes from the film interspersed with colorful squares.) Despite the differences and superficial similarities, the films ultimately have the same notion of how we interact with others and what makes up an individual, namely that we must discover what is at the center of our being before we can properly relate to the rest of the world or participate in any sort of relationship with others.

The Journey in *I "Heart" Huckabees*

It is hard to discuss one part of *Huckabees* without getting caught up in other parts of the film. This is mainly due to the myriad theories floating around and the oft used tactic of having various characters scream at each other all at the same time instead of speaking in turn. Near the beginning of the film existential detective Bernard explains existence and perception to Albert using the example of a blanket. Holding up the blanket, he says, "… this blanket represents all the matter and energy in the universe, okay? You, me, everything–nothing has been left out … this is everything." (All quotes from *I "Heart" Huckabees* and *Eternal Sunshine of the Spotless Mind* are transcribed by the author from the film.) In Bernard's world everything is connected, all matter is part of one grand scheme–giving meaning and purpose to all parts of life. Both Albert and Tommy rebel against this theory opting instead for nihilism and the idea that nothing is connected and that there is no meaning to anything. At the core of both of the theories, however, is the idea that you need to "dismantle your day to day reality to see the big picture." In other words, you need to break down your identity into its various components, finding what the essential element is, so that you can see how it does–or doesn't–relate to the rest of humanity and the world.

When Bernard confronts the rebelling Tommy with the ideas of connectivity in the universe, Tommy counters, saying that the world is actually chaos, "identity is an illusion," and "we are all alone." It is in his journey to find the "reality" of his identity, along with corporate shill Brad's journey, where the most interesting points for our discussion lie. Brad and Tommy begin as seemingly polar opposites. Tommy feels as though nothing makes sense and he constantly questions every aspect of his world. Brad, however, does not see himself as questioning or unhappy at the beginning of the film–he approaches the existential detectives simply out of spite for Albert, not for a deeper meaning or soul search. Brad has the perfect girlfriend, Dawn, the perfect house, the perfect car, and the perfect job. Tommy and Brad appear to be on separate journeys, but end up at similar realizations.

At the end of the film, Tommy finds that he is not alone in the world and that he needs people, but it takes him losing it all to discover this. His "other," Albert, the person that he is supposed to share his journey with, betrays and deserts him for a woman. Tommy decides that he must feel pain, including the physical pain of hitting himself in the head with a giant ball, and raw emotion to ultimately find who he is and how he interacts with the rest of the individuals in the universe.

Brad also finds that he must lose the things he thought important before he can discover his true identity. It is when the detectives question his perfect life that Brad's reality and identity starts to disintegrate. Vivian plays an audio tape of Brad telling the same celebrity story multiple times over several months, and with that Brad realizes that he is playing out a role, not being himself. Brad then asks, "how am I not myself?" This question, first asked to the detectives and then to himself over and over and then echoed back to him by the detectives, becomes the mantra not just for Brad, but also for the film. In the next few scenes Brad offends his bosses in the middle of a meeting–thereby most likely losing his job, loses his girlfriend to Tommy, and loses his house to a fire. All of the external trappings he used to define himself are removed, and he is forced to confront his emotions. For both Tommy and Brad, it is in confronting emotion and "dismantling" themselves to an essential part that they are able to find their true identities and start acting in the world. Brad is then able to speak with Albert as an equal while Tommy and Dawn discover that they have more in common than they originally thought.

The Core of *Eternal Sunshine of the Spotless Mind*

Eternal Sunshine is a bit easier to discuss than *Huckabees*, though it certainly has its own interconnected theories in each frame. While ostensibly being a story about love–how we fall into and out of it–this film is also about how we lose our identity and what it takes to get it back. In *Eternal Sunshine*, Dr. Mierzwiak (Tom Wilkinson) is the inventor of a process that erases selected memories from the brain. Explaining the process to Joel, which will occur while Joel sleeps, he notes: "We start from your most recent memories and work backwards from there, more or less. There's an emotional core to each of our memories and when you eradicate that core, it starts its degradation process. By the time you wake up in the morning, all of the memories we have targeted will have withered and disappeared. As in a dream upon waking." Once we find and remove that core, the memory is gone and that experience–and emotion–is no longer part of who we are. In his theory, this means that a person never has to live with painful memories or emotions. Life can just be happy!

Even after Joel and Clementine erase each other from their respective memories there is still some lingering part of each other there. The film begins with Joel and Clementine meeting on the beach at Montauk in the middle of February–the morning after Joel's procedure, which the audience learns was the location of their original meeting two years prior. Despite the removal of this memory, the two are drawn to each other and the resilience of the past. We see also that this is not an isolated case. Dr. Mierzwiak's assistant Mary (Kirsten Dunst) is quite obviously obsessed with him, and at one point near the end of the film painfully confesses this to him and they kiss. The audience quickly discovers that the doctor and assistant have already had an affair, but Mary had the procedure done to erase the relationship, so she has no memory of it. The emotional core of each person and personal history remains intact despite the surrounding emotions and memory having been deleted. Perhaps then, Dr. Mierzwiak's theory of the emotional core is correct to an extent. We all have an identifiable emotional core, and it lies at the center of who we are. It cannot be removed, and is difficult to pinpoint, but it is when we can find that emotional core–of a memory, of a thought, of a relationship–that we can discover our true identity. If we try to irradiate these emotional cores instead of learning from them, however, we run the risk of losing our identity, as the emotions are so tightly entwined with who a person is.

Joel finds his main emotional core just before waking, in one of the last memories to be erased, one of the first originally created. As mentioned, the technicians erase his memories from the most recent to the oldest, so this is a memory of Joel and Clementine's first meeting. The scene starts with them meeting at a winter beach party, both outcasts by choice, not quite being able to fit in with the rest of the crowd. Throughout the film the audience has seen Joel fight to save Clementine and their relationship, something he failed to do in real life, but now he has given up for the second time. He knows that the memories are about to be gone permanently. Clementine, or Joel's impression of her, interrupts his remembrance, saying "this is it, Joel. It's going to be gone soon."

As Joel's memory continues to play out to the end of their first meeting, the audience sees Joel and Clementine break into a house on the beach's edge. Clementine searches for the liquor cabinet and then runs upstairs to search for clothing, while Joel gets nervous and debates leaving. Clementine yells down "so go." As Joel paces, about to run out of the house, the memory starts to disintegrate. Large chunks of the house fall away. The floor is replaced with sand and the ocean rushes in around Joel's feet. Clementine can no longer be seen, but her voice surrounds Joel as they discuss what happened

Clementine: I wish you'd stayed.
Joel: I wish I had stayed, too. Now I wish I'd stayed. I wish I had done a lot of things. I wish I … I wish I had stayed. I do.
Clementine: Well, I came back downstairs and you were gone.
Joel: I walked out. I walked out the door.
Clementine: Why?
Joel: I don't know. I felt like a scared little kid. I was, like, above my head; I don't know.
Clementine: You were scared?
Joel: Yeah. I thought you knew that about me. I ran back to the bonfire trying to outrun my humiliation, I think.
Clementine: Was it something I said?
Joel: Yeah. You said, "So go" with such disdain, you know?

Clementine: Oh, I'm sorry.
Joel: It's okay. (Runs out the door as he did in the actual memory.)
Clementine: Joely? What if you stayed this time? (Appears at top of stairs)
Joel: I walked out the door. There's no memory left.
Clementine: Come back and make up a goodbye at least. Let's pretend we had one. . (Joel returns and kisses Clementine.) Bye Joel.
Joel: I love you.
Clementine: (whispered) Meet me at Montauk.

It is not just the memory of Clementine that he has lost here–he has lost it all–but at the same time he has discovered the core of the memory/emotion. It is at this moment, with his memory crumbling around him and at the point where he is most alone and lost, that can find his own identity.

Here Joel is most himself. The memory, even more visually present as the crumbling house and ocean rushing in, crashes around him. He admits he is scared; he is nervous within his skin, unable to stand still; and that he needs someone. At this point Clementine re-appears in the memory, something that did not happen in "reality." Now that he has been "dismantled" as the folks in *Huckabees* would say, Joel is open to the emotions and pain of life, and realizes that it is necessary before he can relate and live in the world. As this is a love story, we see that his love of Clementine is very much related to his emotional core that cannot be erased without losing his identity. In reality Joel let Clementine walk out of his life, just as in this final/first memory, he walks out of her life. In his altered memory, they both stay, making up a goodbye they never had. Joel and Clementine–or at least the Clementine of his memory– acknowledge that life and relations will bring pain, but it's the rest of it that makes it worth it. (In a sign that their cores are intertwined, something not discussed at length in the paper, both parties end up obeying memory Clementine and go to Montauk the next day.) Joel and Clementine eventually find out about their past relationship, thanks to Mary who mailed back all files to their owners, and decide that, despite knowing that their relationship fell apart before, they want to try again.

Who Am I?

Tommy, Brad, and Joel all chose to break down their identities to find who they really were and help make sense of the world. They see the flaws and faults in their lives, the excess, and are able to react to the environment through an emotional core. Once this core has been found, they can find who they are and interact with others. Tommy realizes he should be, and can be, with Dawn, Brad becomes friends–or at least stops fighting–with his previous enemy Albert, and Joel is able to start again with Clementine.

This comes back to the two quotes listed at the beginning of this essay: Brad's question/mantra, "how am I not myself?" and Clementine's admonishment to Joel, that she is "just a fu**ed up girl looking for [her] own peace of mind." It is in these two statements that we return to Horkhemier's claim that it is through philosophy that we can shed light on the most mundane and seemingly innocuous problems of life, that, in fact, "today our task is rather to ensure that, in the future, the capacity for theory will never again disappear" (272). By not just passively viewing film, but actively watching and intellectually participating in cinema, the audience can take up the task and keep philosophical inquiry as part of our daily struggle to discover identity and our place in the world.

The characters in *I "Heart" Huckabees* and *Eternal Sunshine of the Spotless Mind* question everything, from the use of petroleum, to the betrayal of love and self. Through their journeys and pain we can perhaps attempt to better understand how we can focus our own identities and live in the world.

CHAPTER TWO

BLOOMSBURY BLUES:
VIRGINIA WOOLF'S MOMENTS
AND MICHAEL CUNNINGHAM'S *HOURS*

by Suzette Henke

Stephen Daldry's award-winning 2002 film version of *The Hours* makes use of a brilliant screenplay by David Hare to adapt Michael Cunningham's novel of the same name for a cinematic audience, thus proving the "permeability of the borders between high and popular culture" (Chatman 269). Both film and novel use Virginia Woolf's *Mrs. Dalloway* as the substratum for a multifaceted narrative and celluloid framing of 20th-century malaise—from Woolf's own manic-depressive battle with headaches and haunting voices, through a housewife's suburban entrapment in postwar America at mid-century, to the millennial *angst* of a homosexual artist battling the ravages of AIDS. All the principal characters confront, in different ways, the vacuous hours that threaten to engulf their psyches and asphyxiate their spirits. They take refuge from perilous hours of anxiety or boredom in the exhilarating sensations provided by those heightened "moments of being" described by Woolf in "A Sketch of the Past." Woolf had originally entitled the working manuscript of her novel *The Hours*, and various manuscripts of the draft versions of *Mrs. Dalloway* have been collected and edited by Helen Wussow in a scholarly volume (now out of print) called *The Hours*—a doubling of titular reference geared to baffle readers and reference librarians for years. As Karen Levenbeck points out, Cunningham has omitted this germinal text from the bibliography supplied at the end of his novel.

As a Woolf devotee and a literary scholar currently co-editing a collection of essays on *Woolf and Trauma*, I have spent a great deal of time over the past several years immersed in Woolf's biography, essays, letters (6 volumes), diaries (5 volumes), and literary texts. Consequently, I find my response to Cunningham's double(d) narrative, as well as to Daldry's film, highly perplexed and uneven. I cannot help sharing Hermione Lee's "squeamish reluctance to see a real person made over into a fictional character, with made-up thoughts and speeches" (50), especially in light of the many thousands of words that Woolf herself penned. Lee complains in *Virginia Woolf's Nose* that both novel and film encourage their audiences to interpret Woolf's life backwards from her suicide and perpetuate tragic, distorted, highly sentimental and melodramatic portraits of the artist as a middle-aged woman. The film suppresses Virginia's "gleeful comedy" and "evacuates her life of political intelligence or social acumen, returning her to the position of doomed, fey, mad victim" (Lee 54-55). To an uninformed reader or spectator, it would seem that Woolf was a neurotic, hysterical authoress who killed herself immediately after completing *Mrs. Dalloway*; whereas, in reality, she remained relatively stable until her final psychological crisis in 1941. What strikes me as extraordinary about Woolf's biography is the fact that from 1915 until 1941—a period of 26 years—she suffered from persistent migraine headaches, flu, pulmonary distress, and recurrent toothaches. She did not, however, have a severe breakdown during that period, and she endured the vicissitudes of chronic illness while continuing a prolific reading program, travel and social engagements, grueling labor alongside Leonard at the Hogarth Press, and most importantly, literary creation.

Cunningham's novel moves into the tormented mind of the suicidal author and follows her to the banks of the River Ouse, whose amniotic torrents would devour her 59-year-old body. He re-creates, with sensitivity and compassion, the pain of her panicky consciousness seeking solace in death by water. And he quotes, in full, the suicide letter that Virginia left for Leonard in the sitting room of Monk's House the day of her death.[i] Both novel and film vividly portray the anguish and conflicted emotions that must have motivated Woolf's desperate decision to put stones in her pockets and drown herself. Neither novel nor film, however, truly represents Virginia's suicide in the context of British politics in 1941. Cunningham makes a few laconic references to Woolf's anxiety now that "[a]nother war has begun" and "the bombers have appeared again in the sky" (3-4). But readers have little cognizance that a war is being waged on the continent and German planes are buzzing overhead. Virginia's diaries and letters offer abundant evidence of her severe psychological distress in reaction to impending catastrophe. The Woolfs' house in London was bombed and burned during the infamous *Sitzkreig* that preceded Hitler's more aggressive *Blitz*. Bombs were exploding around Monk's House, and Virginia and Leonard, along with the majority of the British public, feared invasion by Germany. As a Jew, Leonard could anticipate deportation or death. And Virginia, along with Freud and E. M.

---

[i] For information about the dating of the three suicide notes, see Nicolson and Trautman's edition of the last volume of Virginia Woolf's *Letters*, as well as Panthea Reid's 1996 book *Art and Affection*, which challenges the premises of Nicolson and Trautman and offers a speculative "Redating of Virginia Woolf's Suicide Letters" in an Appendix. I discuss Virginia's three suicide notes in the "Afterword" to a forthcoming co-edited volume on *Virginia Woolf and Trauma*. In terms of genre, Bret Keeling labels Cunningham's novel a postmodern homage and "continuation" of Woolf's original text.

Forster, was on Hitler's "blacklist" of subversive intellectuals to be executed after occupation. The couple made a suicide pact and kept a supply of gasoline in the garage, with plans to asphyxiate themselves through carbon monoxide poisoning should German storm-troopers reach the British mainland. On 28 March, 1941, a month after her 59th birthday, Virgina plunged into a river torrent that would spare her the threat of Nazi occupation.[i]

As Hermione Lee complains, Woolf's "death has been simplified, or Ophelia-ised, by the film of *The Hours*, as the romantic immersion of a young woman with a very long nose in beautiful still waters, with music playing" (121). We see Nicole Kidman "slowly entering ... the green, sun-and-shade-dappled waters of a gently flowing river, to the accompaniment of birds calling and a pulsating, emotional score by Philip Glass" (40). Like Lee, I take exception to Cunningham's nostalgic evocation of the author's lyrical extinction in *The Hours*, as well as to Daldry's .romantic rendition of her death. The reality of Virginia's drowning must have been otherwise. The water of the River Ouse would have been frigidly cold in March; the sludge of the riverbank viscous and muddy; the stones, desperately gathered, solid anchors to oblivion. Surely Virginia's helpless body struggled against fluid suffocation and her lungs gasped for air, as she would have instinctively fought the engulfing current that swept away a lifetime of traumatic memories.[ii]

Paradoxically, Woolf's novel about a tormented war veteran and a sensitive British matron would serve as the "pre-text" (or inspirational text) for Cunningham's fictitious character, Laura Brown, to abandon her husband and children in a postwar Los Angeles suburb at mid-century. When Laura's grown-up son Richard capriciously labels his friend and bisexual lover, Clarissa Vaughn, with the monicker "Mrs. Dalloway," Cunningham invokes a *tour de force* that binds Virginia, Laura, and Clarissa in a seamless web of love and loss, tragedy and bereavement, homosexual desire and personal regeneration. As Lee explains, "Septimus's hallucinations are re-enacted in Richard Brown's terminal illness: shellshock and the traumatic aftermath of the Great War are translated into the trauma of the AIDS epidemic and its effect on individuals. Woolf's own struggle against suicidal depression colours the story of Laura Brown" (Lee 50-51). Lee judges Hare's screenplay "more polemical" than Cunningham's novel, in which the three kisses prominently exchanged by women suggest that bisexuality is the "normal condition of life" (54).

---

[i] Hermione Lee confirms that Virginia "and Leonard knew they were on Hitler's blacklist, and . . . had made suicide plans" (120).

[ii] When Lee challenged Daldry about the inaccuracy of the film's representation of Virginia's death, he protested: "We only had Kidman for four weeks in June, and we couldn't exactly strip the trees" (56).

Both novel and film arbitrarily situate Virginia Woolf's bisexual impulses in the scenario of her sororal affection for the more flamboyant Stephen sibling, Vanessa Bell. From an affectionate kiss shared with her vivacious and voluptuous sister, Virginia feels inspired to portray the incipient, somewhat muted lesbian relationship between Clarissa Parry and Sally Seton. In *Mrs. Dalloway*, their budding female friendship would be eclipsed by Clarissa's ostensibly "safe" marriage to Richard Dalloway, a conservative member of Parliament. In contrast, Cunningham's Clarissa defines her sexual identity principally through her "stable and affectionate [lesbian] marriage" (*H* 97) to a long-term partner named Sally Lester—a relationship romantically overshadowed by Clarissa's youthful moment of passionate affection for Richard Brown, a gay writer with omnivorous appetites and youthful bisexual inclinations. Their liaison transpired in the Cape Cod village of Wellfleet in 1965, when Clarissa Vaughn's bedtime reading conspicuously included Doris Lessing's feminist classic, *The Golden Notebook*. From this inspiring text, she apparently managed to wrench a late-century script for personal liberation and the free choice of (homo)sexual identity. Such literary intertextuality would seem slightly ironic, insofar as Lessing provides a penetrating critique of western society's limitations with respect to traditional marriage, conservative politics, and cultural conventions of every kind, but she exhibits a glaring blind spot in her representation of homosexuality as a deviant, clichéd, and emotionally suspect life-style. In contrast, Cunningham presents a more balanced perspective when he remarks in an interview with James Schiff that "the notion of human sexuality is titanically complicated, enormously idiosyncratic. No one person's sexuality in any real way resembles somebody else's, and the terms 'gay,' 'straight,' or 'bisexual' are so inexact and crude as to be virtually meaningless. In *The Hours* I am pleased with the fact that ... there is no character who can accurately be described as gay or straight" (126).

Both Cunningham's *Hours* and Daldry's .adaptation offer a contradictory and somewhat paradoxical representation of the highly conventional conjugal partnership shared by Clarissa and Sally, though both suggest traditional patterns of monogamous affiliation, which are challenged in the novel by Clarissa's daughter Julia and her queer feminist mentor, Mary Krull (a cruel pun). "You respect Mary Krull," Clarissa muses, "living as she does on the verge of poverty, going to jail for her various causes, lecturing passionately at NYU about the sorry masquerade known as gender, ... but she is finally too despotic in her intellectual and moral intensity, her endless demonstration of cutting-edge, leather-jacketed righteousness" (*H* 23). Krull, in turn, condemns Clarissa as a fool and considers her a smug, "self-satisfied witch." She despises the lesbian couple for being "queers of the old school, ... bourgeois to the bone" (*H* 160). For the sake of cinematic economy, Daldry has deleted Cunningham's embittered "dyke" from his film adaptation. It might seem to middle-class or midwestern American audiences that only in New York City at the turn of the 21st century could such gay conjugal liaisons prove so easily acceptable and, indeed, normal to the point of reactionary critique. Mary Krull feels that Clarissa and her partner have "sold out" to the Establishment by self-consciously replicating traditional connubial arrangements. In contrast, Richard Brown's self-pitying narcissism sets him apart as a suffering soul both mentally and physically afflicted and traumatized by his mother's seemingly heartless desertion of her prepubescent son, without a word of explanation to soothe his heightened filial sensitivities and obsessive Oedipal attachment to Mom. As a boy, Richie "is transparently smitten with her; he is comic and tragic in his hopeless love" (*H* 44). And Laura herself entertains voracious fantasies about the cannibalistic incorporation of her son: "she could devour him, not ravenously but adoringly, infinitely gently, the way she used to take the [Catholic] Host into her mouth" (*H* 76).

One can appreciate *The Hours* as Cunningham's gracious tribute to Virginia Woolf as lyrical author, modernist prophet, and spiritual guru to men and women of the 20th century. The author explains to James Schiff: "I never thought of myself as rewriting *Mrs. Dalloway* .... What I wanted to do was more akin to music, to jazz, ... to both honor it and try to make other art out of an existing work of art" (Interview 113). One feels gratified that Daldry's cinematic adaptation called attention to Woolf's 1920's masterpiece and made it a best-selling paperback in America in March 2003. Reluctantly, I confess a personal preference for certain aspects of Daldry's film adaptation over the fictional text on which it is based.[i]

The Laura Zielski Brown sections of Cunningham's novel, for instance, though modeled on the author's own mother, seemed to me extremely *boring*, especially in contrast to Virginia Woolf's rich, palimpsestic prose. In what appears to be a torturous version of Ivor Winters' pet peeve, the myth of imitative form, Cunningham has replicated the tedium and asphyxiating boredom of middle-class American life at mid-century by using a narratological style of such utter, deadpan simplicity that it might strike a contemporary reader as bland and uninteresting—though Seymour Chatman judges these sections the most successful in the novel. Laura's impassive but depressed consciousness rarely transcends the drabness of her suburban Los Angeles surroundings, despite Cunningham's intention "to do for [his] neighborhood in Los Angeles

---

[i] Lee argues that the film of *The Hours* "is much more vulnerable to charges of vulgarization, inaccuracy, and sentimentalisation" (53). She complains that Nicole Kidman, "doesn't look very much like Virginia Woolf. She looks like Nicole Kidman wearing a nose" (53). A fairly quiet discussion between Leonard and Virginia about moving back to London becomes, in the film, a histrionic conjugal battle.

[where he grew up] something like what Woolf did for London in the '20's" (Interview 127). It might prove difficult for readers to generate significant interest in the minor domestic drama of Laura's (twice) baking a birthday cake, fleeing to a local hotel to find sanctuary for her bibliophilic compulsions, ministering to the Oedipal anxieties of a devoted but pathologically sensitive son, and successfully, perhaps artistically, staging a birthday celebration for her boyish and libidinally voracious husband, who comes across as a shell-shocked veteran of World War II.[i] Sporting a meaty frame and *Vitalis*-slickened hair, he exudes "a deep and distracted innocence, with sex coiled inside like a spring"(*H* 213), a snake, or a jack-in-the-box—startling, and ready to attack.

In Daldry's .cinematic *Hours,* Julianne Moore, luminescent in her second pregnancy, adds vivacity and interest to an otherwise dull, insipid role by conveying a schizoid fragility that emanates neediness and a sense of the utter futility of her subject position as a 1950's housewife. Trapped in a life of quiet desperation, she "can't always remember how a mother would act" (*H* 47). She feels helpless and alone—a victim of the unnamed and unnamable "housewife's disease" diagnosed by Betty Friedan in her 1960's classic, *The Feminine Mystique*. But before Betty Friedan and Gloria Steinem, before the second wave of the women's movement and the inauguration of the National Organization for Women, a thoughtful, independent female ensconced in American suburbia at mid-century might very well, like the isolated artist depicted by Woolf in *A Room of One's Own*, have gone mad, been labeled a deviant, or felt tempted to commit suicide. Cunningham's Laura Brown fits all these categories. She goes to a hotel, where she considers ending her life. In the film version of *The Hours*, the visual impact of oceanic engulfment during Laura's afternoon hotel adventure beautifully and powerfully conveys the urgency of her suicidal impulses. But unlike Septimus Smith,, Laura is inspired to "choose life" by an auspicious reading of *Mrs. Dalloway*, a novel that engenders the kind of redemptive egotism requisite for her escape from suburban claustrophobia. Laura realizes that, like Woolf's Clarissa, she "loves life, loves it hopelessly" and feels reassured, through her bibliophilic tryst with *Mrs. Dalloway*, that she can find "comfort in facing the full range of options; in considering all your choices, fearlessly and without guile" (152).

In the "Mrs. Dalloway" sections of *The Hours*, Cunningham models his prose on Woolf's limited omniscient authorial point of view and "indirect free

---

[i] For a provocative essay on Cunningham and Daldry's mutual emulation of Virginia Woolf's "pragmatic" aesthetics, see Birgit Spengler, who argues that both novel and film "provide instances of 'versioning' Woolf" via "an updated version of Woolf's novel that modernizes and liberalizes its hypotext" (52, 53-4). *The Hours*, Spengler argues, in both textual and cinematic incarnations, reflects "an egalitarian and pragmatic concept of art that recalls John Dewey's theory of art as aesthetic experience" (63).

style" of writing, but translates particular scenes from Woolf's modernist novel into a contemporary scenario. The crowd's mindless awe and reverence at following the progress of what purportedly appears to be the Prime Minister's car in *Mrs. Dalloway* is replicated in Cunningham's text when curious spectators watch, with predatory fascination, trailers set up in Greenwich village to house celebrities for the onsite shooting of a film that captures the attention of mesmerized pedestrians.[i] Late 20th-century film stars, the author suggests, have appropriated the glamour and brio that once emanated from political figures decades earlier, in the patriotic wake of World War I. In *Mrs. Dalloway*, Woolf pulls her authorial lens far back, to delineate a panoramic perspective on evolutionary eons engulfing the few fragile hours of each human lifespan on a godless planet vertiginously spinning out of control. Her modernist meditation on human mortality proves poignant and somber, though somewhat lugubrious. In contrast, Cunningham's postmodern rendition of the evanescence of human life seems trivialized by its contemporary gloss on meteoric celebrity. Although this particular scene has been omitted in the film, the fictional spectators' query about the identity of the star, similar to the British crowd's tentative identification of the Prime Minister's car, raises convoluted postmodern speculation about the woman emerging from the trailer—putatively Meryl Streep, who does, in fact, play Clarissa Vaughn in Daldry's .rendition of the story.

My question, however, echoes some perplexing issues investigated by Seymour Chatman: how does one distinguish mimetic reverence from sardonic pastiche? How should one analyze the tone of Cunningham's imitative prose, as well as the aesthetic impact of Daldry's adaptation? Is Cunningham celebrating Woolf's prophetic vision or satirizing her modernist naivety, even as he flagrantly adapts her lyrical meditations to the parameters of late 20th-century American society? Do the extravagant metaphors he invokes bear the weight and serious tenor implied in Woolf's text? Or does such literary intertextuality inadvertently mock and minimize the serious resonance produced in the modernist prose model so cunningly, and ingeniously, revised? In other words, is Cunningham's contemporary novel *The Hours* related to Woolf's *Mrs. Dalloway* in the same way that Henry Fielding's parodic *Shamela* echoes Samuel Richardson's *Pamela*?[ii]

---

[i] For a discussion of Woolf's fragmentary novella, which became a first-draft version of *Mrs. Dalloway*'s opening scenes, see Henke, "The Prime Minister." Cunningham seems oblivious of Woolf's germinal text.

[ii] See Chatman for a provocative narratological analysis of complex distinctions among terms such as "parody," "pastiche," "caricature," "satire," "travesty," "imitation," "*forgerie*," "transformation," "transposition," and "rewriting."

Chatman poses similar queries in his essay on "*Mrs. Dalloway's* Progeny" and places Cunningham's novel in the schema of "what Gerard Genette has dubbed 'second-degree' narratives, those bearing a more than passing resemblance to some original" (269). *The Hours*, Chatman suggests, might be considered a "serious transformation" that "imitates another text on sustained and explicit grounds" (270). It "announces a contract with Woolf's novel" to "preserve serious elements of the *story*, but move it to a new spatiotemporal world, a new *diegesis*" (270). Although Cunningham himself prefers the term "rewriting," Chatman categorizes *The Hours* as an "extension," "*complement*," or "complementary transposition" of *Mrs. Dalloway*. "What goes oddly unexplained, however, is why Clarissa Vaughn, despite her manifold associations with Clarissa Dalloway, including Richard's calling her by that name, should be oblivious of these parallels" (Chatman 273).

Can a late 20th-century author successfully adapt and revise a modernist prose model by vividly plagiarizing a text whose reiteration must necessarily be repeated and remodeled in the mode of sophisticated satire? Jonathan Dee thinks not and, in an article entitled "The Reanimators," likens the "coincidences that pile up" in Cunningham's text to a "particularly highbrow episode of *The Twilight Zone*" (76). He complains that the postmodern "practice of conscripting flesh-and-blood people into novels has become a veritable epidemic" and that "every psycho-historical novel furthers fiction's abdication of its own uniquely, transcendently unreal power to apprehend, and meditate on, the nature of our existence" (77, 84). Roberta Rubenstein echoes this objection by complaining that such reanimating practices offer audiences melodramatic versions of what she acerbically calls "Virginia Woolf lite" (3).

How, finally, can one translate into contemporary fiction—or film—the shimmering instability of Woolf's masterpiece? Can the indefinite deferral of an open-ended plot be transferred to the postmodern stage and repackaged under the ambiguous aegis of poststructural *différance*? In deferring to Woolf as his model, Cunningham has replicated a modernist text in the haunting shadow of late 20th-century skepticism. In so doing, he re-inscribes *Mrs. Dalloway* into the contemporary register of postmodern pastiche. And Daldry, it would seem, perpetuates that ambiance in his cinematic adaptation. Are these bold artistic experiments, in both film and fiction, intended as tributes or satire, laudatory elegies or brash examples of literary appropriation? For Cunningham's fictionalized Virginia, "sanity involves a certain measure of impersonation" (*H* 83). Imagining Woolf impersonating one of her fictional characters, then becoming a character in his own text, Cunningham, via "the androgyneity of authorship," creates radical art from the perspective of a "homosexual male writer impersonating a bisexual woman writer and writing about the lives of lesbians and homosexuals" (Lee 50-51)

Like Woolf's war veteran, Septimus Smith, Cunningham's scapegoat-protagonist, Richard Brown, leaps from a window to free himself from the weight of a body tormented and a mind ravaged by the effects of AIDS—a role played brilliantly by Ed Harris in the film, in response to a universal health crisis that reached pandemic proportions in the last decades of the 20th century. In responding to both film and fiction, however, I find it difficult to generate empathic concern for this truculent, narcissistic, character, who plays the role of sociopathic artist with unnerving pathos. Daldry's film further accentuates the passive aggression motivating a suicidal act that shatters and defies the genuine hospitality behind the party that Clarissa so tenderly prepares for her erstwhile lover. She discerns in Richard "some combination of monumental ego and a kind of savantism" and realizes that other people are, for him, "essentially fictional character[s]" (*H* 60-61). The feast, the well-wishers, the prize, and the celebration are overshadowed by Richard's defiant act of self-destruction. Friends and former lovers feel devastated by the tragedy and painfully disappointed that their doomed comrade refused to persevere for the few additional hours that would have offered them the most precious gift of all, the space of time required to utter an affectionate "good-bye." Woolf's Septimus Smith, was threatened by two authoritarian physicians, Dr. Holmes and Sir William Bradshaw, and feared incarceration in a sanatorium that he perceived as a penitentiary for lunatics. Richard Brown, in contrast, has nothing to fear from the evening's festivities but roses, crab dip, and a literary prize. When Richard angrily refuses these offerings of love, laurels, garlands and celebrity, it becomes challenging for either the reader or the film spectator to feel the kind of compassionate identification that his tragic suicide should warrant. Even in death, he has alienated far too many people, both fictional and spectatorial, to evoke bereavement or tears.

Two other aspects of the novel and film trouble me, and both are related to the political unselfconsciousness of Cunningham's experimental text. Hermione Lee, in *Virginia Woolf's Nose*, and Seymour Chatman, in *"Mrs. Dalloway's Progeny,"* raise similar objections. As Sue Thomas observes, *Mrs. Dalloway* was probably composed as an "angry response to the *Report of the War Office Committee of Enquiry into 'Shell-shock,'* presented to the British Parliamentin August 1922, and to the publicity given the *Report* in *The Times* in August and September, 1922" (49). The novel was, among other things, a work of protest against the jingoist politics that sent idealistic young men like Septimus Smith, Rupert Brooke, Wilfred Owen, and Siegfried Sassoon to fight in the Great War of 1914-1918—a conflict emblematic of the mass psychosis that fuelled the tragic slaughter of a generation. *Mrs. Dalloway* is not simply a private meditation on suicide. It is a politically prescient text that decries the psychological consequences of military aggression and "calls into question any rosy prognosis of the British empire's future" (Chatman 279). The role of shell-shocked veteran is transferred, by Cunningham and Daldry, to Laura Brown's brutish and unselfconscious husband, who returns from the second World War to claim domestic and conjugal privileges in a 1950's America about to explode in the cultural dysphoria characteristic of the turbulent 1960's. It is not Brown *pater* who is suffering symptoms of constriction and mental dissociation, but Laura, the suburban housewife who struggles with psychological asphyxiation in a postwar, pre-feminist era.

Cunningham's *Hours* suffers, uncannily, from the author's reluctance to embed the "beautiful caves" of his characters' biopics, revealed through memory and flashback, into the dense historical reality of America in the second half of the twentieth century.[i] As Chatman complains, "his novel lacks Woolf's breadth of social and political resonance .... *The Hours* seems so much less a social critique than *Mrs. Dalloway*" (279). He goes on to observe that "Cunningham does not achieve the broad cultural sweep of *Mrs. Dalloway*," whose "purview is the whole of London's population, indeed the whole of a British empire in decline" (280). In contrast, "*The Hours* seems too sealed off .... And while it may be true that the AIDS epidemic has been as great a scourge as World War I, it has not led to the sort of political and social consequences that afflicted Britain in the 1920's" (280-81). Chatman concludes that "to match the scope of the original, Cunningham needed a broader canvas and a set of Woolfian techniques he didn't utilize" (281).

When teaching this text a year ago, I realized, to my shock and chagrin, that Richard Brown (born in 1946) and Clarissa Vaughn (born in 1947), would virtually be my contemporaries. They belong to the generation of "baby-boomers" who came of age in the late 1960's and early 1970's and whose youthful concerns were situated squarely within the cultural cataclysm provoked by the Vietnam War. For anyone of my generation, male or female, the military draft was a primary, pressing, and overwhelming concern—either a serious personal threat, or a source of severe anxiety for one's friends and life partners. How did Richard and his mate Louis avoid the army? Did they "come out" as homosexuals in protest of service to Uncle Sam? And how could characters as astute as Clarissa and Richard harbor pastoral memories of heterosexual experimentation without once remembering the pervasive anti-war sentiments that inflected this controversial period of U. S. history? A "generation gap" was the epoch's watchword, and revolution against Nixonian authority the *cri de coeur* of "hippies" and college students.

---

[i] In 1923, Woolf expressed her excitement at discovering an innovative technique for psychological exploration: "how I dig out beautiful caves [of memory] behind my characters" (*D* 2:263).

My last cavil is a minor one, but I cannot help wondering whether a book like *The Hours*, with so many scenes transpiring in the urban landscape of New York City at century's end, could have been successfully promoted after the global tragedy of 9/11/01. In my own opinion, this 1998 novel seems too politically naïve to have the kind of sensational impact it generated prior to terrorist bombings of the World Trade Center. Cunningham's end-of-century narrative is imbued with a meticulous, sometimes snobbish attention to sartorial correctness and an overweening concern, on the part of Clarissa, for clothes, dress, fashion, and sophisticated taste. At one point in the novel (but not the film), she makes a mental note that Sally ought to retire her mustard-colored jacket. In light of the communal tragedy of 9/11/01, who in New York, beyond the cast of a spin-off television program called "Queer Eye for the Lesbian Gal," would care? And if they did, could one respect such a snob as the protagonist of a 21st-century novel?

Why, despite all these apparent flaws, did Daldry's film prove so popular and win a number of Academy Awards? Certainly, the acting on the part of all three female protagonists, as well as by the fiery and impassioned Stephen Dillane as Leonard Woolf, is superb. The drama rises, at times, to poignant (melo)dramatic crescendos that just barely fall short of tragic catharsis. Ed Harris is magnificent in the role of the suffering, demented AIDS victim, another version of the "mad artist" that Woolf herself was often purported to be. The score by Philip Glass" is eerie and emotionally stirring. And anyone who has failed to read the novel prior to seeing the film might be caught by surprise when he or she realizes that the wide-eyed son of Laura Brown is none other than the angry, tormented Richard. One has to commend an ingenious costume department for managing, at the end of the film, cleverly to disguise Moore's, pregnant figure in loose garments cloaking the dowdy and aged Laura, who reappears in New York as a beleaguered woman who has lost husband, daughter, and self-murdered son. "So Laura Brown ... is alive now, after her ex-husband has been carried off by liver cancer, after her daughter has been killed by a drunk driver. She is alive after Richard has jumped from a window" (*H* 222). She, like two of the Clarissas—Woolf's and Cunningham's, but not like the fictional mother-surrogate Richard creates in his novel—is a survivor. Clarissa Vaughn realizes that "Clarissa, the figure in a novel, will vanish, as well Laura Brown, the lost mother, the martyr and fiend" (*H* 225). But meanwhile, the vestigial remnants of a party foreshortened by disaster make the ongoing art of life a "party for the not-yet-dead; for the relatively undamaged; for those who for mysterious reasons have the fortune to be alive" (*H* 226).

To paraphrase Samuel Beckett, there's nothing more interesting than unhappiness. Or, to quote Cunningham, "Death and resurrection are always mesmerizing" (*H* 180). By the end of the film, the spectator can wallow in the pleasurable sensations of *Schadenfreude* and celebrate the joys of both sanity and survival in an otherwise chaotic, pain-filled, treacherous environment. Both novel and film end on a note of provisional consolation. Cunningham's Clarissa takes comfort from "an hour here or there when our lives seem, against all odds and expectations, to burst open and give us everything we've ever imagined," and we dare to "hope, more than anything, for more" (*H* 225). In Daldry's film, a script by David Hare indulges in cinematic *prosopopoeia*, resuscitating Virginia's spirit to reassure the audience that the answer to the overwhelming challenges of human experience is "to look life in the face and to know it for what it is; to love it for what it is, and then to put it away" (Lee 56). Hare might more profitably have turned to Woolf's own writing for a different, more powerful and lyrical message from the grave, such as when, content with the consolations of an atheistic humanism, she declares in "A Sketch of the Past" that the "whole world is a work of art .... But ... certainly and emphatically there is no God; we are the words; we are the music; we are the thing itself" (*MOB* 72).

CHAPTER THREE

SEEING WHAT'S *NOT* THERE INSTEAD OF WHAT *IS*: CHILDLESSNESS AND INFERTILITY IN THE ADAPTATION OF *WHO'S AFRAID OF VIRGINIA WOOLF?*

by Jody W. Pennington

Edward Albee's *Who's Afraid of Virginia Woolf?* is the story of two childless couples and one of the couple's imaginary son.[i] Critics immediately noted the centrality of the fictive son to the play's theme of truth and illusion. The theme of illusion is woven into the narrative by a series of acts that turn out to be something other than what the viewer has been led to expect them to be such as the false shotgun with which George "shoots" Martha and George and Martha's son. One critic, Robert Brustein, writing in *The New Republic*, referred to this aspect of the play as "three and a half hours of prestidigitation" (30). Interestingly, by focusing on what was illusory and what was *not* there (the child), critics seem to have been blind to what *was* there: the two couples' childlessness. When the play was adapted to the cinema, the fictive child presented difficulties to Mike Nichols and Ernest Lehman, not least because they understood the imaginary child and ignored the importance of the theme of childlessness in the way critics had already established.

The collective critical and creative silence on childlessness and infertility speaks, I argue, to the near invisibility of the issue of childlessness and infertility in popular discourse at the time of both the play's Broadway debut in 1962 and the film's release in 1966. In contrast to traditional figurative readings of the imaginary child, I will argue that the play and film's representation of involuntary and voluntary childlessness was a critique of pronatalism. I will argue that the fictive son, as the product of fictive procreation, offered both a

---

[i] Childlessness can be categorized in terms of the intentions of the childless couple—voluntary or involuntary. Each kind of childlessness seems to be represented in *Who's Afraid of Virginia Woolf?* George and Martha, we eventually learn, are involuntarily childless; Nick and Honey, the narrative eventually seems to reveal, are voluntarily childless.

critique of the mainstream consensus on sexual attitudes and the family in the late 1950s and early 1960s and a strategy George and Martha employ to cope with being childlessness during the baby boom.

While a theoretical analysis of how perceptions of plays and film adaptations are shaped by their institutional context is beyond the scope of this paper, I will examine how certain limits to adaptation are imposed not only by the aesthetic work itself but by critical reception and social norms as well. To that end, I will first examine the critical reaction to the play and the way in which critics tended to interpret the imaginary child. The idea that the themes of childlessness and infertility represented crucial social and personal issues did not occur to either the play's critics or to any of those involved in the play's adaptation even though the imaginary child was so important to the narrative, a thorn in the side of many critics, and an aesthetic dilemma for the filmmakers. Next, I will look at the role played by the imaginary child in the play's adaptation to the cinema. Nichols and Lehman were unable to change the understanding of the imaginary child, I argue, not only for the aesthetic reasons the two put forth but also because of the two institutional factors: the fossilization of interpretation that occurred between the play's debut and the film's adaptation and the muzzling effect of social norms about childlessness and infertility on popular discourse at the time of the film's adaptation. Lastly, I will look at examples of the themes of childlessness and infertility in *Who's Afraid of Virginia Woolf?* and offer an alternative, non-figurative, reading of the imaginary child.

Traditional Readings of the Imaginary Child

Reactions to the childlessness reveal a dichotomy in the critical reception of the play and the play's adaptation to film: a tremendous amount of commentary on the imaginary son but a dearth of commentary on the issue of childlessness, except in figurative—*mythological*, *symbolic*, or *allegorical*—readings of the play, which interpret George and Martha's infertility as symbolic or allegorical for the state of the union of the United States in the early 1960s. That is, numerous critics and scholars have analyzed the role of the fictive child and have commented on childlessness in the play and film, but these analyses have invariably tended to see the childlessness in *Who's Afraid of Virginia Woolf?* as a broad criticism of American life, society, and culture. Matthew Roudané summarizes the way in which much criticism of the play pivoted on the imaginary son:

> Perhaps the most hotly debated issue concerns the son-myth and the attendant exorcism. Three decades of critical exegesis may be roughly divided into two schools of thought regarding this issue: those who feel the son-myth and

exorcism fail and are much ado about little, and those who see in the play's ending a purgative, cleansing process that is both structurally and thematically decorous. ... Although scholars establish many distinctions relative to the degree of artistic success ascribed to the son-myth and exorcism, nearly all the authors of the (at last count) fourteen book-length studies on Albee address the idea of the possibility of redemption as engendered in the son-myth and exorcism. (23–24).

As Roudané's point suggests, there are numerous examples of mythological, symbolic, or allegorical readings but I will give two. A classic example of the interpretation of childlessness as a metaphor for the sterility of American society and culture can be found in Ronald Hayman's *Edward Albee* (1973). In Hayman's view, Albee "makes childlessness work as a symbol of emotional and spiritual sterility" (41). In Hayman's reading of the play, George and Martha have an opportunity at the end of the play to "become less sterile" after they have admitted "the fact of their sterility" (47). Obviously, Hayman is not suggesting that George and Martha could literally become fecund simply by acknowledging their condition or that they could attempt to have children through the assisted reproduction technologies available in 1962. Rather, he understands their sterility figuratively, seeing George and Martha's "personal failures" as "representative of the failures of a whole society, a whole culture" (65).

A second example comes from British literary scholar C. W. E. Bigsby. Bigsby takes both George and Nick to be impotent, arguing that "the impotence of the male is a particularly accurate symbol of what he takes to be the sterility of contemporary society," (47). Bigsby's equation of mail infertility with the inability to perform sexually exemplifies the negative perception of infertility as such and the tendency to ignore male infertility as a cause of childlessness. Rather than pursuing the literal implications of his claim, Bigsby instead read the play's setting as following a figurative textual line from St. Augustine's *Confessions* through T. S. Eliot's *The Waste Land* (1922). He believed the play conveyed "a sense of the false standards of a sterile society in which personal values had become degraded. So Albee's play, set in a Carthage of the New World, is similarly dedicated to an insistence on the falsity of the values adhered to by that society" (48).

The playwright himself contributed to figurative readings of his work. In a mid-1960s interview, Albee said that the effect of naming the two main characters after George and Martha Washington was to implicate the whole of American culture in his critique: a minor element of the play was "an attempt to examine the success or failure of American revolutionary principles" (110–111). Such readings are understandable and (no pun intended) fruitful. Indeed, it is not only drama, literary, or film criticism that highlights the mythological or allegorical qualities of concrete aspects of human life such as infertility. In their brief history of infertility in various societies, Philippe Morice and his co-authors note that "[t]hroughout history and its various civilizations, woman has always been the symbol of fertility" (497). The social provides the basis for mythological, allegorical, or symbolic readings of the history of medical science as well as for humanists.

There is something odd, though, about critics' ignoring the possibility that the imaginary child and the childlessness that begat it were a critique of pronatalism. It seems to have been a case of now they see it, now they don't. Despite commenting on the fictive child and George and Martha's inability to have children, none of Albee's critics or the filmmakers considered its implications in the context of the postwar baby boom within which they were writing or adapting the play to the screen respectively. The baby boom started in 1946 and lasted until 1964, as dated by the U.S. Bureau of the Census. During those two decades, there were seventy-six million births in the United States. The surge in childbirths, following as it did the low rates of the 1930s and 1940s, "confounded demographers" (Westoff et al. 5). It was unprecedented and largely unpredicted. Max Lerner, noting the flippancy of the expression *baby boom*, argued that it "half revealed and half concealed a dramatic revolution that overturned many accepted ideas and expectations about American population trends" (114). The demographic shift was accompanied by an ideological shift in views of the family and a revival of the domestic sphere ideology. Lerner's insight suggests the way in which normative consensus naturalizes behavior and attitudes and "half-conceals" them.

The reproductive consensus during the boom was sustained and driven by an ideology or social norm that has been given various labels: the religious term the *procreative imperative*, , the demographer's *pronatalism*; and Jean Veevers' *parenthood prescription* (1–14). Pronatalism can been seen in two fertility norms: first, that all married couples should have children and, second, that they should *want* to have them (Veevers 3). The norm of bearing children was strong during the postwar baby boom; in their analysis of what the United States would look like in the 1960s, Daniel Seligman and Lawrence A. Mayer noted that the "ideal" number of children according to American women was 3.4 (14). Elaine Tyler May has argued that "Procreation in the cold war era took on almost mythic proportions" and was promoted as "a way to express civic values" (135). This view can be seen in a sociology text on marriage and the family published around the time of the release of the film. The text described the various shades of pronatalism

> On the desirability of having children ... traditionalists are inclined to think of the bearing of children as a duty to God, church, and country. Liberals ... think of children as the natural outcome of a happy marriage. Those in the middle

range of orientation may have mixed reasons for desiring children, but ... they do tend to favor them (Stroup 349).

The norm against *not* bearing children was equally strong during the boom decades. Analyzing data gathered in the summer of 1960, the authors of *Fertility and Family Planning in the United States* wrote "Nearly all American couples now in the childbearing ages have a strong aversion to childlessness" (Whelpton et al. 162). They estimated that around six to eight percent of American couples would remain childless but that the large majority of these would do so involuntarily: "Voluntary childlessness," they concluded, "is nearly extinct" (163). In his article "Childlessness, Intentional and Unintentional," Edward Pohlman reported that less that 1% of couples surveyed since World War II said that remaining childless was ideal (3). Furthermore, he claimed, parenthood was more important than marriage to most adults (2). In any case, by the time Albee wrote his play, demographers and sociologists who studied the family and birth rates agreed that the United States "[was] a peculiarly child-oriented society" (Seligman and Mayer 12). In fact, the ideals and behavior of the reproductive consensus were more or less aligned: the average number of children was 3.2 and birthrates rose among all social groups. As May points out, the pronatalist ideology "found expression in Hollywood, in the political culture, in the prescriptive literature, and in the thoughts and aspirations of women and men at the time" (160). But not, I argue, in *Who's Afraid of Virginia Woolf?*

Adapting the Imaginary

Edward Albee's first Broadway play debuted at the Billy Rose Theatre on October 13, 1962, directed by Alan Schneider and starring Uta Hagen as Martha and Arthur Hill as George, roles played by Elizabeth Taylor, who won an Academy Award for Best Actress, and Richard Burton, respectively, in the Warner Brothers release four years later. George Grizzard played Nick on Broadway, a role George Segal had in Nichols' adaptation. Melinda Dillo was Honey on Broadway while Sandy Dennis won Best Supporting Actress, for her portrayal of Honey in the film. The play was a tremendous critical and commercial success, and Jack Warner bought the rights to it for $500,000 and a percentage of the gross in March 1964 (Leff and Simmons 243–44). Veteran screenwriter Ernest Lehman and director Mike Nichols were given the task of adapting Albee's play for the screen. Most critical attention has fallen on the issue of language in the play's move from the stage to the screen. Warner "expected Lehman and Nichols 'to substitute potent and pungent dialogue' for the profanity and blasphemy ... " (Leff and Simmons 248). Instead, Lehman and Nichols left the manuscript of the screenplay very close to the text of the original play. They "labored for more than six months on the script and finally decided they were being dishonest," *Life* reported in a cover story on the film (Thompson, "Liz in a Film Shocker" 92).

Particularly troublesome for Nichols and Lehman was figuring out what to do with George and Martha's imaginary child, which had generally been panned by theater critics. The influence of the critical response on Nichols and Lehman is in part evident from the way in which their interpretations of the imaginary son parallel that of critics. In an interview given while directing *Catch-22* (1970), Nichols said he had wanted to film *Who's Afraid of Virginia Woolf?* because of his own experience as a stage director. He believed that he "understood it quite well" and that he could remain true to Albee's material. He thought he would be able to "protect it from being turned into God knows what—'the child is real, but had committed suicide' or whatever else might have been done to it" (Gelmis 275). Lehman had actually written an early draft of the screenplay in which the child was not imaginary but real and dead from suicide (Leff 456). Suicide was an unsatisfactory solution to Nichols, though, and he rejected it.

While Nichols' attitude suggests a director who appreciated and wanted to bridge the contrasting demands of the theater and motion pictures, he might have been less than completely forthcoming. According to Ernest Lehman, Nichols had called him in the middle of the night at one point during the re-write phase and suggested excising the imaginary child from the play altogether (Madsen 27). Lehman was an uncertain about the imaginary child as Nichols. He had attempted to make the child real because he read the imaginary child as "a latent homosexual fantasy," which, he told Axel Madsen for *Sight and Sound*, was "his toughest nut" (27). Axel Madsen described what he perceived to be "the play's homosexuality" an "open secret" [*secret de polichinelle*] and he noted that students at the UCLA Theater Arts Department had produced a gay rendition of the play's third act in 1967 with the two main characters changed to George and Marty (27).

Indeed, numerous critics endorsed the idea that George and Martha's infertility was a symbol of hidden homosexuality, even though Albee rejected it. Albee consistently denied that the two couples were surrogates for gay couples.[i] Nichols called the idea that the imaginary child symbolized latent homosexuality "nonsense." He argued, overly optimistically given the cultural climate of Broadway in the early 1960s, that if Albee had wanted to write a play

---

[i] The idea raises interesting questions concerning the intersection of fertility, gay marriage, and the role of the institutions of marriage and the family as the centers of reproduction.

about four gay men, then "would and he could" (Gelmis 277). In the end, the imaginary child remained since removing it, Nichols and Lehman agreed, would have been akin to committing "literary treason" (Madsen 27). That critics breached the idea that the two couples' childlessness was actually a symbolic substitute the characters' gender and sexual orientation—that they were in some way two gay couples—indicates how completely they missed the point of the play possibly critiquing the reproductive consensus. The interpretation of childlessness as latent (or hidden) homosexuality, reveals furthermore how ingrained the assumption of having children was. A heterosexual couple, the widespread assumption seems to have been, could not have been childless. Rather than see George and Martha as a childless heterosexual couple, critics chose to ignore its relevance, at least in literal terms.

Childlessness in *Who's Afraid of Virginia Woolf?*

The theme of childlessness appears in the first Act when George and Nick are alone. After commenting on Honey's slim hips, George asks Nick whether he has children: "You have any kids?" Nick hesitantly replies, "... no ... not yet." Nick's hesitancy indicates that he is aware that he and Honey are in violation of the reproductive consensus. Being childlessness was seen as deviant Erving Goffman categorized childless married couples "who disavail themselves of the opportunity to raise family" as social deviants (154). Nick asks George the same question, and George responds by saying "That's for me to know and you to find out." Later in the play but not the film, George asks Nick if the reason he and Honey do not have any children is because Honey is "slim-hipped," and Nick replies that he does not know whether that has anything to do with it. The question indicates that the matter is on George's mind. It also indicates that a young couple's not having children demands an explanation, perhaps a physiological one. When asked if he wants children, Nick assures George, "Yes ... certainly. We ... want to wait ... a little ... until we're settled." The exchange captures the considerable societal pressures against voluntary childlessness during the baby boom. Families and friends applied subtle and direct forms of social pressure. The way in which the topic of children recurs in *Who's Afraid of Virginia Woolf?* suggests a critique of pronatalism. The privacy normally afforded by the marital relationship is invaded by inquisitive relatives, friends, and acquaintances. This appears in the play and film in the questions George and Nick ask one another (and Honey probably asked Martha, which prompted Martha to tell Honey that she and George had a son).

The film adaptation retains the exchange between George and Nick takes place but employs significant camera work: George leans into the camera for a close-up and asks, "No kids? What's the matter?" (in almost as a whisper). After talking briefly about Martha's father, George asks Nick, "How many kids are you gonna have?" The shot cuts to a close-up of Honey (out of the men's line of sight) on the stairs and her facial reaction to George's question. Nick answers: "I don't know. My wife has ...." George finishes his sentence: "Slim hips." Honey looks slightly anguished and comes down the stairs when George sees her, saying "You must see this house dear. This is such a *wonderful* old house," attempting to return the dialogue to the surface concerns of new acquaintances. The shot suggests, however briefly, that Nichols might have pursued a more literal reading of the couples' childlessness, although he chose not to do so.

Throughout the narrative, Albee plays with the close relationship between the regulation of sexual behavior, paternity, and reproduction. The fictive child is placed in conjunction with adultery twice in the play and film. First, when Honey comes down from the second floor before Martha and tells the two men that Martha's changing (stage directions: *with a nervous little laugh*): "I imagine she wants to be ... comfortable." Thus, George is dealt two blows almost simultaneously, both of which are closely related to sexuality, marriage, and procreation. , On the one hand, Martha signals that she will *brazenly* seduce Nick despite George and Honey's presence; on the other, Martha has revealed the existence of a child (known to Martha and George to be fictive, assumed by Nick and Honey and the audience at this point to be real). That blow to George is also a blow to the dominant sexual morality of the period: George's inability to have procreative marital sexual behavior is contrasted with Martha's threat to engage in non-procreative, non-marital (adulterous) sexual behavior with Nick. Incensed by his coming betrayal, George subtly attacks his guests just before Martha comes down the stairs in her new attire: When Honey says she and Nick should be leaving, George asks: "For what? You keeping the babysitter up, or something" to which Nick testily replies, "I told you we didn't have children."

Later in the play, the fictive child again becomes a site for critiquing sexuality, marriage, and procreation. , Honey brings up George and Martha's son, but Martha no longer wants to discuss him while George insists that she do so. Martha then angrily claims that George has "a problem" with their son: "he's not completely sure it's his own kid." George seems genuinely hurt by this blow and tells Martha she is a "deeply wicked person." Nick proposes, in vain, that George's paternity ought not to be discussed in his and Honey's company. Martha's derision can also be read as her blaming George for being infertile. George had mocked Martha's inability to have children earlier in another context during Act II in the play, when George and Nick are alone in the backyard in the film. George alludes to Martha's possible sterility when he tells Nick that "Martha doesn't have pregnancies at all"; Nick assumes that George means *after* the birth of their son. Whether Martha's lack of pregnancies is because of her fertility or George's is not clear. At the end of the play, though, it is made clear that George and Martha wanted to have children but couldn't when Nick asks George whether they couldn't have children. George replies "*We* couldn't," and Martha echoes "*We* couldn't." The manuscript to the play includes: "stage directions: *a hint of communion in this.*"

Once Nick sees that the child is merely fictive, he repeats "I think I understand this" as if he has been shaken by this last revelation on the part of George and Martha. Nick's awkward expression of empathy at the end of the play and film, when *he* attempts to communicate, to "to ... reach you ... to ... make contact," suggests (as do the numerous other contexts in which a great deal of explicit or implied emphasis is placed on having children) that childlessness is perceived to be a great tragedy. The seriousness of childlessness is also visible in Nick's strong response when he figures out that George and Martha's son is imaginary. The hostilities cease immediately. His reaction is not to the possibility of Martha being psychologically unstable but rather to the couple's childlessness: "You couldn't ...." He seems so shaken by their infertility that, just before leaving, he awkwardly attempts to exhibit empathy and compassion. It doesn't seem perfunctory even if it is formal.

Voluntary Childlessness

Just as it represents the involuntarily childless couple, *Who's Afraid of Virginia Woolf?* also critiques the motherhood mandate at the level of popular discourse, motherhood was idealized, and women "were expected to achieve their greatest fulfillment in parenthood" (May 149). Women who expressed ambivalence about motherhood were labeled neurotic. Most importantly, infertility was said to result from women being "conflicted or ambivalent about motherhood" (Burns 359). In other words, failure to live up to the biological demands presumed by the motherhood mandate was interpreted to be symptomatic of a failure to adapt psychologically to the motherhood mandate. Honey, it slowly becomes clear, is evading the motherhood mandate.

An indication of this comes in the second act when George and Nick are alone, and Nick tells George that he thinks George and Martha ought to be more discrete and not argue in from of him and Honey. Then, despite having just implored George not to reveal his marriage's fault lines in public, Nick proceeds to confess that he married Honey because he thought she was pregnant. He calls it a "hysterical pregnancy." While Albee has chosen to portray Honey's premarital pseudopregnancy in Freudian terms, the condition is recognized as *pseudocyesis*, sometimes referred to as *delusional pregnancy* and *pseudopregnancy*, a condition some physicians believe to be a variant of Munchausen's Syndrome. It is not clear whether Honey really experienced pseudocyesis or whether she perhaps had had an abortion. Either way, Honey's voluntary childlessness was a form of deviant behavior. If this is the case and whether or not Nick knows what she is doing or not is never made clear either. It is never made clear whether Nick is maintaining a social façade when he tells George they want to have children but are simply waiting until they are more settled or that Honey has convinced him that she can't have children.

Later in the film, after George glances up and sees the silhouetted image of Martha and Nick through the window of the recently tidied upstairs bedroom, he encounters Honey screaming "I DON'T WANT ANY CHILDREN! I'm afraid, I don't want to be hurt." If Honey is indeed afraid of childbirth (she might be afraid of being a mother, a point about which the play is ambiguous) it was not a condition outside the range of concerns of the medical community. Indeed, there was a small but growing literature on fear of pregnancy and childbirth when Albee wrote his play.

Albee was not alone in representing childlessness as resulting from a woman's fear of pregnancy. Kroger and Freed summarize the views current in psychoanalysis at mid-century and find a variety of psychoanalytic explanations. One view posited that chronic anxieties led to sterility in women who were "endocrinologically normal" while another assumed that fear of pregnancy combined with an unconscious awareness of the time of ovulation, which led the woman to avoid coitus to avoid pregnancy, while yet another theory posited the dominant wife, a masculine woman who remained infertile to avoid the femininity imposed by pregnancy and motherhood. They even presented reports of women who became fertile only after renouncing their careers as evidence of the psychogenic problems that prevent pregnancy (Kroger and Freed 870).

George infers from what Nick has confided to him earlier—that she privately denies and represses everything related to her own barrenness and her husband's impotency—as she tells her own tale of marital woe. She is terrified of bearing children, a symbol of her own inauthentic and illusory relationship with Nick. Honey wakes up with no idea of what's going on and says that she does not want to have any children because she's afraid of getting hurt. George infers that the nausea and headaches are the result of her practicing some sort of birth control:

> I should have known ... the whole business ... the whining ... How do you make your secret little murders stud-boy doesn't know about, hunh? Pills? PILLS? You got a secret supply of pills?

Honey is thus a hidden deviant in that she conceals (again, presumably, from her husband as well as others—until she drunkenly confesses her fear of having children to George) her desire to remain childless. Although it is not entirely clear whether Honey is afraid of childbirth or childrearing, her reference to being hurt suggests it is the former that she dreads. Honey's choice to keep her voluntary childlessness under wraps fits with her personality and the impression management that she engages in throughout the film (her efforts to present herself as the "perfect little wife" (or as George describes her, "a wifey little type" of a successful academic) although she is less than successful at doing this since she continually drinks (George: "gargles brandy all the time") and her behavior otherwise leads George to remark that Nick's concern for her "this mouse, of whom he was solicitous to a point that faileth human understanding, given that she was sort of a simp, in the long run" in his monologue of "Get the Guests" at the roadhouse. At the end of the play, as George explains to Martha that they son is dead, Honey has an apparent change of heart: "I want a child ... (more forcefully) I want a child! ... I want a child. I want a baby."

Conclusion

What is the illusion offered by the fictive child? The fictive son serves to create for George and Martha the illusion of being a nuclear family—of attaining a social ideal. Martha is very much concerned with social status attainment as seen in her frustration with George is often related to her disappointment in his less than stellar academic career. At the same time, the illusion repeats elements of the growing mainstream concerns over the marital institution that see the institution itself as in some ways an illusion of permanence and fidelity and many concrete marriages as being based on illusions of compatibility.

Once George has announced the death of his and Martha's son, Martha tells the other three:

> I've tried to carry pure and unscathed through the sewer of this marriage; through the sick nights and the pathetic stupid days, through the derision and the laughter .... *God*, the laughter, through one failure after another, one failure compounding another failure, each attempt more sickening, more numbing than the one before; the one thing, the one *person* I have tried to protect, to raise above the mire of this vile, crushing marriage; the one light in all this hopeless ... *dark*ness ... OUR SON.

Put simply, reading the representation of childlessness as a critique of the pronatalism of the 1950s rather than as a critique of American society at large provides insights into reproductive ideals otherwise subsumed in generalities about American society and culture. Re-reading the representation of involuntary and voluntary childlessness as a critique of the procreative, , pronatalism that had dominated popular discourse during the postwar baby-boom era rather than the "sterility" of American society and culture helps us understand the shift in views of the family that were taking place at the beginning of the 1960s, including changes in birth control technology and use, changes in attitudes toward and laws regulating abortion, and developments in assisted reproductive technologies. The failure of the filmmakers to see the imaginary son in another light and the neglect of infertility in the adaptation of the play to film suggests the influence of critical response to a work in its original medium on filmmakers when they adapt that work. In sum, although *Who's Afraid of Virginia Woolf?* is normally characterized as an absurd, its representation of involuntary childlessness and the childless couple is realistic.

CHAPTER FOUR

ANTI-THEATRE IN FILM

by Temenuga Trifonova

The historical avant-gardes were instrumental in finalizing the most important paradigm shift in recent history: the decline of the logocentric conception of reality, the shattering of Idealism, the transvaluation of values. In the first decades of the twentieth century, under the increasing influence of philosophies of becoming or vitalism (Bergson) and new discoveries in physics (*e.g.,* the argument that atoms are merely convenient "mental symbols" humans impose on "an energetic universe" in which, however, isolated things do not exist), the logocentric view of reality gave way to an "energetic view of reality" (Sheppard, 2000: 36). That artists were aware of such scientific discoveries is evidenced by the explicit references to the relativity of time or to Brownian movement in Futurist and Dada manifestoes (by Marrinetti and Tristan Tzara). Painters renounced the fixed point of perspective they had inherited from the Renaissance, while writers experimented with limited or unreliable narrators, blurring the distinctions between author, character and narrator, relying on a whole range of intertextual devices, and challenging the privileged mode of relationship to the work of art—contemplation—through various defamiliarization techniques that demanded from spectators a reflective and critical appraisal of their own reception of the work. As Wittgenstein's *Tractatus* unsettled common assumptions about the representational power of language, both poets and fiction writers moved "away from the noun-based syntax that implies the reality of (illusory) things ... [toward] a more active syntax based on transitive verbs"(113), a shift that was intimately related to the Bergsonian idea of reality as governed by an élan vital.

Though Beckett's work can be easily situated in the context of this fragmentation of linguistic confidence, it is also a significant departure from Bergson's belief that the failure to represent reality, to subordinate it to ordinary syntax, linear logic, and the power of reason, is actually a gain as it forces us to humbly open ourselves to a world that far exceeds the limits of rational comprehension, a world that remains ultimately (and fortunately, for Bergson) unsayable. The roots of Beckett's anti-theatre should be sought rather in the Dadaists' and the Futurists' critique of the bourgeois concept of art as high culture destined for the narcissistic, philistine delectation of the middle class; in their intolerance for symbolism; in their emphasis on chance and random events; and especially in their fascination with "functionless machines," language being one of them. In this respect, Beckett is closer to the Dadaists than to the Futurists. Futurist poets, for all their ecstatic references to a "universal dynamism," still subscribed to the belief that there is "a homology between noun-based syntax and thing-based (molecular) reality"(127). Although they recommended using language in a non-instrumental fashion, the Futurists ultimately reaffirmed the belief that poetic language, stripped of its instrumentality, could tap into a spiritual substratum underlying the material world.

Dada nonsense poetry, on the other hand, hovered somewhere in-between linguistic mimesis and pure sound. Dada was motivated by two opposing impulses: on one hand, the Saussurean idea of the arbitrary connection between language and world and, on the other hand, the desire to "create a redeemed, adamic language in which pristine words, untarnished by corrupt misuse, have a necessary connection with the things they name"(136). The difference between Dada nonsense poetry and Beckett's reification of language (especially in the later plays) is that between nonsense and the absurd. Dada nonsense poetry (for instance, Hugo Ball's poem "Karawane" which begins with "jolifanto bambla o falli bambla" and ends with an emphatic "ba–umf") can, no doubt, be characterized as absurdist; however, Beckett's absurdist works are not necessarily nonsensical because the sense of the absurd is grounded in a particularly well-developed (to the point of enervation) moral sense, whereas morality is not constitutive of nonsense. The Dadaists' experiments with language [the Dada poème statiste, the Dada poeme simultane, the optophonetic poem, intonarumori (noise-machines), or bruitist poetry] were designed to shock the *viewers* (these were poem-performances rather than poem-texts); Beckett, on the other hand, sought to unsettle or estrange them. Even as they blatantly destroyed referentiality and meaningfulness, the Dadaists insisted on developing a system of specific rules for the performance of nonsense poems, rules that were, paradoxically, designed to make what seemed like incomprehensible nonsense actually comprehensible. Berlin Dada poet Raoul Hausemann explained the optophonetic poem in the following way:

> Every unit of this poem is purely independent and acquires an aural value according to whether the letter, the sounds, the concentrations of consonants are handled using a higher or lower pitch, more loudly or more quietly. In order to be able to depict this typographically, I chose letters of differing sizes or strengths as substitutes for musical notes. (qtd. in Sheppard, 2000: 140)

Reading or experiencing a Dada poem was predicated on the understanding that certain semantic boundaries had been crossed, *i.e.,* there was a certain suspension of disbelief at work that actually counterbalanced the intended shock effect.

The Dadaists' discordant performances figured nonsense as the other side of language and kept the absurd at a safe distance. Beckett, Ionesco, and the nouveau roman writers (Marguerite Duras, Alain Robbe-Grillet, Michel Butor, Nathalie Sarraute) did not have to chant "Umba! Umba!"—as Zurich Dada poet Huelsenbeck did in his poem "Negergedichte"—if they wanted to convey the absurdity of language. Beckett and Ionesco were not concerned with transforming nonsense into a new, self-sufficient language. Instead of transporting the reader/viewer to "the other side of language," from where its arbitrariness could be observed, they forced him to become estranged *within* language, and often within the most banal uses of language. Rather than inverting, subverting, or refusing sense, Beckett and Ionesco drew attention to the fact that nonsense is often indistinguishable from sense taken literally. Accordingly, in their works basic dramatic conventions were not discarded but rather literalized: the characters in *The Bald Soprano* do not signify or refer to the failure of communication (simple misunderstanding) but enact this failure in the very act of communicating (they actually find it hard to stop talking). Beckett and Ionesco understood that if they were to comment on the unrepresentability of reality, the inauthenticity of language, or the failure of communication, such comments would have to be enacted *i.e., techniques* of representations would have to be continually reexamined as *objects* of representation.

Despite the anti-aesthetic agenda it shares with Dada (*e.g.,* exposing the arbitrariness of language, challenging the classical idea of reality as essentially anthropomorphic and, particularly in the case of Ionesco, the traces of Dada primitivism, *i.e.,* the interest in mundane situations provoking extreme, even murderous emotions), anti-theatre invites a closer comparison with nouveau roman's minimalism. The minimalism of Beckett's later fictive and dramatic works—"the decrease in length, number of characters and physical space" (Oppenheim, 2003: 56), the "ghosting of language," or the gradual displacement of language onto the increasing "poeticization of mise-en-scène"(24)—demonstrates Beckett's growing preoccupation with the visual as a dramatic prototype. Not only does Oppenheim interpret minimalism literally, as "fewer words," but he considers it proof of the truthfulness of Hegel's dictum that "art is a thing of the past," a thesis "resurrected" recently by Arthur Danto. According to Hegel, art has reached its end when it self-consciously internalizes its own history, when, in an attempt to return to its own origins, it asks "What Is Art?" Art dissolves into philosophy of art or aesthetics when it reproduces within itself its most fundamental problem, the problem of representation *i.e.,* when it transforms *techniques* of representation into *objects* of representation.

Oppenheim considers the resistance to narrativity and the domination of image over word in Beckett's later plays analogous to Pop art's problematization of representation (note the well disguised, unexamined assumption on which Oppenheim's entire argument rests: of course in order to argue that minimal language and emphasis on the visual is a sign of the "problematization of representation" in theatre, Oppenhein must assume that the "essence" of theatre is precisely language so that any deviation from it, such as "the ghosting of language" in Beckett's later plays, automatically becomes a symptom of the end of art, or, in this case, the end of theatre). From Oppenheim's point of view, then, the dissolution of the differences between the arts prefigures the end of art. Thus, he concludes that wherever the visual paradigm dominates, as in Pop art or in Beckett's late minimalist works, "the result is a self-reflexivity that impedes expression in both"(59). This argument rests on extremely rigid and ultimately indefensible definitions of "image" and "word."

Although Oppenheim upholds the binary understanding of word and image, his critical study has contributed to a significant shift in Beckett criticism—from poststructuralist to phenomenological readings—by drawing attention to "the visual paradigm" in Beckett's later plays and novels, many of which often fall silent and become concentrated in a single, usually immobile, stage-image sculpted through extremely specific stage directions and subtle interactions of light and darkness. Beckett's growing interest in the visual (the space of the stage and the image of the actor's body on the stage), which he shares with the nouveau roman writers, is an attempt to distill the events on the page/stage from the influence of any prior constructs of reality, to diminish the relevance of narrative and verisimilitude, and to foreground the presence of the observing subject which often remains hidden in naturalist fiction and drama, "to reunite the object of perception with a visually perceiving subject"(Oppenheim, 2003: 30). However, this stress on the visual as a prototype is best described "as the substitution of an ontological for an objective (or descriptive) vision"(34), for these writers are not interested in dutifully describing objective reality but in creating concentrated images of existential states. Accordingly, Martin Esslin describes the theatre of the absurd as "a theatre of situation as against a theatre of events in sequence, and therefore it uses language based on patterns of concrete images rather than argument and discursive speech. ... The action in the play of the Theatre of the Absurd is not intended to tell a story but to communicate a pattern of poetic images"(Esslin, 1983: 402-403).

Most Beckett criticism has focused almost exclusively on Beckett's language "variously exposed as anti-language, metalanguage, or metatheatrical language"(Essif, 2001: 3), ignoring the most essential aspect of nouveau théâtre, "the textual design of the character as a corporeal presence and visual image on the stage"(3). Essif proposes a phenomenological approach to Beckett's plays, one that takes into consideration the corporeal existence of the theatrical image in place of the dominant semiotic one. Such an approach is better equipped to examine what Essif regards as the most important contribution of twentieth century dramatists to theatre—their development of "a new poetics of space for the text, one based on emptiness" (19) and the connection that postwar French avant-garde theatre in particular established between empty theatrical space and an empty inner space. This empty inner space accounts for the curiously backward nature of actors' performances in Beckett stage productions: "It is true ... that a surprising number of excellent performances develop, as it were, backwards—beginning with external physical techniques and working inward toward psychological centers"(Kalb, 1989: 39). Beckett's conception of character, which one also recognizes in New Wave cinemas of the 60s, especially in Godard's films, is rooted in the existentialist notion of the subject. Robbe-Grillet's discussion of *Waiting for Godot* points to the existentialist underpinnings of this new conception of character/subject as absolutely free:

> The dramatic character, in most cases, merely plays a role, like the people around us who evade their own existence. In Beckett's play, on the contrary, everything happens as if the two tramps were on stage without having a role. They are there; they must explain themselves. But they do not seem to have a text prepared beforehand and scrupulously learned by heart, to support them. *They must invent. They are free.* (Robbe-Grillet, 1965: 120-121 my italics)

The subject/the fictional character is not the sum of pre-existing motivations of which it is perfectly aware; rather the subject reveals itself through gestures and concrete actions the motives for which, as Sartre argues in *Being and Nothingness*, are posited only retrospectively. Beckett's refusal to answer any questions about the motivation of his characters is a tacit admission that the sheer presence of the actors' bodies on stage, particularly of bodies presented as physically confined and extremely vulnerable, *is* the significant situation.

Beckett's growing preoccupation with the visual or corporeal nature of the stage image, his growing "respect for " 'the naked stage' "(Essif 25), and his minimalist or anti-psychological understanding of character were all part of a general process of self-purging that the arts undertook in the decades after the war, a process that involved the critical re-examination of dramatic, cinematic, and painting conventions, an attempt on the part of each art to return to its origins and evaluate the criteria based on which it had so far differentiated itself from the other arts. Painting investigated its own gestural nature, the phenomenology of color, and the uses of the canvas. Experimental cinema engaged in a sort of obsessive self-cataloging of film techniques, which became its newly found subject matter. Painters stared at the canvas rather than through it, filmmakers stared at the zoom lens instead of seeing the object they were zooming in on, and dramatists stared at the stage rather than at the scene they were supposed to be staging. This fascination with emptiness can be traced back to symbolist theatre (Maurice Maeterlinck's bare stage and minimal sets) and surrealist theatre (the articulation of the empty psyche in Antonin Artaud and Andre Breton).

Ironically, such self-proclaimed abstinence produced an effect that was the exact opposite of the one intended: superself-conscious, self-reflexive works *about* painting (*e.g.,* abstract expressionism), *about* cinema (*e.g.,* structural film), *about* literature (the literature of exhaustion, metafiction), *about* theatre (Beckett's and Ionesco's anti-theatre). While the purpose of this self-purification had been to reaffirm the "essential" differences between the arts, the return to the "origin" merely exposed the falsity of any rigid distinctions between the arts. As cinema took to examining what it believed to be purely cinematic techniques, it deviated from the dominant idea of cinema—a visual medium for telling stories—and explored its own painterly and poetic potential; theatre moved away from the prioritization of characterization through speech and action and, following cinema's example, explored the visual, corporeal aspect of the theatrical image; finally, painting sought to imagine a kind of off-screen (off-frame) space similar to that in cinema (*e.g.,* by foregrounding the act of painting, as in action painting, or by trying to make the spectator's visceral experience of color into a work of art itself). In other words, the so called temporal arts (*e.g.,* cinema and theatre) were in the process of redefining themselves as spatial/visual arts (cinema refused to tell stories and theatre became interested in the architecture of the stage and in the creation of images out of words), while a plastic or spatial art like painting was trying to reclaim its temporal dimension (*e.g.,* abstract expressionism reconceived the painting as an event rather than an object).

Thus, the very preconditions for sense experience—a reader's or spectator's sense of time and space—became the new subject matter of the arts. The result? A "surly discourse" exemplified by Beckett's "inhibited reading" ("a writer who may not wish to be read"), Rothko's "blocked vision" ("a painter, who may not wish to be seen"), and Resnais's "stalled movement" ("a maker of movies in which movement seems designed to immobilize us"(Bersani and Dutoit 4). The "surliness" in question refers to the deliberate de-narrativization of time and space in avant-garde art. Beckett's plays are catalogs of techniques for falsely narrativizing time, sustaining talk despite the absence of anything to talk about. Similarly, space becomes de-narrativized when the very precondition for painting objects—the belief in our ability to distinguish between separate bodies—turns into the object of representation. Under these circumstances, the object of representation merely distracts the viewer from the true work of art, namely the very conditions that make the work of art possible in the first place:

By painting nothing but variations on the form of his surface, Rothko appeared to be making a choice for a visuality from which no subject could distract us: neither the implied narratives of traditional art nor the implicit perceptual realism of cubist distortions nor even, as in Pollock and Kline, the gestural work of the painter himself. It is as if Rothko were taking the painter's framing of space as literally as possible, as an act preparatory to nothing more substantial than a visual focusing ... [thus drawing our attention to] the difficulty of the very act of seeing. (Bersani and Dutoit, 1993: 104)

The new object of avant-garde painting, cinema, and drama is the act of seeing itself.

A long-standing argument in film studies is the idea that movement is essential to cinema. Even more influential has been the belief, often associated with the Soviet school of montage (Eisenstein, Pudovkin, Kuleshov), that editing (rather than simply the movement of people and things before the camera) constitutes the essence of movement in cinema:

I claim that every object, taken from a given viewpoint and shown on the screen to spectators, is a dead object, even though it has moved before the camera. The proper movement of an object before the camera is yet no movement on the screen, it is no more than raw material for the future building-up, by editing, of the movement that is conveyed by the assemblage of the various strips of film. Only if the object be placed together among a number of separate objects, only if it be presented as part of a synthesis of different separate visual images, is it endowed with filmic life. (Pudovkin xiv-xv)

If the supposed "essence" of the cinematic medium has often been identified with editing, the prevalent conception of theatre has given priority to the dramatic significance of language *i.e.,* to its narrative and expressive function. From this point of view, which essentially applies Pudovkin's line of reasoning to theatre, it is only when the words and sentences in a play are assembled in a specific way—so that they express the characters' psychology and push forward the action—that language has been used dramatically. Thus, we find the same implicit assumption underlying the conception of both arts: in both cinema and theatre "development" or "progression" is assumed to be of the utmost importance, whether in the sense of an assemblage of individual shots that acquire their meaning only in virtue of their relationship to other shots (cinema) or in the more oblique sense of dramatic development (theatre).

It is precisely this subordination of the part to the whole, an allegorical conception of art, that the avant-gardes have challenged. The task of avant-garde cinema and theatre has been to liberate the particular—individual shots and sentences—from the expectation of signifying something other than itself.

Paradoxically, precisely by foregrounding the particular image, word, or sentence as meaningful in themselves, avant-garde cinema and theatre aspire to, and achieve, a level of abstraction that would have been impossible to achieve by means of the conventional subordination of the particular to the universal (*e.g.,* of the shot to the sequence, or of the scene to the overall dramatic structure of a play). The reason for this paradox is that by privileging the particular (images and language as "things" rather than as means of representation) avant-garde cinema and theatre become self-reflexive and, therefore, abstract.

When Ionesco wrote *The Bald Soprano* in 1950, he called it an "anti-play," automatically posing the question "What is theatre?" The question "What is ... (cinema, theatre, painting etc.)?" can be paraphrased as "What are the conventions that have developed and determined a particular art, distinguishing it from the other arts?" Faced with the daunting task of defining something as broad as "cinema," "theatre," or "art," it would be helpful to narrow down the object of our definition. Defining first the concept of genre, as a subset of conventions, would illuminate the evolution of a whole art form (cinema or theatre) as a set of conventions. According to one common model of film genre evolution, every genre has its own *lifecycle*: "[G]enres are regularly said to develop, to react, to become self-conscious and to self-destruct"(Schatz, 1981: 21). A genre passes through a phase of self-definition (an experimental phase during which the conventions of the genre are established), followed by a classical stage (relying on audience expectations or, in hermeneutic terms, on existing horizons of interpretations) until, arriving at a self-reflective stage, it grows tired of its own predictability and collapses into self-parody and intertextuality. At this stage a genre tends to exploit the cinematic medium *as a medium*:

> [When] the genre's straightforward message has "saturated" the audience ... the genre evolves into ... the age of refinement ... [and] its transparency gradually gives way to *opacity*: we no longer look *through* the form ... rather we look *at the form itself* to examine and appreciate its structure and its cultural appeal. (38, emphasis in the original)

Self-consciousness is always a later stage in the evolution of a genre or an art form (the development of human consciousness follows the same model: from unreflected to reflected consciousness).

This model of genre evolution can be mapped onto the relationship between theatre and anti-theatre, the difference between which can be conceived as that between showing and telling or between narrating and describing. Given that art becomes self-reflexive when it treats its own material or medium as subject matter, theatre seems to follow this progression from absorption to alienation: anti-theatre, which chronologically follows theatre, works through various techniques of alienation, intentionally not allowing the audience to become absorbed in the spectacle. The evolution of cinema, however, goes not from absorption to alienation, but from alienation (theatricality, pictorialism) to absorption (the narrativization of cinema as a result of the development of editing), with elements of pictorialism or theatricality popping up at later stages (*e.g.,* special effects as a sort of throwback to the pictorialism of silent cinema). What facilitates the absorption of the audience in a temporal piece of art is time itself or, more precisely, delay. Both narrative cinema and traditional theatre work through delay, the delay of future events and thus of the significance of events currently represented. To be "absorbed" means to experience filmic or dramatic time on analogy with one's own duration (one's unreflective experience of time). Whenever the flow of time is arrested on the stage or on the screen, the spectator is prevented from spontaneously drawing such an analogy and instead is made aware of his own duration. When time is arrested in anti-plays, the effect is, therefore, unavoidably paradoxical: time "stops" or one has the impression that nothing is happening but, at the same time, one becomes aware of one's internal time which usually remains outside reflective consciousness. *Waiting for Godot* dramatizes this experience (in this sense Beckett's play is a kind of meta-play). Usually, when we are waiting for something, our attention is directed towards the thing we are waiting for. In an anti-play, however, the act of waiting shifts our attention from the object of waiting to that which prevents us from getting to it. Insofar as waiting already implies an object or a goal, while, on the other hand, an anti-play provides no such object or goal, one could say that an anti-play focuses our attention on that which *prevents us from waiting even as we are waiting,* namely language.

Despite the different paths cinema and theatre have followed—from absorption to alienation (theatre) and from alienation to absorption (cinema)—film history and criticism have always been inextricably connected to theatre history and criticism. In her essay "Film and Theatre" Susan Sontag writes:

> The history of cinema is often treated as the history of its emancipation from theatrical models. First of all from theatrical "frontality" (the unmoving camera reproducing the situation of the spectator of a play fixed in his seat), then from theatrical acting (gestures needlessly stylized, exaggerated—needlessly because now the actor could be seen 'close up'), then from theatrical furnishings (unnecessary "distancing" of the audience's emotions, disregarding the opportunity to immerse the audience in reality). Movies are regarded as advancing from theatrical stasis to cinematic fluidity, from theatrical artificiality to cinematic naturalness and immediacy. (Sontag, 1979: 359)

She goes on to argue against the common, biased view of cinema as "the art of the authentic"(362) and of theatre as the art of pretense. Although these ideas are meant to support Sontag's larger argument—a defense of experimental film—her reflections on the theatrical and the cinematic prefigure Tom Gunning's more recent critique of the evolutionary approach to the history and theory of cinema according to which "the development of film ... usually takes the dramatic form of a liberation of film from a false homology that restricted it to the technological reproduction of theatre"(Gunning, 2004: 42). Gunning's work on silent cinema aims at disabusing viewers and film scholars of what he calls the "cinematic" and "narrative" assumptions that have thus far dominated film scholarship, especially that portion of it which explores the relationship between cinema and theatre. According to the cinematic assumption, cinema discovered its purely cinematic essence only when filmmakers began moving the camera thereby transcending the artlessness of early films, which were nothing more than static shots of a single, continuous, usually repetitive action (for example, waves breaking on the beach, workers leaving the factory, passengers waiting for the train, etc). According to the narrative assumption, which became dominant through Christian Metz's semiological writing on cinema, "cinema only truly appeared when it discovered the mission of telling stories"(Gunning 42). Jean Mitry was instrumental in establishing the narrative assumption when he defined silent cinema "as a struggle between theatricality and narrativity" (Mitry qtd. in Gunning 42).

"Theatricality" in silent cinema refers to the "foregrounding of the act of display" (42) at the expense of narrative development. Classical (narrative) cinema and "the cinema of attractions" (Gunning's term "attractions" refers to any non-narrative material) address and construct the spectator very differently. In the classical paradigm, "the spectator is rarely acknowledged, an attitude exemplified by the stricture against the actor's look or gestures at the camera/spectator"(43-44). The classical spectator is thus "modeled on the voyeur, who watches in secret, without the scene he watches acknowledging his presence"(44). A perfect instance of this would be the construction of the spectator through the continuity system of editing in Hitchcock's *Rear Window*. On the other hand, "attractions" "invoke an exhibitionist rather than a voyeuristic regime"(44). The "attractions" of silent cinema—for example, the extreme close up of the gun in *The Great Train Robbery*—are "displayed with the immediacy of a 'Here it is! Look at it!'"(44). They draw attention to themselves by refusing to be subordinated to, and dissolved in, a narrative structure. It is namely in this respect that anti-theatre—specifically Beckett's and Ionesco's anti-theatre or theatre of the absurd—is reminiscent of silent cinema: images in silent cinema do not obey the law of narrative and, similarly, language in anti-theatre does not obey the law of dramatic, narrative development. While "[a]ttractions' fundamental hold on spectators depends on arousing and satisfying visual curiosity through a direct and acknowledged act of display, rather than following a narrative enigma within a diagetic site into which the spectator peers invisibly"(Gunning 44) , the hold anti-theatre has on spectators depends on arousing and satisfying their linguistic curiosity through foregrounding the structure, form, and rhythm of words, phrases, sentences and their relationship with one another (most often a jarring one, as in non sequiturs, puns, repetitions, etc.)

This is not to say that in anti-theatre there is no narrative enigma or no dramatic action; rather, the drama no longer takes place on the level of character psychology but on the level of language itself. When we are following a typical narrative enigma (one driven by character psychology and, at the same time, driving character development) we ask "what happens next?" We make predictions about possible outcomes based on our knowledge of the characters and the story so far. But can we still talk of "events" when the drama takes place on the level of language? Is an event necessarily something that happens to a character and demands interpretation? An "event," in the common sense of the term, carries with it a certain understanding of temporality. An event presupposes a "before" and an "after," and an implicit distinction between objective and subjective, or real and unreal: there is always more than one possible interpretation of an event. However, when we are reading or watching anti-plays like those of Ionesco or Beckett, we cannot really say that we are waiting for something and this is precisely the paradox of a play like *Waiting for Godot*. What we are doing while we are reading Beckett's play is the very opposite of waiting: because we have no knowledge of the characters, we cannot predict what they will do next, or explain why they are doing whatever it is they are doing. What we are waiting for in *The Bald Soprano* is for a certain line of reasoning to unfold, not for characters to communicate something to one another. For instance, in the scene in which the Martins are trying to remember where they have seen each other, it is the momentum of language itself that drives the story forward rather than the motivation of the two characters. There is an entirely different temporality at play here: our attention is on the present (and thus on the "material" of the play *i.e.,* its language); our attention span is foreshortened. Insofar as an interpretation of an event is the difference between the anticipation and the memory of the event, in an anti-play, which does not make this sort of distinction, events coincide with their interpretations. One cannot "interpret," in the common sense of the word, lines such as the following:

Potatoes are very good fried in fat; the salad oil was not rancid. The oil from the grocer at the corner is of better quality than the oil from the grocer across the street. It is even better than the oil from the grocer at the bottom of the street. (Ionesco, 1958: 9).

There is nothing ambiguous about these lines. The anti-play achieves a level of specificity and transparency atypical of traditional drama: since everything is in the language, and language is on display, there are no hidden meanings or interpretations. And yet, there is something diffuse in this kind of signification. It is generally agreed, among film semioticians, that cinematic signifieds are far more diffuse or less articulated than literary ones. Statements in an anti-play are very specific, not revealing a deeper meaning, not withholding anything from us, but because of the lack of traditional cause and effect relations between them it is difficult to say what the play as a whole "means." Thus, despite the transparency and specificity of its language, the way in which an anti-play "means" is closer to cinematic than to literary signification. However, this sort of diffuseness is different from ambiguity: ambiguity implies the proliferation and destabilization of meanings whereas diffuseness implies the impossibility to phrase a meaning. The paradox of the anti-play lies in the fact that although it works through fairly discrete and recognizable units—specific, self-evident statements—it nevertheless produces the impression of something vague and abstract. Thus, if we were to summarize a play by Ionesco, we would be forced to make a very general and ultimately meaningless statement such as, for example, "*The Lesson* is about the impossibility of communication."

If it's true that an anti-play tends towards cinematic (rather than linguistic) signification, perhaps it's not so strange that what Ionesco calls anti-theatre bears a striking resemblance to Gunning's "cinema of attractions." Someone might object to approaching post-war theatre as a kind of a "reference" or "return" to the origins of a much younger art, cinema. However, a similar argument has been made by various film critics with respect to avant-garde films. For instance, in "Primitivism and the Avant-Gardes: A Dialectical Approach" Noël Burch lists some of the elements avant-garde films share with so called "primitive" (silent) cinema: the acentered image (no single portion of the image is privileged over others); the "artlessness" or "flatness" of the image due to the immobility of the camera and the minimal variation in the angle or distance from which subjects are shot; the merely "behavioral" (rather than psychological) presence of the people on screen; the nonclosure of films most of which were often looped during exhibition (Burch, 1986: 486-488). Beckett's and Ionesco's anti-plays employ many of these "primitive" strategies, though in a self-conscious manner: acentered language (no single portion of a statement or no piece of dialogue is privileged over others *i.e.,* all statements have equal dramatic significance); acentered performance (no gesture is priviliged over others: the old dictum "the movements of the body express the movements of the soul" is absolutely foreign to anti-theatre which refuses to treat the body as a mere signifier of "internal" psychological development); indeterminate ending (reminiscent of the film loop); and, finally, interchangeable characters and/or a lack of character development—the theatrical "equivalent" of the minimal variation in the angle and distance from which cinematic subjects are shot and of their purely behavioral presence.

The objectification of the human body in "primitive" cinema, especially in slapstick comedy (the human body treated as purely material rather than as an expression of a particular mental space) is structurally similar to the objectification of language in anti-theatre, which frequently treats words literally rather than as vehicles of some transcendental meaning or as expressions of a particular personality. Chaplin and Keaton often produce the effect of the absurd by attributing the same functions and/or personal expectations to a range of different objects and people: they treat everything and everyone as if they were the same, mixing and mismatching objects and their functions (*e.g.,* Chaplin's *The Pawnshop*). Thus, both slapstick comedy and the anti-play rely on the continuous dissociation of objects (material objects, words, or bodies) from their functions (the uses specific to an object, the meaning specific to a word, the voice embodied in a particular body). However, while slapstick comedy performs such dissociations playfully, the anti-play refuses to "return" functions to their respective objects/words/bodies. In the work of Ionesco and Beckett the carnivalesque never fulfills its liberating promise the way it does in Chaplin's films and in Dada nonsense poetry. Although the carnivalesque and the grotesque have their place in anti-theatre (hence the importance of the clown figure in Beckett's work), they remain trapped within an existentialist framework that obstructs the celebration of the absurd. Nonsense or flights of absurdity and ridiculousness in Dada poetry conceal a therapeutic purpose that is ultimately missing from anti-theatre.

While in Beckett's anti-plays there is a strong connection between the corporeal presence on the stage (in Essif's terms "an empty figure on an empty stage") and the empty mental space of characters (as opposed to realistic psychological portraits "stuffed" with clear character motivations), the corporeality of early cinema does not make this connection: it is simply interested in what must have, at least in the beginning, appeared as an almost magical process of the technical reproduction of three-dimensional bodies on a two-dimensional surface. The corporeality of silent cinema does not suggest the metaphysical and psychological emptiness that pervades nouveau theatre, but simply celebrates the realistic reproduction of bodies apart from any mental space that can be associated with them. Chaplin's and Keaton's clownish characters do not yet anticipate Beckett's hyperconscious marionette-character, the "übermarionette" whose essential characteristics include "its relative immobility (instead of either dynamic acrobatics or "normal" social or biological motion and gesture); its central … detached and highlighted presence on stage (instead of an interactive relationship with other characters); and consequently, its focus on the head as a metaphorical empty space (instead of the mimetic—ideological or psychological—focus on the whole body"(Essif 184).

Joining forces with Tom Gunning and Noël Burch in challenging the traditional analysis of silent cinema as a "primitive" phase in the evolution of cinema, Thomas Elsaesser notes that what is striking about silent cinema, particularly the films of Lumière, "was neither the realism nor the magic of the images, but [their] extreme artificiality ... their sophisticated mise-en-scene, the exactly calculated camera placements"(Elsaesser, 1998: 52), in a word their highly stylized or theatrical aspect. Two of the features of early Lumière films to which Elsaesser draws our attention are the use of depth and space and the distinction between off-screen and off-frame or between imaginary space and real space (56). What appear to be simple films, for instance *Arrival of a Train*, are in fact not plotless at all; their narrative emerges from the purely visual manipulation of space and depth of field. Similarly, even if it seems as though nothing happens in Beckett's or Ionesco's anti-plays, they are not undramatic. In *The Bald Soprano*, which consists of purely declarative statements (in fact, it's a kind of meta-dialogue: Mrs. Smith, for example, speaks in the first person singular but her speech sounds as first and third person singular *at the same time*; she, and all the other characters, always seem to be talking *about* what they are talking about, as if they were their own literary critics), the drama is precisely the falling apart of declarative speech, the impossibility of declarative statements to link to one another. The opaqueness of language is dramatized, paradoxically, through its reduction to its most basic, supposedly unproblematic use (the declarative one). Another feature of early films Elsaesser points to is what he calls "the structural principle" (exemplified in the film *Boat Leaving the Harbour*), which forces the viewer to distinguish between off-screen and off-frame. The opaqueness of language in Ionesco's plays has an analogous effect of making us aware of the distinction between language as a thing and language as a means of communication.

Another interesting parallel between early films and anti-plays is their circularity or nonclosure. Elsaesser explains circularity in early cinema by pointing to a specific socio-historical fact, namely the fact that Lumière's films were exhibited as part of a variety programme *i.e.,* they were supposed to be seen over and over again (57). Many of Beckett's and Ionesco's plays also rely on repetition or looping: in *Waiting for Godot* the protagonists decide to move and then do not move, over and over again; the two sets of families in *The Bald Soprano* become interchangeable at the end of the play; the professor gets ready to kill, in the course of a lesson in philology, the next student in *The Lesson*. The nonclosure of such plays is anti-theatre's own way of approximating what André Bazin considers the basic principle of cinema, "the denial of any frontiers to action"(Bazin, 1967: 105). (Bazin is referring to the infinity of off-screen space, which he contrasts with the circumscribed space of the stage flanked by wings and thus foregrounding the machinery of illusion.) The plays' flagrant disregard for any kind of an ending or resolution, on the level of narrative, mimics the infinity of action that cinema achieves on the level of space. Thus, a feature of the cinematic medium itself (the ontology of the film image) becomes a theme in anti-theatre: as we cross from one art to another, a technique of representation transforms into an object of representation.

The continuity between silent cinema and theatre is the subject of Ben Brewster's and Lea Jacobs' recent book *Theatre to Cinema*, in which they argue that "much nineteenth and early twentieth century theatre was characterized by a situational and pictorial approach to narrative"(Brewster and Jacobs, 1997: 212). The authors take up A. Nicholas Vardac's argument, in *Stage to Screen: Theatrical Origins of Early Film From Garrick to Griffith*, that "a large part of nineteenth-century theatre was cinema manqué"(Brewster and Jacobs 6). Considering theatre as part of a larger cultural project which demands a greater realism in the arts, Vardac argues that the development of cinematic technologies has resolved the problems of achieving a realistic representation in theatre. Brewster and Jacobs (like Susan Sontag) challenge the idea that the history of cinema is one of a steady emancipation from theatrical models:

> [R]ather than seeing the theatre as striving to be cinematic [as Vardac did], to be what the cinema was, as it were, automatically, we believe that the cinema strove to be theatrical, or to assimilate a particular theatrical tradition, that of pictorialism (214).

They insist that both theatre and cinema demand spectacle as such, rather than realism:

> 'Spectacle' described a kind of staging that appealed primarily to the eye, and what appealed to the eye was conceived in terms of painting rather than photography (8).

Challenging the dominant idea that the most essential part of theatre is the dramatic text (a view as old as Aristotle), the authors demonstrate the way in which the pictorial effect in theatre informed the evolution of silent cinema. Using the term "theatrical pictorialism" to describe a certain kind of address in which the spectator is not absorbed by the play or the film, they take issue with Diderot's idea of the absorbing tableau, and claim instead that nineteenth century theatre—and later silent cinema "solicit attention ... either apparently engaging the viewers (addressing them by look or gesture), or revealing the self-consciousness that suggests an awareness of the regard of an unacknowledged viewer"(10). Insofar as Brewster's and Jacobs' purpose is to liberate this sort of "theatricality"—what they call "the coup de théâtre"—from its disparaging interpretation, in their discourse "tableau" or "picture" become associated with the anti-absorptive sense of the word that emerged in the eighteenth century. Not surprisingly, Gunning's notion of "a cinema of attractions" figures prominently in Brewster's and Jacobs' discussion of "theatrical pictorialism. " The connection between anti-theatre and theatrical pictorialism might not be obvious. There are two ways in which such a connection can be established. First, like silent cinema, anti-theatre is anti-absorptive. Second, whereas in the case of silent cinema "theatrical display" refers literally to the visual aspect of cinema, to the foregrounding of the image (in the absence of editing techniques which will eventually push cinema in the direction of narrative), in anti-theatre the effect of "theatricality" is metaphorical. Language is foregrounded, rather than images, and yet the foregrounding of language has the effect of "flattening" it in such as way that it becomes "pictorial" in a metaphorical sense; it becomes opaque or decorative rather than expressive or dramatic.

Another term Brewster and Jacobs use to talk about theatre and early cinema, in conjunction with the notion of "tableau" or "picture," is "situation." Situations are not actions:

> Situations exist on the cusp of actions; they give rise to actions and are in turn altered by them. ... To think of a story in terms of situations, as opposed to a series of obstacles, grants a certain autonomy to each discrete state of affairs (23-24).

Actions have a past (actions that led up to them) and a future (actions that will follow from them), while a situation is more episodic and thus more self-sufficient. Insofar as situation cannot be subsumed under the laws of narrative, I would argue that in anti-theatre language follows a situational kind of logic: we are presented with a certain linguistic situation—for example, repetition—which then simply unfolds to its (ir)rational conclusion. This happens quite often in Ionesco's *The Bald Soprano*, a play rich in "linguistic situations": analogy, inversion, deduction, induction, contradiction, etc. Ionesco is more interested in enumerating possible outcomes of various logical procedures (drawing an analogy, formulating a hypothesis based on inductive or deductive reasoning, etc.) than in characterization. By analogy with Brewster's and Jacobs' idea of "situation dramaturgy," Ionesco's plays provide us with an example of "linguistic dramaturgy": the drama originates not in the characters' minds but in the structure of the language they use. Characters are "individualized" through the particular kinds of linguistic situations assigned to them in what seems to be a random fashion. For example, if we sense a tension between Mr. and Mrs. Smith when they argue whether or not there is always someone, or never anyone, outside the door when the door bell rings (aha, we say to ourselves, here is a psychological—marital—problem), this is merely the tension inherent in any self-contradictory hypothesis produced through inductive reasoning. What appears to be a "conflict" between husband and wife has nothing to do with their personalities but results from the inevitable failure of language to represent, and thus account for, the messy, self-contradictory empirical evidence with which we are confronted every day.

In traditional theatre characters are endowed with a certain psychological make up, which becomes transparent through their performance on the stage (gestures, voice, etc.) and through the narrative their performance puts in motion. In anti-theatre language no longer expresses the inner life of characters and neither does it move forward a chain of causally related events. The excessive verbosity of anti-plays assigns language a pictorial function and locates the drama in the excessive banality of the situation. In *The Bald Soprano*, for instance, the drama originates in the banal (purely adjectival) situation with which we are presented in the stage directions for the first scene, which describe both the characters and the setting simply as "English." Insofar as a "situation" foreshortens time, it is similar to Lessing's notion of "the pregnant moment": it contains in itself the causes that led up to it and the possible consequences that will follow from it (Brewster and Jacobs 11). Like "tableau," with which it is closely related, a "situation" interrupts the narrative: it freezes time into an image that captures the significance (emotional, narrative, or allegorical) of the entire work. A "tableau" or a "situation" are characterized by flatness and self-sufficiency, as opposed to depth and transparency. Inasmuch as in a tableau everything is given, displayed, foregrounded, the tableau is anti-absorbing: by drawing attention to itself, it addresses the spectator in such a way as to make him self-conscious of his own act of looking (conversely, any sort of narrative development absorbs the spectator: editing distracts our attention from the individual shots, from their pictorial nature, directing it instead to the relation between them).

In the anti-plays of Ionesco and Beckett, then, language becomes pictorial or tableau-esque. One might object that a tableau freezes time whereas many of these plays rely on the trope of repetition, which seems to be temporal in nature. In fact, repetition is the perfect example of the freezing of language, analogous to the freezing of narrative action in a tableau. Take the exchange between Mr. and Mrs. Smith in *The Bald Soprano*, for instance. Following a long series of coincidences, recounted in exhaustive and exhausting detail and in an intentionally annoying repetitive pattern (the same sentence structure, even the same sentences are repeated: "How curious! How bizarre! What a coincidence!") the two come to the logical conclusion that they are married. If we have been attentive enough, we realize early on that they are married, so that the rest of the exchange adds nothing to what we already suspect. As a result, the words the Smiths keep repeating become opaque, no longer transmitting information or pushing the action forward, but simply foregrounding more and more the absurdity of the situation. The characters realize that they are married only because of the force of logic (which is to say language) *i.e.* they are married only if (and insofar as) their marriage can be logically deduced rather than lived. Reading or hearing their exchange does not provide us with a sense of discovery (either that they are gradually discovering their identities or that we are gradually discovering their identities) but rather with a sense of a self-fulfilling prophecy: given the logical connections between successive statements, it is inevitable that the two characters will turn out to be married. The correct grammatical structure of sentences outweighs in importance the meaning of what is being said. Thus, Mrs. Smith talks, in the same breath, of her children and the food she had for dinner ("Helen is like me: she's a good manager, thrifty, plays the piano. She never asks to drink English beer. She's like our little daughter who drinks only milk and eats only porridge .... She's named Peggy. The quince and bean pie was marvelous"(Ionesco 10)) , mixes words of different semantic registers in a grammatically correct way ("Yogurt is excellent for the stomach, the kidneys, the appendicitis, and apotheosis"(10) (the place of a word in a sentence is more important than the word itself: apotheosis is a noun, like appendicitis), and reasons in a circle (when her husband asks why Parker died whereas his doctor lived, she answers ("Because the operation was successful in the doctor's case and it was not in Parker's"(10)) (the implication being that as long as a statement is formulated as an answer—"Because …"—it is an answer, even if doesn't answer the question at all). Throughout the play the validity and significance of what is said is determined by the vague appearance of logic, which rests on the grammatical correctness of statements. When a character is asked to draw a conclusion from a set of facts, what matters is that his/her ideas take the believable form of a conclusion ("All doctors are quacks. And all patients too. Only the Royal Navy is honest in England"); the content of the conclusion itself is unimportant. Similarly, when Mr. Smith draws an analogy between the doctor's relationship to his patients and the captain's relationship to his ship, one need only announce that one is drawing an analogy in order to accept the conclusion, however false, based on the analogy.

A situation is complete from the very beginning. Consider the opening of *The Bald Soprano*:

> There, it's nine o'clock. We've drunk the soup, and eaten the fish and chips, and the English salad. The children have drunk English water. We've eaten well this evening. That's because we live in the suburbs of London and because our name is Smith"(Ionesco 9).

Although these lines of dialogue make reference to several "events" (the family members have had dinner: a specific list of unspecific food items is provided as "evidence") these events are not "actions" in the traditional sense of the term. The attribution of the same adjective-"English" -to all of them renders the events representative of a whole lifestyle rather than being specific events that have taken place on a particular day. A situation can be summarized: there are dictionaries listing possible situations. The situation with which *The Bald Soprano* opens can be summarized as "middle class life in the English suburbs." Not only are the characters themselves merely representative of a particular social class, rather than individuals, but (and here lies the absurdity) they are aware of their own abstract, representative nature ("That's because we live in the suburbs of London and because our name is Smith"). Thus, the situation, like the tableau on the level of language, also works on the principle of foregrounding. In the example above, the description of the scene includes its own interpretation (in fact, the author's interpretation, which he presents as the characters' own self-awareness). A "situation," unlike an "action," is self-reflexive precisely on account of its generality.

***

Between 1998 and 2001 a team of nineteen filmmakers were involved in the project *Beckett on Film*, whose ambitious purpose was to put Beckett's nineteen plays on film. Fortunately, none of the films suffer from what André Bazin disapprovingly calls "the urge 'to make cinema'"(Bazin, 1967: 86). The filmmakers involved in the project do not pretend to be making movies; they do not ask us to forget the conventions of theatre. Here it is useful to recall Bazin's comment on Laurence Olivier's film adaptation of *Henry V*: "We are not in the play, we are in an historical film about the Elizabethan theatre. ... Our enjoyment of the play however is not of the kind we would get from an historical documentary"(88). Similarly, *Beckett on Film* makes us feel as though we were watching a film about Beckett's theatre. Cinema is used to foreground, rather than hide, theatrical conventions, the result of which is, as Bazin says of Jean Cocteau's films, that "[o]ne is no longer adapting a subject. One is staging a play by means of cinema"(93). These film adaptations are premised on the understanding that Beckett's stage directions are part of the text itself, that the text is already performative. Beckett's plays are synthetic: intonation, gesture, rhythm, speed of delivery, light, shadow, projection of voice, movement are all integrally connected: slightly altering one shifts the overall effect of the play. In this respect, Beckett as a playwright comes very close to the film auteur.

One of the arguments put forward by the critics of the project *Beckett on Film* is that the film director imposes his or her own interpretation of the play by merely choosing one particular kind of shot over another, one particular angle over another, etc. The filmmaker can crop the image of the actor whichever way he or she wants so that what the film viewer gets is a reinterpretation of the play rather than the play itself. Interestingly, all examples the critic gives in support of his argument have something to do with the representation of the human body on screen. Supposedly, the film version of a play is more subjective than its stage production and a large part of this difference is due to the filmmaker's greater freedom to manipulate the actors' bodies. The implication is that since an actor's body is always in full view on stage, a common ground is established between the points of views of all theatre goers: even if they see the body from different perspectives, depending on where they are sitting, they still see the same body in its entirety. This least common denominator supposedly grants a certain fundamental objectivity to the representation and its reception. Starting from an erroneous assumption—that the way in which a body behaves on stage is not a matter of directorial choice but something "given"—this criticism suggests that cinema is intrinsically more subjective than theatre. This line of reasoning suffers from the same faults that undermine the Bazinian notion of cinema as having a purely indexical relationship to reality: the idea that the human body on stage does not differ from the human body off stage, that it is an objectively existing thing rather than a representation, is not, in the end, very different from the idea that the film image is an "imprint" of reality rather than a representation.

The intriguing thing about the argument put forward by the detractors of the project *Beckett on Film* is that it reverses the relationship between cinema and theatre: contrary to the popular belief that cinema is less "theatrical" than theatre, it suggests that theatre is more realistic than cinema, that cinema is more "theatrical" than theatre because on top of the supposedly "raw" material with which theatre works, cinema adds a second level of articulation or signification, that of film techniques. This implies that while there can be a semiotics of cinema, there cannot be a semiotics of theatre (or at least that the semiotics of theatre is "borrowed" from the semiotics of the written text from which the stage production, supposedly, never strays) simply because theatre "deals" with real human bodies and bodies, supposedly, cannot function as signs. Leaving aside the fact that a stage production of a play is as far removed from the text of the play as the film adaptation is removed from the stage production, I want to argue not only that a semiotics of the theatre is possible but, more specifically, that the aesthetic of anti-theatre (the theatre of Ionesco and Beckett) recalls the aesthetic of silent cinema, although there is also an important distinction to be made between the two art forms: the pictorial nature of silent cinema is a sort of display that provokes in the viewer a sense of pleasure and control over the representation, whereas the pictorial nature of anti-theatre underscores the opacity of the representation and the frustration we feel in trying to penetrate it.

In other words, a distinction needs to be made between the naïvely pictorial and the self-reflexively pictorial.

How do we explain the similarities between *silent* cinema, on one hand, and the *garrulous* plays of an author like Beckett? Are the film adaptations of Beckett's plays merely silent films with added sound or is there something of the aesthetic of silent cinema in the plays themselves? The plays share with silent cinema a preoccupation with the very material of each respective art form: images in silent cinema, language in Beckett's plays. Thus, despite the verbal nature of Beckett's work, language in his plays achieves a pictorial effect not unlike that produced by the foregrounding of the visible (rather than the signifying) aspect in silent cinema. Beckett's verbal excess borders on a kind of muteness, perhaps an effect of the typically Beckettian approach to drama and performance, which, as Enoch Brater argues, are never separated in Beckett's work: "'Text' ... at least as Beckett has been redefining it since *Not I*, collapses our traditional way of thinking about drama as something separate and distinct from performance" (Brater, 1987: 4). As long as what is said (drama) remains separate from the act of saying it (performance) we are still in the domain of signification. It's only when speech and its delivery become one that language becomes "mute": it is mute precisely because it says everything, including the fact that it is saying it.

The film adaptations of Beckett's plays are reminiscent of silent cinema in the faithfulness with which they avoid intricate camera movements or, as some of them do, any sort of camera movement at all. It's generally agreed that what separates film from theatre is the mobility of the point of view in film, a mobility that filmmakers, however, did not immediately explore: for the first decade in the development of cinema, the camera remained stationary, recreating the fixed point of view of the theatre viewer. The film adaptations of Beckett's plays do not attempt to dynamize or mobilize the spectator's point of view (panning or traveling shots are almost entirely absent). The camera does not explore the film space but remains distanced from it, underscoring further the pictorial effect of the film image. And this makes perfect sense when one considers what the plays are trying to represent: by intentionally immobilizing the film viewer's point of view and ignoring the wide range of tools available to the filmmaker to achieve a peripatetic point of view, the films facilitate our identification with the intellectually, emotionally and physically immobilized characters of Beckett's plays. Of course, one would argue that the stage productions of these plays achieve the same effect much more easily since the point of view of the theatre viewer is naturally immobilized. And this is precisely the point: in theatre the spectator's immobilized viewpoint is taken for granted, but when it's employed in cinema, an art that works precisely through the opposite means of mobilizing the spectator's viewpoint, it draws attention to itself and heightens our identification with the characters.

The artlessness of silent cinema Noël Burch analyzes in his article on avant-garde cinema is readily observable in the film adaptation of Beckett's *Happy Days*, for example. Throughout the film—the film consists of a long monologue, which the protagonist delivers half-buried in the sand in the middle of the desert with nothing else in sight but her bag, an umbrella, and a gun—there are absolutely no camera movements. We cut from extreme long shots of the protagonist buried in the sand, to medium shots and, toward the end of the film, to extreme close ups of her face. The image remains intentionally flat—the foreground and the background are always in perfect focus. The only cutting takes place between shots of different distances or different angles but there is no expressive cutting, for example cutting on a certain sentence or word to underscore its significance. Thus there is nothing to guide the viewer, to tell him where to look or when to pay more attention. Just as in silent cinema images are noncentered—no portion of an image is more significant than another—so in this film adaptation of Beckett's play, no cut (be it from a long shot to a medium shot, or from a low angle to a higher angle) is more significant than another. The lack of expressiveness in cutting is matched by a similar lack of expressiveness or suggestiveness in the manipulation of image and sound. As we cut from a longer shot to a medium one and then go back to a longer shot, the protagonist's monologue continues: it becomes separated from the character and sounds as distant from her as it is from us. Since the voice continues to be heard even when the protagonist is barely visible in the distance (in a very long shot), it loses its expressiveness and begins to sound like a voiceover. This de-linking of sound and image is reminiscent of the use of captions in silent cinema.

Even though *Happy Days* is a long monologue, and in this sense an instance of verbosity rather than muteness, it resembles silent cinema in terms of acting style. In silent cinema, the actor uses his or her whole body (in a sense the body in silent cinema fulfills the function of the voice in sound cinema). In *Happy Days*, there are no "events" in the traditional sense of the word: the events happen only on the level of language and are thus registered only as imperceptible shifts in the protagonist's facial expression, in the intonation of her voice, in the rhythm of her delivery. Thus, while in silent cinema the entire body of the actor compensates for the lack of sound, in the film adaptation of Beckett's play the face of the protagonist compensates for the lack of narrative action in the traditional sense of the word. Similarly, in Ionesco's plays drama is rhetorical rather than psychological: *The Bald Soprano* escalates into a cacophony of meaningless dialogue while *The Chairs* ends in muteness.

Anthony Minghella's adaptation of Beckett's play entitled *Play* (a sort of love triangle melodrama consisting of three characters' monologues carefully edited together) opens with an overtly self-referential gesture that mimics the meta-theatre or anti-theatre aspect of Beckett's own play: the film opens with a long film leader, cut and scratched here and there, until we get to the first shot, an omniscient crane shot of a field of enormous urns in which are trapped men and women incessantly talking, whispering, or yelling their banal story of marital infidelity. Again mimicking the act of foregrounding that is constitutive of Beckett's meta-theatre (the play is called *Play*), the film keeps foregrounding its own status as a film by interrupting itself to insert another long piece of film leader and by foregrounding the sound of the film equipment used in the shooting of the film (the monologues of the three characters are accompanied by the unmistakable sounds of cameras clicking and/or zooming). The same act of foregrounding takes place in *Acts Without Words I*. "Action" in this film take place literally on a film roll which we watch unroll across the screen (with the equally literal soundtrack of a film projector) in the beginning of the film. Three film frames spread across the screen and two characters take turns moving, literally, from one film frame to the next, even as their literal, foregrounded movement reminds us of the same movement of film shots that we don't notice but thanks to which we are able to watch the film within the film. The film within the film mimics the aesthetic of early silent film: faded colors, spasmodic and mechanical physical movements, repetitive soundtrack.

Another way in which Beckett's plays, and their film adaptations, return to silent cinema than to theatre has to do with the role of the actor. According to Bazin, "in the theater the drama proceeds from the actor, in the cinema it goes from the décor to man"(102). This distinction does not apply to Ionesco's and Beckett's anti-plays, in which character psychology plays such a minor role, or no role at all, and characters become as important—or rather as unimportant— as the mise-en-scene. This becomes particularly evident in plays that underscore the characters' literal (and metaphorical) immobility. Characters are presented as trapped, either in certain linguistic structures (such as the structure of repetition in *The Bald Soprano*) or literally trapped (as the protagonist in *Happy Days*, buried half-way in the sand, or the characters in *Play*, trapped in ancient urns). The décor in these plays no longer fulfills a secondary, decorative function: it functions both as the immediate setting for the unfolding action and, at the same time, as a sort of character in its own right. The relegation of the actor to a secondary role is taken to the extreme in the film version of *Not I*, where we see the actress (Julianne Moore) , only for a second, the rest of the film consisting of a series of close ups of her mouth. In a way Beckett's plays disprove Bazin's argument that the human, which he identifies with the verbal, play a central role in theatre and a secondary one in cinema. Discussing Racine, Shakespeare and Molière, Bazin notes that "[w]hat is specifically theatrical about these tragedies is not their action so much as the human, that is to say the verbal, priority given to their dramatic structure"(106). While it is correct to emphasize the verbal priority given to the dramatic structure of Beckett's plays, the verbal is by no means equivalent to the human. The verbosity of Beckett's characters does not have the effect of producing highly individual human beings who want to express themselves. In fact, the more a character speaks—even about himself or herself—the less we know about them (thus, many of Beckett's characters are interchangeable). We focus on the cadences of their speech, on its rhetorical features, and we know next to nothing about their motivation, or their individual past. We are interested in the speech, not in who is speaking. This is why privileging the verbal is not necessarily privileging the human. The more performative drama becomes (and in Beckett's case drama and performance are one), the less it is concerned with individual psychology. In this sense, performance (and performative speech) is pictorial: it does not aim at revealing the interior life of characters.

When asked how the film versions of Beckett's plays differ from the stage productions, most actors and directors involved in the project *Beckett on Film* underscore the differences in terms of acting: whereas on stage actors are expected to project their voices in order to be heard, on the screen, a more "intimate" medium, their performance is toned down, sounding more "naturalistic." For example, the female protagonist of *Happy Days* does not project her voice but rather chatters to herself. A common thread running through the actors' and directors' comments is a general agreement that a film version of a Beckett play is more intense, more dynamic, more intimate than a stage version. Interestingly, the intensity in question is that of the human voice. For example, Neil Jordan points out that a stage production of a play like *Not I*, which is concerned with speech, cannot produce the same intensity as the film simply because a mouth on the stage would be too small and inaudible, whereas the film can isolate the mouth in an extreme close up. In the film *Not I* the dramatic action of the play unfolds through abrupt cuts between a series of close ups of the mouth, shot from different angles, the subtle contortions of facial muscles, the movements of the lips, the rhythm of the mouth opening and closing. Insofar as we can make the generalization that Beckett's plays are about language, the film *Not I* captures what is most essentially theatrical about Beckett's play better than the stage production. On stage the foregrounding of language as a thing rather than as a means of expression and communication can be achieved only indirectly, for example through intentionally minimizing the role of other elements such as the set design or the actors' physical movement. Minimal physical movement and a minimal set force the viewer to focus on the verbal exchange between characters (of course one could argue the other way around as well: it's because characters talk interminably that everything else sinks into the background). The close up in cinema, however, allows this interminable chatter to be presented directly, with a greater intensity.

This is the case not only in *Not I*, but also in other monologues such as *Rockeby* (which consists of a steady, rhythmical cutting back and forth between a close up and a medium shot of the heroine, and between a frontal and side shot of her, the rhythm of the cutting mirroring the rhythm of the rocking chair), *Ohio Impromptu* (in which the camera starts outside the room and gradually waltzes closer and closer around the character(s)), *Play* (which works through spasmodic cuts between close ups of the three characters), and *Happy Days* (which begins with an extreme long shot and ends with an extreme close up of the heroine's face, the drama unfolding not only through the heroine's speech but also through the variation in the length of the shots). In the documentary included in the first volume of the project, Alan Rickman, who plays "M" in *Play*, observes that Beckett's instructions for the way in which M's lines are meant to be delivered—"in an ash and abstract voice"—would be impossible to follow on stage but are easily realized on the screen thanks to the close up, which renders the actors' voices more audible, more expressive or intimate.

One of the directors working on the project summarizes Beckett's minimalist method in the following way: if Beckett has to tell a story about a man who falls in love with a woman but things don't work out and he makes a fool of himself, he would strip the story of all circumstantial details, get it down to the bare necessities, probably ending up with a stage direction such as "the character takes three steps forward and shrieks." Beckett's intention is to condense or compress the dramatic action, which raises the question: What is the minimal requirement for a play, that which cannot be bracketed out, to use a phenomenological term, after everything else has been bracketed out? I would say for Beckett it's the human voice. The physical entrapment of many of his characters liberates the voice and immediately locates the drama in the characters' speech, more specifically in the characters' monologues. The monologue is certainly one of Beckett's preferred forms. But what is a monologue? It is an intimate conversation one has with oneself, a kind of thinking aloud that we are engaged in all the time, sometimes unconsciously and sometimes not. Here an important distinction needs to be made. Too often Beckett's plays are referred to as "wordy." However, the interminability of speech, the barrage of words that washes over us when we read a Beckett play, is simply the normal, everyday monologue that runs through our heads, most of the time silently and not very coherently. There is nothing "wordy," "rhetorical" or "theatrical" about it. That it appears to be wordy and rhetorical is due to the specific nature of the stage, on which actors are supposed to project their voices, pause between lines, exaggerate their intonation, etc. From this point of view, the film medium seems better suited than theatre at presenting the spontaneous chatter that fills our minds.

Beckett has been alternatively "claimed for" both modernism and postmodernism, with critics like Richard Sheppard proposing a middle path by arguing that postmodernism has inherited its problematics both from the avant-garde wing of modernism and from high modernists like Joyce, Eliot, Conrad, Proust, Le Corbusier, and Picasso (Sheppard, 2000: 356-357). Even if Beckett's plays could still be seen as anti-art, their film adaptations participate in the postmodernpractice of appropriation rather than in a modernist oppositional practice. On one hand, paradoxically, it is precisely because they are so faithful to their literary and dramatic source, because they patently refuse to translate the theatrical into the cinematic, because they refuse to "make cinema," that these film adaptations participate in the art of appropriation: they cleverly appropriate Beckett for the film audience of the twenty-first century, an audience well-educated in ideas of theatricality, stylization, Brechtian distanciation, unsuturing the spectator, foregrounding the film apparatus, etc. And yet, there is something anachronistic or un-postmodernist about this very insistence on respecting the autonomy of the two arts (theatre and cinema), this refreshing lack of interest in producing yet another postmodern pastiche of dramatic and film techniques.

CHAPTER FIVE

AS HOLLYWOOD TEACHES:
TRACING THE CULTURAL IMPACT OF
LOLITA AND ITS ADAPTATIONS TO FILM

by Kellie Dawson

Lolita: the title of a novel and of two films. Lolita: a particular sort of little girl.

We pay a lot of attention, in this culture, to our complicated feelings about little girls. Exposés in newspapers and periodicals, segments of news magazine programs on television, documentary films, articles in academic journals, and even entire books are devoted to examining the issue of America's fascination with the sexualization of ever-younger girls. We agonize over the causes of this phenomenon and wonder how we can help the children who start, at ages ten, nine, eight, dressing and behaving in ways they are not psychologically prepared to support. Less nuanced and less visible has been the discourse surrounding the nymphet's partner in crime: the adult male who responds to the sexualization she exudes. When we have discussed such men, our tendency has been to let the conversation fall fairly quickly into name calling. The tendency has been to call them monsters—but this tendency may be changing.

An examination of the differences between Stanley Kubrick's constrained adaptation of Vladimir Nabokov's novel, *Lolita*, in 1962 and Adrian Lyne's 1998 re-telling—with some attention to the films that come in between and after these filmic milestones—will demonstrate quite a bit of change in American culture in regard not only to our tolerance for pedophilic themes, but also toward the pedophile himself. Here I will follow a line of pedophilic discourse in film and will highlight a trend toward humanizing the person we've been used to think of as the villainous demon pedophile.

Although it is still considered impolite to raise the questions Nabokov did in his *Lolita* and that I will take up here, we know that films often tell us things about ourselves that we aren't always ready to admit we know—and it is that submerged knowledge I will fish for here. It will not be my business to offer solutions to our social ills. I will simply point to a particular line of discourse running through the highly influential medium of film and suggest that we consider what it may mean. Whether the trend I will trace here is a backlash against the discourse of demonization that has dominated most discussions of pedophilia or whether it is merely a tempering of the heights of hysteria we reached during the McMartin Preschool scandal of the early 1980s, it is worth our while to re-take up one of the challenges Nabokov set us with his novel: to ask ourselves how far we get when we insist upon seeing issues in simplistic terms, ignoring the actual human beings involved.

Romantic Slosh: Kubrick's *Lolita*

The teaser for Stanley Kubrick's film version of *Lolita* was "How *did they* ever make a movie of *Lolita*?" According to film critic, Richard Corliss, the "general critical opinion" in answer to this question was that "they hadn't" (34). We must acknowledge, however, that it is a tribute to Stanley Kubrick's talent and determination that he managed to bring *Lolita* to the screen at all, let alone created a fine film despite the limitations imposed upon him by the cultural atmosphere of his time. Unfortunately however, even as we appreciate his accomplishment, we must also admit his failure. Since he was forced to make so many concessions to contemporary standards, Kubrick made a fascinating film that misses, almost entirely, the point of Nabokov's novel.

Lolita, as Nabokov wrote it, is a complex examination of difficult issues. Although it resists reduction to a single point or message, it is clear, as I have argued elsewhere [citation forthcoming], that the sympathy Nabokov elicits from the reader for his pedophile is not merely a nasty side-effect, but is an important key to the very essence of the novel. Without asking his readers to excuse Humbert Humbert of his crimes, Nabokov challenges his readers to sympathize with his very human suffering.

And yet, rather than truly examining Humbert's plight, instead of testing the delicate balance between love and obsession, between adherence to norms and attention to idiosyncratic desires that is the crux of Nabokov's *Lolita*, Kubrick's film comes off as a quirky murder mystery framed by a puerile romance. Instead of laying bare the agony of a middle-aged man's obsession with a pre-pubescent girl, Kubrick opens his film with the comedically overblown murder of Clare Quilty and then proceeds to explain how this death came about. Although this plotline is in keeping with Nabokov's novel—in which Humbert writes his memoirs to explain how he has landed in prison for murder—Nabokov's version keeps Quilty so far in the background that it is very late in the novel before the reader realizes that he is an important part of the tale—let alone that it is he whom Humbert has killed. Nabokov's biographer, Brian Boyd writes that in the reading of the novel *Lolita* readers "face not a whodunnit, but a "whocoppedit" (243). Kubrick's version, however, plays more like a "whycoppedit" and features Quilty so heavily that it ends up being more a vehicle for the actor who portrays him than an adaptation of Nabokov's novel. Peter Sellers is wonderfully funny in the role of Quilty and gives a fine sense of the character's general creepiness, but his unrelenting presence in this film distracts greatly from Nabokov's original focus. As a matter of fact, the nature of the relationship between Humbert and Lolita is so downplayed by Kubrick that it may be confusing to one who has not read the book. This confusion is exacerbated by the fact that James Mason is playing against type as Humbert Humbert.

Usually cast as a desirable and debonair man of worldly sophistication, Mason appears in Kubrick's *Lolita* as a tragically befuddled and sophomoric puppy-lover. As Lance Olsen puts it, Mason's Humbert is "no longer the sinister, obsessed pervert from the pages of Nabokov's novel." Instead he "comes closer to an elegantly accented, love-smitten fool" (39). This perception is heightened by the fact that Humbert is given no past in this film. In the novel, Humbert explains that his sexual obsession with little girls can be traced back to a grand passion he experienced when he was thirteen years old—with Annabel Leigh, a girl his age. Their longing for each other, both thwarted and inflamed by the watchfulness of their guardians, finally culminates in an awkward and interrupted attempt at coitus, which is described in the same sentence that reports the girl's death of typhus four months later. The drift of this episode in Nabokov's novel is that Humbert believes that it is the trauma of this unresolved passion that forces him to attempt to recreate it with another girl. However, since Kubrick doesn't offer this or any other excuse for Humbert's behavior, they have no basis for interpreting his sudden and strange infatuation with his landlady's young daughter. Furthermore, since no mention is ever made of his lifelong struggles with "nympholepsy," this Humbert's inexplicable attachment seems to "commute into airier love, or perhaps simply into a midlife crush on a young woman half ... his age" (Olsen 40).

Another concession to public sentiment that Kubrick considered making but ultimately avoided was to end his film with the wedding of Humbert and Lolita in whatever state has the lowest marriageable age. The vestige of this consideration survives in his film in the fact that Sue Lyons was "17 going on 23" (Olsen 38) when she played Lolita—and if she ever had been a nymphet, those days were far behind her by the time she was cast in this film. This Lolita's exact age is left ambiguous, but she does have a boyfriend prior to meeting Humbert and is clearly a young lady—not at all a little girl. There is nothing giggly and very little that is immature about her. Furthermore, she is far too reserved and meticulously coifed to be sexual. Kubrick does try to compensate for the lack of actual sexuality in his film by resorting to suggestive wordplay and by foregrounding Lyon's legs in a shot or two—and there is also, of course, the famous toe-nail painting business. But nowhere, despite what is said about her or how she is shot, does Lyon come off as sexual. She's pretty and arch and inexplicably willing to tolerate Mason's bumbling Humbert—but never sexual. Of course, the reputation of the novel would have preceded Kubrick's film, so the implications of the vague intimacies he presents would have been clear to its first audiences. Overall however, this film is so leery of even these opaque allusions that for one thing it is left entirely unclear what this aloof and mostly untouchable Lolita sees in this goofily love-addled Humbert—and for another it is difficult to conceive their relationship as reaching anywhere near the level of grand passion that would justify the murder of the rival Quilty.

In all fairness to Kubrick, his film does acknowledge its own deficiencies in that it focuses on proving that Quilty deserves to die because he is a hopeless degenerate rather than because he trifled with an epic romance. Peter Sellers' Quilty is a snivellingly corrupt uber-miscreant whose actual propensities Kubrick leaves tantalizingly undefined even as he implies that they run the entire gamut of sins. For example, during his encounter with Humbert at the Enchanted Hunters (the hotel to which Humbert has taken Lolita for their first night together), Quilty is twitchy and anything but "normal," even though his speech is compulsively peppered with that word. The oblique generality of his implied deviance is even capped with a hint of homosexuality in his conversation with the hotel desk clerk, Mr. Swine, who caresses his hand with a pen as he confesses his aspirations to be an actor. Quilty all but simpers as Swine suggests that maybe, as a playwright, Quilty could "use" him sometime.

All of this implicit depravity adds up to the assurance that Quilty deserved to die in the opening scene—and in fact the jokey quality of this death accomplishes two purposes. First, it teaches the audience to laugh at Quilty, not to take him seriously—for not only is he, himself, a comic figure, but his surroundings further undercut any claim he may try to make on our sympathies. His home seems to be a mansion filled with the arty spoils of his irresponsible wealth, and the mess indicates that it could also be home to orgiastic parties. Quilty's use of a sheet as a toga ties the cues together. He is a comedic figure of Romanesque decadence and we are not to be disturbed by his death. Second, this scene sets the moral tone of the film. It tells the audience that here is a tale in which deviance will not be tolerated. In full, this opening scene serves to assure the audience that despite what they may have heard, this is not going to be an alarming and uncomfortable movie about pedophilia. It is going to be a breeze—and perversity will not be allowed to triumph. True to this promise, the film ends with a return to the opening scene—but instead of playing through to the murder of Quilty it now fades before he even appears to reveal an announcement of the death of the other bad guy. Onscreen lettering reads: *Epilogue: Humbert Humbert died of coronary thrombosis in prison awaiting trial for the murder of Clare Quilty.* Although Lolita's death is reported in the novel, no mention is made of it here because here she is the Innocent. She has wafted through the film, sly and untouchable, serenely accepting pedicures as her queenly due. She has not touched and no inappropriate touch has penetrated her haughty veneer. The bad guys, on the other hand, are dealt the death penalty contemporary standards demanded. Pedophilia, admittedly not the point of Nabokov's novel, has not even been an issue in Kubrick's film. If there had been a child in his *Lolita* she would have been left to live happily ever after.

The Curious Pattern of Simultaneous or Overlapping Moves: Films Between Kubrick & Lyne

Directly after Kubrick's *Lolita* came Elia Kazan's *Baby Doll* (1956), which from its very title would seem to relate it to the trail we are following here. And yet, despite its title and despite its being condemned by the Legion of Decency, this film is not really about what it goes so far out of its way to pretend to be about. Although it features a grown woman who is known by the nickname "Baby Doll" and who sleeps in a tiny bed that looks very much like a crib, she is, as the film opens, two days away from her twentieth birthday. So, although this film does depend upon infantalization of a hyper-sexualized female, and does play with pedophilic fantasies, it can't rightly be said to be about pedophilia. By evoking pedophilia however, this film cleverly taps into a contested theme without directly confronting it, exploiting an interest raised by Nabokov and toyed with but ultimately left unexamined by Kubrick.

The next major landmark on our tour comes over twenty years later with Louis Malle's *Pretty Baby* (1978), a film that is even more straightforward than any treatment of *Lolita* in its unapologetic sexualization of a 12-year-old girl. In this film, Violet, the daughter of a prostitute raised by her mother in a New Orleans brothel, has grown to understand sex as a transaction wherein both parties get what they want. So when she is abandoned by her mother, left alone in the brothel which is then shut down by the police, she, needing a new home presents herself (quite naturally, according to the logic of this film), to a man to live in his house as his mistress. What is interesting about this film for our purposes is that Bellocq, the man in question, cannot really be blamed for anything we would normally accuse pedophiles of. Although he clearly finds her attractive, Bellocq never makes any untoward move on Violet before *she* presents herself to *him*. Further, he makes it clear that he doesn't consider her a "whore." Not only does he reject her attempts to continue to act toward him in the ways the brothel has trained her to behave toward men, he marries her. Uncomfortably, this film leaves us no one to blame for a situation we so vocally proclaim as blameworthy. In fact, by the end of the film, Bellocq is left in the position of innocent victim as Violet's mother re-appears with her new husband to reclaim her and he is left pathetically begging these "parents" to be allowed to keep his child-bride. His innocence is then compounded as the audience is left weighing his relatively honorable treatment of Violet in comparison to the predatory gaze of the stepfather who, in the last moments of the film, is meant to be taking a picture of his newly intact family. As he frames Violet, her mother, and her toddler brother for the photo, the stepfather's focus creeps menacingly toward Violet, leaving the viewer a clear clue as to his actual motives in regaining his beautiful young stepdaughter.

Four years after the release of this calmly presented exploration of the complications of the matter we know as pedophilia, the McMartin Preschool scandal broke, making anything of the *Pretty Baby* sort unthinkable. Incredibly, the nation was now willing to believe that the entire staff of a preschool had been systematically and unrelentingly abusing its charges in sexually sadistic ways—all right under the noses of parents who would have had to have been astoundingly oblivious. As with the rest of the nation, it took the film industry quite some time to recover from the psychic wounds inflicted by this bizarre episode. It was not until the1990s that the trail I am following can be picked up again.

In 1994, Luc Bresson's *The Professional* re-introduced the theme of a love relationship between a grown man (Leon) and a 12-year-old girl (Mathilda). What makes this film a poignant wonder is that although Mathilda clearly expresses her desire to be Leon's lover and although they both express (in word and deed) their love for each other, there is never any indication that anything we could label as pedophilia occurs between them. In fact, this film portrays the most romantic of loves: the sort that remains unsullied by the sexuality our culture thinks of as at least semi-dirty—even when shared between consenting adults.

As Michel Foucault makes clear, the discourse of repression does not equal actual repression and as James R. Kincaid argues in his book, *Erotic Innocence: The Culture of Child Molesting*, the excessive discourse over pedophilia in our culture shows that we are more interested in *discussing* the problem than in *solving* it. As the trend I am tracing shows, for whatever reason, and whether we like to admit it out loud or not, America has been increasingly willing to engage with narratives treating of pedophilia. And that willingness seems to have been building since Nabokov's *Lolita* inspired Kubrick's tentative attempt to bring such issues to the screen.

The Stark Act: Lyne's *Lolita*

Kubrick knew what he could and could not get away with in his film: he never even bothered to shoot a love scene. Adrian Lyne, almost forty years later, is equally aware. The fact that he shot Nabokov's sofa episode—during which

Humbert masturbates to orgasm with Lolita (supposedly unaware) on his lap, as well as several other sex scenes—shows that he knew that late 1990s America was willing to witness a pedophilic relationship. Even though Lyne had to cut most of these scenes from the final product (due, mostly, to the Child Pornography Protection Act of 1996), he wasn't wrong about his cultural climate. A climate in which we eagerly consume images of sexualized children in all sorts of media, and yet continue to pretend that children are innocent and that they don't notice that their everyday environment is saturated with sexuality. As Corliss astutely points out, "The excisions forced on Lyne say a lot about our two-faced age, when the rankest pornography is available to every kid with a laptop and fingers, while grownup filmmakers (and filmgoers) must see works of serious ambition diluted, derailed, never made" (35).

Indeed, it is indicative of something very strange in our culture that the Child Pornography Protection Act notwithstanding, we *are* willing to see representations of pedophilia—as long as we can rest our minds that we are not seeing the real thing: which in itself is odd since we know that everyone we see on screen is an actor. Shirley Temple didn't live with a grandfather in the Swiss alps any more than Linda Blair was ever possessed by demons. The production of *Heidi* didn't cause Shirley to be orphaned, acting in *The Exorcist* didn't result in Satan inhabiting the soul of little Linda Blair, and despite her performance in *Scream*, Drew Barrymore lives on, uneviscerated. Of course, at least two of the three example I've just given are not without complication—people do object to children acting in such scenes as I evoke with the mention of *The Exorcist* and *Scream*—but the point is that whether they are acting in stories in which children are blissful or in which they suffer the most gruesome tortures imaginable, we do let children *act*. We allow them to perform in movies that require them to enact the most nauseating scenes of emotional and physical horror—and we flock to see the movies in which they do so. It's an old argument, not my own, but it's worth repeating here: We are willing to see films in which children are tortured and killed in ways we hope no human will ever have to endure, we get squeamish about seeing children in sexual situations—even when the acts depicted are consensual.

Be this squeemishness as it may, however, while Kubrick was forced to excise all sexuality and all but the goofiest sense of romance from his film, Lyne's audience is more used to seeing twelve-year-old girls as sexually desirable and knows (if from nowhere else, then from teen pregnancy statistics) that they are often sexually active. So he was able to be less coy and could allow his actors to be sexy while still retaining fidelity to Nabokov's original characters. Jeremy Irons' Humbert is sometimes pathetic, sometimes comedic—but ends up turning just these vulnerabilities into an admirably human sexiness. Dominique Swain, as Lolita, is just as Nabokov wrote her: a little girl beginning to realize her own sexual potential. And Frank Langella's Quilty is a masterpiece of the weirdly attractive and repugnant-yet-compelling sexuality Nabokov created in this character.

Not only does he restore sexiness to Nabokov's characters, Lyne goes even further to introduce the added complication of love to his version. Nabokov gives no indication that Lolita was ever in love with Humbert. She goes from the girlishly playful crush played out in her mother's house to resistant participation in sexual captivity. Lyne, however, is convinced that there was love between them. In his commentary on the film he says of the scene in which Lolita runs upstairs to kiss Humbert before leaving for camp that it is a key moment in that it shows a sort of love between them that "after this ... goes rapidly downhill." Not only is he convinced that this is proof of love on Lolita's part—and not simply a continuation of her childish flirtation with Humbert—but he believes (despite evidence to the contrary in the novel) that Lolita continues to enjoy sex with him after that first morning in the Enchanted Hunters.

In order to sell his film for distribution and exhibition, Lyne was forced to cut many of the scenes of consensual sexuality he filmed between Lolita and Humbert—but one is preserved in the final cut. In the novel, Nabokov describes Humbert sitting naked with Lolita on his lap. "There she would be," Humbert complains, "a typical kid picking her nose while engrossed in the lighter sections of the newspaper, as indifferent to my ecstasy as if it were something she had sat upon, a shoe, a doll, the handle of a tennis racket, and was too indolent to remove" (165). In Lyne's reproduction of this scene he has Lolita reacting with pleasure. The point here is not Lyne's departure from Nabokov's original, but that this departure is possible. Whereas Kubrick knew better than to even allow his Humbert to share a bed with his Lolita at the Enchanted Hunters, Lyne not only filmed sex scenes between an adult and a child, but one of them—showing a child enjoying sex—actually made it to the final cut, to be presented to audiences.

And yet, Lyne is savvy enough to realize that movie audiences need a back story upon which to hang uncomfortable concepts—and this must be what is behind his straightforward presentation of the Annabel Leigh affair. Whereas Kubrick simply ignores the question of why his Humbert is so thunderstruck by the bratty elegance of his young lady, Lyne recognizes that although American culture may have arrived at a point where we are (perhaps grudgingly) prepared to admit that young girls may be sexually attractive we still seem to prefer to have the apology of a childhood trauma to blame it on. Therefore he not only presents the Annabel Leigh affair as a straightforward explanation of what is to come, but also adds to this excuse, particularizing the glamour and romance of Humbert's attraction to Lolita, by leaving out any suggestion of generalized pedophilia. In his film, Humbert seems to go directly from Annabel to her replacement, Lolita, with nary a thought of any other little girl in between. This undeviating progression sets Humbert up as the classic romantic movie hero. According to Humbert, he has been "poisoned" with love for a girl who has died. He cannot, therefore, rest until he resurrects her in another—we wouldn't forgive him if he did. Furthermore, by showing Lolita as a direct replacement for Annabel—with no one (and certainly no pedophilia) in between—Lyne co-opts the notion of love as fate. Humbert couldn't help falling in love with Annabel, couldn't help being "poisoned" by the interruption of their passion and then by the death that prematurely severed their love. Therefore he can't help falling in love with a girl who is just like his tragically lost sweetheart.

Unfortunately, despite Nabokov's well-known disgust for Freud and his theories, Lyne is so convinced by them that in addition to his misinterpretation of the Annabel Leigh episode, he actually alters Nabokov's text to refer to Freud's theories in a way that would have made Nabokov shudder. Nabokov writes that in Lolita's bedroom she has an advertisement featuring a handsome model pinned up above her bed. She has indicated her belief that the model resembles Humbert by writing the initials "HH" and drawing an arrow pointing to the model's head. Lyne uses the essence of this scene, but transforms it. In his version the advertisement shows a smiling father figure carrying a happy little girl in his arms as a mother figure waves goodbye to them from deep in the background. Between the father's and the little girl's heads someone (presumably Lolita) has drawn (in what appears to be lipstick) a heart with the initials "HH" inside of it. Not content with this, Lyne has his camera pan to this tableau from the picture of a bride immediately above it. The implications of this juxtaposition are obvious and it is doubtful that Nabokov would have liked it. Not only does it demonstrate common acceptance of the theories of his archenemy, but it also misses the point. Lolita, at this moment in the novel, sees Humbert as a romantic—not as a father—figure. She does eventually call him "dad," but this is for the most part said ironically, or for appearances' sake—or to finalize her rejection of him as a lover in the end. No matter the prevalence of little girls as sexual objects in our culture then, and no matter our interest in seeing them so portrayed, Lyne knows that his audience is still not comfortable with actual pedophilic relationships—so he provides both of his protagonists with an excuse. Humbert is the victim of a childhood trauma and Lolita, without a father of her own, has fit Humbert into her family romance.

Of course, Lyne's progress from production to exhibition was not without spectacular difficulties, but the fact that it made it to public light at all shows that our culture has changed a great deal since Kubrick made his inhibited film. Intergenerational love may still be perceived as a problem and may still be bound to the issues of child sexual abuse and perversion that is the legacy of the opinions we inherited from early theorists on sexology and adolescence, but the current pervasiveness of even this negative discourse made Lyne's adaptation possible. As a matter of fact, the current climate is, apparently, so amenable to such discourses that he was free not only to produce a faithful adaptation of *Lolita*, but to go even further than Nabokov cared to go. Where Nabokov's story ends with an unreciprocated obsessional love, Lyne's version goes on to show the possibility of mutual love (and even sexual enjoyment) between an adult and a child.

Above and Over Everything There is—*Lolita*: Her Legacy

Lyne was not alone in bringing pedophilic themes to the screen at the turn of this century. In fact, mentions of pedophilia began to be prevalent in film at this time. They were particularly common as excuses/explanations for the bad behavior of adults. An especially egregious example of this trend occurs in the film *One Hour Photo* (2002), wherein a vague reference to sexual abuse in his childhood is meant to account for the bizarre behavior of a character whose actions have had very little to do with sex—and even less with pedophilia. More recently, 2004's *Butterfly Effect* offers reference to pedophilia as an unquestionable explanation for suicide. Oddly however, several films have not only made pedophilia a central issue but have complicated the matter in ways that hearken back to Nabokov.

Lyne's *Lolita*, faithful to the conclusion of Nabokov's novel, ends with Humbert's poignant acknowledgement of the horrible harm he has done Lolita. Standing on a precipice overlooking an idyllic little town in the valley below him, Humbert, in voice over, tells the audience: "What I heard then was the melody of children at play. Nothing but that. And I knew that the hopelessly poignant thing was not Lolita's absence from my side, but the absence of her voice from the chorus." Corliss suggests that "If [this] speech doesn't absolve Humbert, it reinforces his frazzled humanity and allows the viewer to forgive him" (Corliss 39). Some would protest that "forgive" may be too strong a word, but most would admit that we are able, at this moment, to feel sorry for the pain of this miserably wretched creature even though he has brought that pain upon himself through his own actions.

Released surprisingly quickly after Lyne's battle to distribute his *Lolita* is the independent film, *Happiness* (1999), which goes even further with the sympathetic theme in its exploration of the trauma experienced by an active homosexual child-rapist and his family. Without excusing the pedophile for his rape of two of his eleven-year-old son's classmates, this film focuses on the horror of being the perpetrator of such a hideous crime. In keeping with the disconcerting sympathy Nabokov achieves for Humbert in his novel and which Lyne preserves in his film, director Todd Solondz, asks his audience to consider the pain experienced by a man tortured by a sexual obsession with children the age of his own son.

American Beauty (2000) follows hot on the heels of Solondz's film and goes as far as a mass market film can go with the nymphet theme while remaining within the boundaries of an "R" rating. It is also the most popular and successful film linked with a pedophilic theme—which makes it all the more surprising that here the viewer is thrust not only into sympathy for, but identification with a middle-aged man, Lester, whose fantasies make it vividly (even if metaphorically) clear that he would like to have sex with his daughter's manipulative and flirty and brash and vulnerable and ultimately virginal friend, Angela.

Katherine Rowe Karlyn has argued that *America Beauty* is a film about re-directed incest, writing that "popular narratives [tend to] disguise the theme [of incest] through the process of displacement. When the father's desire is explicit, as it is in *American Beauty*, the target is displaced onto a daughter substitute" (70). But why is this convolution necessary? Karlyn's reading of this film boils down to her assertion that "whenever a film ... centers on a midlife male, a young girl who arouses his sexual ... interest, and a mother who is missing or otherwise characterized as inadequate, the incest theme is likely to be lurking in the background" (71). Her argument is that

Incest provides a narrative structure—derived from Freud's work on the subject—that ideologically inverts the social realities of white male privilege. This structure redirects sympathy toward beleaguered mid-life heroes by portraying them as victims of unhinged and vengeful wives, seductive and manipulative daughters, or both (71).

My point in disagreeing with Karlyn as to the theme of this film is to reclaim it, to suggest that sympathy for Lester does not align one with patriarchy, but merely with humanity.

By identifying the problem of this film more precisely, we can make it available again to those of us who appreciate it because we see something very human and pathetic in it. This is not, of course, to say that incest is not a pathetic human problem: it is only to say that if we drop the incest reading of this film, a woman doesn't have to be a contrite shrew to sympathize with Lester. Men don't have to be cringing potential daughter-rapists. If they don't have to defend themselves against charges of covert incest, men can even admit their affinity with Lester. They can smile at their own worries of becoming middle-aged, middle-class schlubs who are now faced with the fact that they never did (and now never will) get the hot car and the hot girlfriend they so desperately coveted in High School. And I believe this is a more productive place to start. If we look this film squarely in the we can sympathize with the confusion of a very young girl who is trying to find her way in a culture she knows finds her pretty and in which she will be sexually sought after and rewarded for her sexuality. And we can do so without blaming a man for responding to the sexuality she is trying on, learning to use. Furthermore, as Nabokov suggested with his novel, acknowledgement of the complications of the issue and sympathy for the actual human beings involved may be more useful than denial and name-calling.

Finally, to exclude the incest reading of *American Beauty* we need only note that Lester ultimately rejects Angela because she doesn't, after all, possess the sexual experience she has been leading everyone to believe she had. She is, in fact, a virgin. Lester, then, was not after the virginal daughter-substitute (unless we assume that he's secretly hoping his daughter's a tramp). He's after the teen fantasy that can survive in any grown man without making him any sort of pervert. He's after the fast and loose girl to whom he will have no responsibility nor commitment. The fact that Lester is living his teen fantasy (rather than indulging an incestuous, or even a pedophilic thrill) is born out by the fast food job he obtains in order to work without any true responsibility, the early 1970s Pontiac Firebird he is finally able to purchase, and the utter liberty he seems to feel in giving his life over to smoking pot and lifting weights. The upshot of all of these changes in Lester's life is that by the time he has access to Angela, it is not as a middle-aged man, it is as the fantasy teen he has remade himself into. It is this encounter, in fact, that bursts the bubble of his fantasy and reminds him that he is a father and husband.

American Beauty is followed in 2003 by *Capturing the Friedmans*, an achingly moving portrait of a man who loved children and who was celebrated for doing so until a law enforcement sting exposed the closet pedophilic interests he was indulging in through mail order magazines. This documentary chronicles the exposure of a previously well-respected teacher, father and husband, who must now admit his inclination and yet who denies having acted upon it in the ways of which he is accused. Viewing this subtle and complex film, it is difficult to not feel the extreme trauma experienced and regret felt by this ruined man who goes to prison still protesting his innocence—and it's hard not to believe that it may be true that he may have loved children and may have been interested in them sexually and yet still may be, ultimately a good man.

More recently we've had 2004's *The Woodsman*, which pulls no punches in its compassionate portrayal of a recovering pedophile. Not only has the protagonist of this film served time for child molestation, but it is clear that he's not, as we meet him, "cured." Will he ever be? This film offers no answer, but it does make clear that the protagonist is trying—and that he's human. It presents a man tormented by a desire he acknowledges is wrong and which he sincerely wishes to control. How can we revile him? We can't. We leave the film sorry and hopeful for this tragic man.

Woman, Thou Art Loosed (2004) complicates the issue of sympathy even further. Written by and starring the charismatic and entrepreneurial Christian leader, Bishop T.D. Jakes, this film comes dangerously close to shifting the final sympathy of the audience from the victim to the pedophile. In a very strange and troubling moment, a young woman, Michelle, driven to the point of desperation by her years of sexual abuse at the hands of her mother's boyfriend, Reggie, her mother's failure to protect her, and the turmoil of the afflicted life that is the legacy of her abuse, shoots her victimizer. Normally we would expect the audience to fully support her in this project. The hitch in this otherwise familiar and straightforward tale comes in the circumstances of Michelle's moment of revenge.

The victim shoots her victimizer. All should be fine and well. But it isn't. Not only does Michelle shoot Reggie in a church, but she does so as he is repenting; sobbing, begging forgiveness not only of her and her mother, but of the God she believes in. At this moment, according to the Christian values that are the underlying logic of this film, the victimizer is absolved of his sin. He has asked forgiveness of the God that governs both himself and his victim and is, therefore, in that God's hands. Taking his life at this exact moment makes his victim at least as guilty as he had ever been, and the audience's loyalties are no longer uncomplicated.

While the audience would have cheered if Michelle had shot her victimizer before he entered the church, while he was still unrepentant and presumably irredeemable (to judge by his unremitting badness throughout the film), his confession, his apparent sorrow and his plea for forgiveness remind us that, like Nabokov's Humbert Humbert, and like the protagonist of *The Woodsman*, even the worst men are human. Killing a sobbing man who is sincerely acknowledging his crime and begging for forgiveness is an act that turns the audience away from the victim and aligns it with the victimizer at the very last moment.

Going even further to drive home the point that even the sort of men we think of as utterly beyond all moral and ethical hope can find salvation, the film steps out of its narrative to present Reggie in direct address to the audience saying, "Don't get me wrong, I've got faults just like the next man. But I was workin' on 'em. I just needed a little more time. I was trying to start a new life .... I just needed a little more time." This speech clinches the moral charges against Michelle—and she, in fact, agrees with them. Directly after Reggie's speech, we hear from her from behind the bars of her prison cell where she is on death row for the murder of Reggie. Herself now the penitent, speaking to Bishop T.D. Jakes himself, she says, "I didn't understand how God could forgive a man like that. I didn't understand why I should forgive a man like that. But now I do .... What I did was wrong. No matter what he did to me, it was wrong. When you talk to God again, ask him to forgive me." Thus, the victim of pedophilia ends on the same level as the pedophile. She has done something unforgivable, irrevocable. She has taken something she had no right to take.

Vladimir Nabokov's *Lolita* does not feature the Innocent beleaguered by the Pervert that American society has thought of as the generic staples of such stories. Instead, his "victim" is a nymphet and his pedophile is a pitiable sufferer of an uncontrollable compulsion to act upon forbidden desires. Nabokov may not have "foresee[n] that by accepting the imaginative and intellectual challenge of inventing values that so thoroughly inverted his own, he would shock the public into taking notice (Boyd 7) , but that was exactly what happened. With *Lolita*, Nabokov did more than challenge his own imagination and intellect, he dared his readers to do the same.

What I have traced here is a trend in film that would seem to contradict public opinion as we assume it to exist. Even as we, in other forms of media, continue to adhere to the Innocent Victim vs Monster Pervert theme that has dominated public discourse on pedophilia, films have been following the model suggested by Vladimir Nabokov over fifty years ago, quietly demonstrating to us that we can and do acknowledge that the matter is much more complicated than that. The films I have examined here have dared to suggest the possibility of sympathy for the sort of person we think of as so inhuman that we often refer to him as a monster. Perhaps this is a more constructive place to start if we really do want to solve the problem rather than simply continuing, endlessly, to discuss it.

CHAPTER SIX

ADAPTATION AS AN ACT OF CONFESSION IN LEPAGE'S *LE CONFESSIONNAL* AND HITCHCOCK'S *I CONFESS*

by Sylvie Bissonnette

Ever since its beginnings, cinema has found its inspiration in many art forms, and its relationship to theatre has always been complex. Alfred Hitchcock showed a sustained interest in this ambiguous love-hate relationship, and explored the boundaries between theatre and film in many film-mediated dramas. Many Hitchcock films based on stage plays foreground their stage origins rather than trying to hide them, which is true of *I Confess* (1952) in particular. Also stage-bound, *Le confessionnal*[i] (Robert Lepage, 1995), which was inspired by the work of Alfred Hitchcock in general, and *I Confess* in particular, pushes back the frontiers of fiction. Indeed, this film deals with the concept of adaptation through intertextual references to *I Confess* and historical rewriting. Ultimately, Lepage's film "confesses" its sources of inspiration while exposing cinematic conventions through historical references and reflexive strategies. Since both films foreground their theatricality in a context of ideological reflexion, this paper will examine how theatricality can refer to the theatrical origins of the films as well as how it can be used to challenge cinematic conventions.

In presenting their views on faith and justice, both *I Confess* and *Le confessionnal* uses Québec of the 1950s as the ideal *topos* of a society religiously clinging to its old values, while its people struggle to escape their fate. Rooted in this religious context, both films offer an interesting opportunity to re-examine the reflection on "faithfulness" of the representation, usually associated with adaptations or intertextual works.

---

[i] *The Confessional*

Being Faithful to the Truth

The discussion about fidelity often occurs in critics of film adaptations of canonical novels, critically acclaimed authors or even Shakespeare's plays. From the point of view of the critics, or even the spectators who appreciated the original play or the original novel, *faithfulness* or *unfaithfulness* to the original becomes an essential subject of debate. However, the issue seems less relevant for films that adapt an obscure work, as in the case of the Hitchcock adaptation of Paul Anthelme's play *Nos deux consciences.*[i] Furthermore, the question of faithfulness seems even less relevant when the adaptation extensively transforms the fundamental narrative and thematic features of its source, so that it becomes an original work on its own. However, as I will suggest later, the question of faithfulness can still be pertinent when dealing with films that reflect upon ideologies in their source, in such case, faithfulness concerns more the comparison/opposition between a set of values in the original and a set of values in the adaptation. Still, when dealing with adaptations that revolve around socio-political issues, such as *I Confess* and *Le confessionnal*[ii], it may seem more interesting to develop an analysis that takes into account cultural, historical, or political concerns than to make a judgmental account about disrespect to the original work.

The intertextual history of a film can enlighten the analysis of the adaptation process, even for films that significantly "update" the original plot. Genette's theory of transtextuality proposes a typology for the relationship between one text and other texts, whether intentional or not, manifest or not. His concept of "text" can be extended to the analysis of the "filmic text" as proposed by Robert Stam in his application of that theory on film adaptations (Stam 2000). Quotation, plagiarism and allusion contribute to form the intertextual matrix of the film, and "adaptation in this sense, participates in a double intertextuality, one literary and the other cinematic" (Stam 2000: 65). In the case of stage play adaptations, theatrical intertextuality refers to either the text of the play or the scenographic elements associated with the performance of the play. Hypertextuality, which is another type of transtextuality, applies more specifically to film adaptation than intertextuality. Referring to Genette's theory, Stam states that "[f]ilmic adaptations [...] are hypertexts derived from preexisting hypotexts. that have been transformed by operations of selection, amplification, concretization, and actualization" (Stam 2000: 66). The hypotexts of *I Confess* include *Nos deux consciences.* (1902), a French play written by

---

[i] Paul Anthelme was the pseudonym of the French journalist, philosopher and historian Paul Bourde (1851-1914).

[ii] *The Confessional*

Paul Anthelme. The hypotexts of *Le confessionnal*[i] include *I Confess*, but also by extension *Nos deux consciences*. Also, in quoting other Hitchcock films such as *Vertigo* (1958), *North by Northwest* (1959) and *Psycho* (1960), intertextual complicity is developed between *Le confessionnal* and the Hitchcockian universe. Threaded together, all these intertextual negotiations form a complex network of significations, which raises new questions while answering older ones. For example, knowing that *I Confess* was adapted from a French play written in 1902, can illuminate the reasons that had influenced Hitchcock to set his film in a francophone, Catholic city. However, it raises some other questions such as: Why not have set the film in France? Or, why not retain the historical time frame of the original? Intertextual references, should they be literary, filmic or historical, complicate the reading of the work and create subtexts that multiply the possible interpretations of the film. Looking at what intertexts have been chosen, or how they have been transformed, can help to deepen the analysis of the adaptation process, but in no way can it offer a totalizing view of the multileveled readings.

When examining films dealing with religious principles and moralities, such as *I Confess* and *Le confessionnal,* looking at the changes made between a hypertext and its hypotexts may shed light on the adaptation process by highlighting ideological changes. Many factors influence those changes: the director's personal beliefs, evolving social behavior, the censorship, the studio system, etc. In comparing *I Confess* with *Nos deux consciences*, analyzing the changes made about characters' motivations and the inversions in their social standing reveals two different worldviews. Comparing narrative changes between *I Confess* and *Le confessionnal* shows different perspectives on the effects that the ascendancy of religion had over Québécois Catholic society.

The narrative of *I Confess* proposes a reflection on private and public confessions, and confronts religious beliefs with moral beliefs. In summary, *I Confess* tells the story of a Catholic priest, Father Logan, who is wrongly accused of the murder of a man after hearing the confession of the actual killer. Sworn to secrecy by the seal of confession, he is prosecuted on the basis that a priest was seen leaving the crime scene. The film reflects on private and public confessions and highlights the polarity between the religious system of justice and the judiciary system. On the one hand, the confession of the murderer occurs in the sacred privacy of the church. On the other hand, the police investigation—which replaces the biblical law with the civil law—becomes the pretext for a series of public testimonies.

The original play also opposed the religious and the judicial, but there was also an evident trust in personal principles, which *I Confess* questions. Without

---

[i] *The Confessional*

sharing the same ideology, both the play and *I Confess* emphasize the harmful consequences of hiding the truth, and suggest that Catholic religion promotes the reign of secrecy. They also both highlight the fallibility of civil justice and expose abuses of power. However, in assigning the same character traits to different social representatives, each work defends its own convictions. In *Nos deux consciences.*, for example, the innocent priest Pioux is blackmailed by a member of the clergy; in *I Confess*, the blackmailer has been replaced by a corrupted lawyer. In *I Confess*, the pragmatic police inspector, which represents in a critical way a heartless moral/civil law, holds the counterpart of the instructional judge in *Nos deux consciences*. However, *I Confess* does not propose a counterpart to the bourgeois doctor, the model of French Revolutionary morality, who sacrifices his political career to exculpate priest Pioux. If *Nos deux consciences* shows doubts about the effectiveness of the judicial institution to exercise justice, it still believes in each person's sense of duty and its power to give victory to truth and justice. On the contrary, *I Confess* draws a rather skeptical portrait about the link between justice and truth. Although the jury innocents the priest in *I Confess*, the trial and the police investigation proved to be ineffective in having the truth revealed. In an alternative ending, Keller could have confessed his crime because he would have felt remorse, or because of a successful police arrest. Instead, in this ending, Keller confesses because he thought that Logan had betrayed his vow of silence by revealing his culpability. This ending expresses mixed feelings about the power of the religious institution, civil justice or moral principles to really exercise justice, contrary to the conclusion of *Nos deux consciences.*, which clearly celebrates moral principles as being the key to a respectable life.

Although *Le confessionnal*[i] shares common narrative elements and thematic links with *I Confess*, their worldviews differ. The historical shooting of *I Confess,* which happened in Quebec City in 1952, inspired Robert Lepage's film *Le confessionnal*, in which actual footage from Hitchcock's film is inserted to stress this reference. However, more interested by the misfortunes of a Québécois family, *Le confessionnal* gives up the thriller plot found in *I Confess*, and chooses to offer a more acerbic look upon the impact of the Catholic religion on Quebec City. Lepage revisits themes from *I Confess*, such as the influence of Catholicism and the transference of guilt. As in Hitchcock's film, incriminating circumstances lead to the accusation of an innocent Catholic priest of a crime that he did not commit. The allegations of having impregnated a sixteen year-old girl, Rachel, will lead the priest to defrock and eventually become a decadent government official. Contrary to Hitchcock's thriller, which focuses on

---

[i] *The Confessional*

Father Logan's struggle, this psychological drama shifts its attention from the priest to Pierre, the adoptive brother of Rachel's child. The baby, called Marc, was adopted by Pierre's mother after her sister committed suicide, because she could not bear the secret of the identity of the father of her son. The film alternates between two different periods, the fifties, when Hitchcock filmed in Quebec City in the church where Marc was born, and the eighties, when Pierre comes back from China to attend his father's funeral. Then he meets his adoptive brother by chance in the Château Frontenac hotel, as Marc was leaving one of his clients' room. As the brothers come to know each other and discover that they are both striving to define their identity, they decide to join their efforts, and set out to unveil the family secrets to finally discover the identity of Marc's father. Identity quests and familial conflicts characterize many Québécois dramas, as Lefebvre suggests:

> [B]y shifting the focus from murder to illegitimate sexuality and family relations or family secrets—a move which has led to the disappearance of the social and public institution of the law in favor of the institution of family [...]—Lepage has managed a *québécisation* of *I Confess* (97).

By removing the court scene and the police investigation, Lepage's film focuses more on the personal tragedies of the members of a family and their difficulty to fit within a society which wants to erase them, to cut them from its social tissue.

Le confessionnal[i] foregrounds the intertextual relationship with *I Confess* by including actual sequences from the film. References to the shooting of *I Confess* in *Le confessionnal* not only represents the past through its historical reference and its filmmaking style, it symbolizes a landmark in Quebec City history. The recurring shifts between the two different film footage accentuates the differences and similarities between the two periods depicted. This dialogue between the two eras initiates a look back to the beginning of Québec's Quiet Revolution, a period associated with ideological changes. In 1952, the Catholic Church's institutions had a very strong influence on Québecois society and still had an essential role in both the educational and health care systems. We learn at the beginning of the film that in 1952, life in Quebec City was marked by three events, the arrival of the first television set, Maurice Duplessis's reelection as provincial premier and the presence of Alfred Hitchcock who had chosen the city as the setting for his new thriller. As noticed by Dundjerovic, "[b]y using a Hitchcock film within his own, Lepage brings the idea of the Hollywood 'dream machine' into 1952 Québec City", and also in a symbolic way, "the increasing importance of American corporations and capital on Québec was

---

[i] *The Confessional*

represented through the making of *I Confess* and the business negotiations conducted by Hitchcock's entrepreneurial assistant" (56). As Lepage suggests, events such as the establishment of television in Québec or the visit of an internationally acclaimed filmmaker may have influenced this closed, almost secretive society. This sudden proximity of the world may have helped to initiate the shift that allowed the society to become more internationally aware and culturally open.

However, *Le confessionnal*[i] draws a non-idealized portrait of the new emerging generation, showing its difficulty to embrace the future (globalization), because it is still stigmatized by its past. The ambiguous ending suggests an unstable future for Marc's son, if he chooses to follow the footsteps of his father's family. The father of Pierre and Marc had gouged his eyes out, because he could not bear to see the suffering he has caused to his family. Rachel, his grandmother, has committed suicide, because she had a child with her sister's husband. His father has cut his wrists during a trip in Japan with Massicotte. We assume that Massicotte has finally told him the identity of his father, which would have provoked his suicide. All these tragic acts bear the signs of the helplessness of a society with a disintegrating value system, and suggests flaws in the familial institution. However, Pierre seems to want to change the child's destiny. After the suicide of Marc, Pierre decides to take care of the boy and turns to Massicotte to ask him money. The motives that lead Massicotte to accept financial responsibility for the child are implied. He may feel guilty about Marc's suicide, but, since he was Marc's sexual partner, he probably fears the implications of a sexual scandal on his political career. The film questions the sense of duty of Massicotte, and of all the members of the family, but without condemning them. Thus leaving to the spectator the responsibility to draw his own conclusions. This ideological view, which totally differs from the ones in *I Confess* and *Nos deux consciences.*, shows how *Le confessionnal*[ii] is deeply rooted in the social and cultural milieu of Québec. Basically, examining the intertextual dialogues between the films has demonstrated that variations on similar themes can lead to different social discourses depending on the choices made during the adaptation process.

Before deepening the intertextual analysis of those two films by exploring their theatrical intertextuality, I will briefly return to the questions of fidelity to the original that the adaptation process raises. As noticed by Robert Stam, the language dealing with the film adaptation has so often being tinted by a moralistic tendency that, in this context, terms like

---

[i] *The Confessional*
[ii] *The Confessional*

[i]nfidelity resonates with overtones of Victorian prudishness; *betrayal* evokes ethical perfidy; *deformation* implies aesthetic disgust; *violation* calls to mind sexual violence; *vulgarization* conjures up class degradation; and *desecration* intimates a kind of religious sacrilege toward the 'sacred word'" (Stam 2000: 54).

Using those terms implies, in some ways, that the process of adaptation is ideologically grounded. A director cannot neutrally update the discourse present in sources that deal with ethical issues such as infidelity, betrayal, justice and truth. During the adaptation process, the screenwriter[i] has to make compromises between reflecting ideologies from the source text, his own beliefs and the different sets of beliefs that are deemed acceptable by society. Therefore, when updating the discourse present in the source, the writer/director has to choose between being *faithful* to it, reflecting his own ideology, or initiating a dialog between both. In asking questions such as, What is the truth?, and What is to be faithful?, *I Confess* and *Le confessionnal*[ii] seem to self-consciously refer to questions asked by the directors when concocting the plot. In this sense, both films can be seen as a meditation on the relativity of the concepts of fidelity and truth, and on the complexity of adapting sources that deal with those fundamental questions. In different ways, both films offer a reflection on the struggle between being faithful or not to the Truth, which can be thought of as a metaphor for the adaptation process itself.

To Confess Origins of Inspiration

Theatricality in *I Confess* and *Le confessionnal* facilitates the intertextual negotiation between the films and their theatrical hypotexts. Through different strategies, both films evoke their theatrical origins, which has the effect of highlighting their production process. In *I Confess*, the mise-en-scène includes references to the stage and evokes the confinement mood often associated with in camera plays. *Le confessionnal* is not an adaptation of a play, but it refers to *I Confess*, which is one. By highlighting the performative nature of making films and watching them, it echoes the theatricality present in *I Confess*. Since

---

[i] Lepage was the screenwriter of the *Le confessionnal* and George Tabori wrote the screenplay for *I Confess*. However, the film on the making of *I Confess*, *Hitchcock's Confession: A Look at "I Confess"* (Laurent Bouzereau, 2004), suggests that Hitchcock had a significant influence on the writing of the film. Bill Krohn, the author of *Hitchcock at Work* confirms that Hitchcock had a hand in the multiple versions of the screenplay. Furthermore, he mentions the existence of a correspondence between Hitchcock and the head of the Production Code Office, the head censor, concerning an appropriate depiction of Logan's ethical behavior under the circumstances.

[ii] *The Confessional*

theatricality is often considered pejoratively in cinema, choosing to use theatrical references may seem risky. Nevertheless, both directors chose to acknowledge their theatrical association as a way to allude to their origins, but also as a way to distantiate their view from those of their predecessors.

Confessing theatricality in the adaptation process requires a skillful dosage of truth/lie, affirmation/confession or authenticity/impurity to refer to the Bazinian concept. In his book *Qu'est ce que le cinéma?* Bazin argues that there is no "pure art". It is not because a film follows step by step the mise-en-scène of a play that it is not cinema, and it is not what necessarily makes it a good adaptation. According to Bazin, the screen welcomes the theatre without betraying it, when "the subject of the adaptation is not the subject of the play, but the play itself with all its scenic specificity" (Bazin 1975: 110 ; my translation). As examples of successful play adaptation, Bazin refers to *Les parents terribles* (Jean Cocteau, 1948) and *Henry V* (Laurence Olivier, 1944). According to him, Cocteau and Olivier succeeded in their attempt to bring theatre to film by demonstrating "a grasp of the language of cinematography equalled only by [their] knowledge of what theater is" (Bazin 1967: 116). For Bazin, those filmmakers have proved that cinema can effectively use its means of expression to bring to the screen its true theatrical value. When considering Hitchcock's adaptation of the play from Paul Anthelme, it is evident that the source text has been considerably altered. However, similarly to the plays adapted by Cocteau and Olivier, I will further argue that in spite of the changes to the plot, the play has transcended the mediums and emerged in the film through cinematic theatricality.

When adapting a play, a filmmaker may prefer to escape theatricality and forget anything specific to the dramatic composition of the original work. Instead, Hitchcock chose to take advantage of the theatrical origins of his movie's scenario and, as Neil Sinyard would put it, to make us "hyperaware" of them (182). Many interior sets, for example, allude to the theatrical origins of the film. Without being locations with a "real" stage, many of them are places for public confessions, testimonies and revelations, such as the courthouse where Logan is interrogated or the office of Crown prosecutor, where Ruth Grandfort has to reveal an affair that she had with Logan before he entered the priesthood, but after her wedding. Basically, *I Confess* highlights the performative nature of confession through its mise-en-scène and art direction.

Moreover, the personal struggle of the tormented priest, and the feeling of entrapment that emerges from the film, echo the tension between the "freedom" of film medium and the confinement of the stage play. Hitchcock opposes cinematic freedom, principally conveyed through the many scenes shot in natural locations, to the interior struggle experienced by the priest. This contrasting pattern can be observed in other film-mediated dramas. As André Loiselle notes,

> [T]he condition of entrapment of the *dramatis personae* is made even more palpable through the depiction of theatrical characters trapped in cinematic spaces. Their situation seems even more dreadful in the films than in the plays as the potential for escape made visible on screen is irrevocably ignored, rejected, forsaken (75).

Also, it seems that Hitchcock chose to adapt Anthelme's play "as a means to tackle the issue of confinement and constraint in terms of both dramatic theme and filmmaking practice" (Loiselle 11). The theme of the falsely accused man, which features in a number of films made by Hitchcock, and the religious thematic in the play gave Hitchcock the opportunity to exploit those issues through Christian symbolism that reflects images of rejection, incomprehension and isolation.

Hitchcock has transformed many aspects of the original play, without renouncing to the theatricality inherent to the characters. Although the numerous on location settings open up the drama, the theatrical character—Logan—appears estranged from the outside world, which seems to condemn him. For example, when Logan exits from the court, the crowd that surrounds him shouts insults even though he has been proved innocent. The filled-up frame squeezes Logan in its middle, emphasizing his powerlessness. Another shot, filmed with a long lens, shows Logan against a stone wall in front of the cinema theatre Capital, and gives the impression that Logan is trapped within the walls of the fortified city. In another scene, the editing suggests that suspicious passengers observe Logan and Madam Grandfort when they secretly meet on the boat. In these examples, the composition or the film's editing create a certain feeling of guilt, which paradoxically annihilates the apparent freedom evoked by the setting.

Like films such as *Murder!* (1930) and *Stage Fright* (1950), the key sequence of *I Confess* takes place on a stage, in the wider sense that stage can take. In the final scene, Keller, the murderer, runs from the courthouse to the ballroom of the Hotel Château Frontenac, and ends up trapped in front of a stage with its curtains wide opened. While threatening to shoot Logan, and called upon by the police to surrender, Keller confesses once again to his crime, but this time he does so in front of an audience. As Alenka Zupancic mentioned it in his article entitled "A Perfect Place to Die", "the truth, *inscribed in the symbolic universe of the film*, is revealed on the stage" (81). He goes on to add: "the culprit has to die, and to die in a literally 'theatrical' way" (81). In front of the stage, the light comes through as the representatives of the law confront the suspect, and the culprit gives himself away, in front of the audience, as in front of the jury. Thus, theatrically condensed in the same scene are the confession, the verdict and the death sentence execution (Zupancic 81).

While this conclusion may seem to reinforce classical conventions, such as the Hollywood "happy ending", the theatrical tone of the finale seems to allude toward a different interpretation. As suggested by Lefebvre, the world view in *I Confess* "belongs in part to post-war America, [which] emphasizes change and self-affirmation, and proposes that the past make way for the present" (97). However, "the choice of a Catholic priest—a traditional figure of conservatism—as hero in this context will appear either as Hitchcockian irony or as unresolved tension between old and new worlds" (Lefebvre 97). I think that the theatrical ending emphasizes this contradiction. Ultimately, the "bad" dies, but, neither the hero nor the judicial system, have succeeded to reestablish justice by the power of their will. Theatricality in *I Confess* challenges classical cinematic conventions by bringing to the fore unresolved tension between moralistic cinema and dramatic theater.

Although theatricality may be used to challenge conventions, this is not why producers are so often reluctant to finance film-mediated dramas or films made by theater directors. On top of the financial risks facing them, producers are usually afraid that the film conveys a sort of "theatrical artificiality". Lepage explains that hesitant producers "think that there is a whole education that needs to be done over again" to properly prepare inexperienced theater directors to work in film (Caron 25; my translation). However, Lepage has affirmed that despite the warnings, he "did not necessarily try to avoid theatricality" and that "theatricality within the film does not corresponds to what this term is usually associated with in cinema. It can be found in characters, in the plot sometimes, but not in a pejorative way" (Caron 25; my translation).

Although *Le confessionnal*[i] is not an adaptation of a play, it evokes the idea of performance, as in many film-mediated dramas. The nude dancers performing in a strip-club, the young girl auditioning for a part in Hitchcock's film, and the actor playing the part of Montgomery Clift during the shooting of the film-within-the-film express theatricality through performance related sequences and characters playing roles. The scenario features also many in camera scenes that recall the stage, such as the intimate scene in the sauna where the brothers meet or the chess game. Also, Lepage explains that his experience in theatre permitted him to experiment "with ideas that cinema people would not necessarily frequently rely on, such as moving the camera two inches aside, and to change the epoch" (Caron 24; my translation). In some ways, these theatrical references not only relate to Lepage's experience as a stage director, but also create a parallel with *I Confess*'s theatricality.

---

[i] *The Confessional*

Theatrical and filmic experience seem to intersect during the projection of *I Confess* within *Le confessionnal*[i], the night of the premiere. The theatricality effect occurs when the camera adopts the point of view of the spectators within the film. At first, Hitchcock's film is filling the screen, so that we—the spectators—are really watching *I Confess* film footage. A subsequent shot presents the back of the spectators within the frame, and then a crane-in shows in perspective the proscenium of the theatre where the film credits are projected. Finally, a following shot shows frontally the characters as they are watching the film. During that whole sequence, spectatorship within the film and outside the film intertwines. A reflexive comment about film-within-a-film interweaves with a reference to the relationship between spectacle and spectators.

Furthermore, in this sequence, the interrelations between the *Le confessionnal* and the excerpts from *I Confess* can simultaneously imply a relationship based on an association and based on a distantiation, as suggested by May Telmissany. Association is created throughout parallelism, as Lepage alternates between 1952 and 1989, which highlights both the continuity and the differences between both periods. The distantiation effect occurs when we realize that we are watching the same film as the spectators within the film. In-between "now" and "then", *I Confess*'s excerpt is both fixed in the past and inscribed in the present—or Lepage's film. We can watch the film as ourselves, today, or identify with the spectators watching the film-within-the-film back then. The tension provoked by the simultaneity of these two states creates a distance, which forces the spectator, us, and especially Quebec spectators, to think about the changes that have occurred since the fifties, a pivotal period of Quebec history. According to Telmissany, the distance provoked by the reference to Hitchcock's film, which has the effect to reverse our relationships with space-time, can also be seen as an anachronism. In summary, the space-time relationships created by the quotation initiates an analogical comparison between both works, while, at the same time, the mise-en-abyme provokes an effect of distantiation.

Theatricality and quotation are means for *I Confess* and *Le confessionnal* [ii]to refer to their source, but also to emphasize the discursive aspect of their narrative. If the quotations in *Le confessionnal* can be interpreted as an homage to Hitchcock, they can also create a distance between both films that suggest a departure from the values conveyed in *I Confess*. On this subject, Telmissany argues that

> all the distantiation interplay, both physique and moral, the parallelism between two worlds (the old and the contemporary, the city and the suburb), the radical

[i] *The Confessional*
[ii] *The Confessional*

transformations of the society (the priest has become a business man), all this interplay is, basically, political, indeed antiestablishment. The modern confessional transforms itself in small rooms for nude dancers and in sauna for marginalized sexual relationships; Lepage's critique toward this transformation is not at a moral level, but at a social level. (260; my translation)

Both films criticize in their own ways societies that are blinded by their own truths or that cannot look past appearances. In that context, theatricality and intertextuality can become ways to confess origins of inspiration, but also means to criticize established social order.

Public and Private Confessions

To push the piety pun further, *I Confess* and *Le confessionnal*[i] can be considered as metaphors for a confessional. In a way, through those films, the directors confess their own play on appearances. In *I Confess*, for example, Hitchcock creates an estranged representation of Québec City in order to show the oppressive effect of concealment. On one hand, the gothic representation of Québec City stresses the oppressive nature of society. During the opening sequence, the crooked low-angle shot of the tower of Hotel Château Frontenac, which looks like a medieval castle on a hill, sets the gothic ambience that prevails throughout the film. The expressionist aesthetic of the opening sequence emphasizes the dual nature of the city, which symbolizes the ambiguity between guilt and innocence, a recurring theme in the film. In the opening scene, little girls walking innocently in the night evoke a peaceful environment. However, the next shots contradict our expectations by suggesting that murderers under priest's cassocks may hide in the streets! On the other hand, the overwhelming usage of Christian iconography emphasizes the personal struggle felt by Father Logan, who knows the murderer, but cannot claim his innocence out of respect for his vow of silence. A long shot of Father Logan walking in the streets after having learned that he is suspected, framed with a statue of the Christ carrying his cross and surrounded by two centurions in the foreground, expresses the torment that weight on the soul of Logan, as well as the cruelty of *justice*. Also, through insert editing, canted church towers repetitively intersperse his path. The diagonal lines in the frame create a tension within the image, while establishing a parallel between the pointed turrets and arrows' points. All this very suggestive iconography may portray Logan as a victim, but can also suggest that guilty feelings torment him. Later in the story, we learn that at the time the crime occurred, Logan had an alibi. He was meeting a former lover, Ruth Grandfort, who is married with a prominent politician. She

---

[i] *The Confessional*

was telling Logan that they were blackmailed by a lawyer that had caught them together years ago, just after her marriage with Pierre Grandfort, but before Logan had joined the priesthood. Although nothing *seems* to have happened between the lovers, Hitchcock has set the appearances against them.[i] The deceptive appearances, which persist until the end, create this moral ambiguity.

On another level, the choice of Québec City, as filming location, echoes the film's theme of deception. Although the original play was set in France, Hitchcock chose Québec City to shoot his film, a French Canadian city. Many reasons seem to justify this choice of location. First, Hitchcock may have wanted to refer to the play's nationality and take advantage of Québec genealogical affiliations with France. Similarity in terms of language and religious practices, combined with an architecture that recalls European cities, certainly contributed to the choice of Québec. The strong clerical presence in the city landscape, reflecting the authority the Catholic Church still had in 1950s on this principally rural society, must have also had an effect. This way, the religious iconography present in the film, such as the multiple leaning church towers, was not only supporting the film's religious themes, but was reflecting a reality of the time. The old fashioned look of the city, with its paved-stoned street and fortified walls, echo the societal attachment to its ancestral traditions. Hence, this North American location remained an opportunity to contemporize the story from 1902, without the expenses necessary for a shooting in Europe[ii], as implied by Martin Lefebvre:

> There can be no question that in choosing Québec City to shoot a French play written in 1902, Hitchcock was aiming at a particular chronotope: that of a backward society not fully in tune – or in time, should I say – with the rest of the industrial world, still clinging to old world values. Had Hitchcock wanted to shoot the film elsewhere, say in an equally urban environment in Europe for example, he most certainly would have had to make this a period or costume film. Duplessis-era Québec City was the perfect site for *I Confess*. (92)

However, choosing to shoot his film in Quebec rather than France could also signal an intention to mislead the audience. Although the first shot of the film pictures a famous Quebec monument, the Château Frontenac, strangers to Quebec culture could easily mistake it for a French castle. Before revealing,

---

[i] Deborah Thomas discusses in her article how Hitchcock deceives the spectators in *I Confess* by withholding some information from them.

[ii] Martineau's article mentions also the economical advantages offered by "the Canadian Co-operation Project—an entente between the Majors and the Canadian government" (18).

through a street sign, the real location, Hitchcock plays with the audience by letting them think that the film could have been set in the 19th century Europe.

Hitchcock uses reflexive strategies to call the attention of the spectator to the game they are playing a part of. When Robert Stam discusses self-conscious novels and films, he mentions that "[r]eflexive fictions defiantly call attention to their own artifice and operations, refusing a transparent self-effacing language that opens quietly onto the world" (Stam 1985: 129). Without trying to deconstruct the filmic language, Hitchcock's way of highlighting the filmic device seeks to involve the spectator in the creative process. From the beginning of the film, Hitchcock makes the spectator aware that he is the one orchestrating the flow of events. His cameo crossing the screen is followed by multiple shots of empty streets and the repeated visual motif of one-way signs with the French word "Direction" written on them. Eventually, an airy camera movement follows the path showed by the authoritative street sign, and reveals that these road signs were strangely leading the way to a murdered man. However, Hitchcock's apparition, followed by this pun, suggests that he wants to play with the word direction and its relationship with *directing*.[i] Furthermore, in those days, and as it is now, only a plain white arrow appears on one-way signs. This alteration to reality further confirms Hitchcock's playful intentions, and invites the spectator to be attuned throughout the film to other symbolic allusions. In fact, Hitchcock continuously plays with false proximity of the locations and even uses the interior of a church and the exterior of another one. At the world premiere of the film in Quebec City, Hitchcock even asked the audience to excuse him for the liberties he had taken with the geography of the city! (*Le Soleil*, Feb. 13, 1953) About Hitchcock's involvement in misleading the audience, Perkins points out that

> [i]n demonstrating that as a vehicle of truth film language must also be capable of falsehood, [...] *I Confess* prepares its ground for what is virtually an inventory of deceptions and concealments within quests for truth and for self-disclosure (35).

In summary, Hitchcock confessed his playing with realism and his *auteur* status through reflexive strategies, drawing our attention to his *direct* involvement in twisting the appearances.

Lepage also plays with appearances in *Le confessionnal*,[ii] but his perspective questions historical representation. As suggested by Erin Manning, Lepage's film incarnates the idea that "the confessional operates as the gnomon around which society configures itself, concealing its secrets in order to sustain

---

[i] Peter Conrad interprets in a similar way the meaning of the French word "Direction" on the road signs (251).

[ii] *The Confessional*

appearances" (Manning 60). Lepage's perspective shows how stories, as history, can *adapt* historical facts to reflect a set of values or a point of view. He also suggests that adapting history, as adapting a text, involves an omission of different events. However, *Le confessionnal*[i] implies also that what has been *cut* from Quebec history has left scars that still have not healed. Through his non-linear narrative and editing, Lepage implies that history needs to be revisited, but also that there should be place for different ways to tell a story.

The form of confession used by Lepage to tell his story foregrounds the fact that history is always told from the point of view of someone, whether it is a historian or a filmmaker. The form of confession that Lepage uses to tell his story questions the ways by which history is written, often choosing to hide secrets that society may prefer to forget. As noticed by Manning, the story of *Le confessionnal* unfolds "through a reading of a gap in history" (52). Manning adds:

> The confession in Robert Lepage's *Le Confessionnal* begins with this dedication to the father: 'À la mémoire de mon père' [, and] takes place twice, in an interval of twenty-seven years. This double confession explores the ways in which the act of confession influences the writing of history and the passing of time. Through the lapse in time, *Le Confessionnal* demonstrates how the act of confession is carried over life, complicating the relationship between telling stories and keeping secrets (Manning 52).

The film structure, mirroring the form of a confession, emphasizes the fact that the story is presented from Lepage's point of view, and foreshadows Lepage's intention to reveal in his film secrets that history has preferred to conceal.

Le confessionnal[ii] invites the spectator to participate in the retelling of Quebec history, by presenting a challenging and labyrinthine structure. As suggested by Larue,

> while the film progresses, more the flashbacks jostle together, and more it appears evident that Lepage tries to stop the *horizontal* flow of the narration, its move forward, in order to give us the possibility to explore it *vertically*; *i.e.*, to think about the meanings that should be given to all the different elements that compose this/these story(ies). (29; my translation)

Therefore, these disruptions during the course of the narrative may suggest that the story requires multiple readings. For example, the old photographs, which leave traces on the walls, can represent ghost memories from the past (Manning

---

[i] *The Confessional*
[ii] *The Confessional*

52).[i] This interpretation may explain that these memories cannot be simply erased with paint. These complex readings and the challenging structure of the film may also reflect changing filmmaking practices. Because people can see a film more than once, Lepage suggests that editing technique should be thought of differently and that "films should allow the spectators to read it straight or upside down, in rewind or in fast-forward, should be verifiable, or, like *Le confessionnal*,[ii] should have a plot structured like a maze" (Larue 27).

This fragmented narrative structure also alludes to postmodern practices in relation to re-presenting the past. As Linda Hutcheon suggests it, postmodern representations of the past "contest the entire notion of continuity in history and its writing" (Hutcheon 63). In *Le confessionnal*, as in postmodern fiction,

> [t]he narrativization of past events is not hidden; the events no longer seem to speak for themselves, but are shown to be consciously composed into a narrative, whose constructed– not found –order is imposed upon them, often overtly by the narrating figure (Hutcheon 63).

Through fragmentation of the narrative and the use of multiple flashbacks that interrupt the narrative progression, Lepage proposes a different way to represent history and seek to challenge the preconceived ideas about the image of Quebec City. Lepage wants to confront the trajectory of the people of Quebec with the ghosts and secrets that still haunt the streets of Quebec City. As if the cuts in the film were representing scars from the past, flashbacks telescope the story in the past in order to offer a reflection on the impact on the present of past-buried secrets.

Through a fragmented plot, Lepage questions the representations of history based on a linear and teleological account of events. Unlike the classical cause-and-effect plot of *I Confess*, or the chronological account of events found in history books, the film's structure is more like a postmodern collage. The film

> has a non-linear structure that interweaves past and present, fact and fiction into four branches that together compose the film narrative: a) the filming and the premiere screening of *I Confess* b) Paul-Emile's family situation in 1952 c) Pierre's discoveries in 1989 d) the circumstances of Marc's life. These sub-narratives are connected by Pierre Lamontagne's search for the father of his adopted brother Marc (Dundjerovic 60).

This hybrid mixture between fact and fiction may be interpreted in different ways. It shows that boundaries between fact and fiction can easily be blurred, when adapting historical facts. But, it can also suggest that history, like

---

[i] Manning's article explores this idea in detail.

[ii] *The Confessional*

Lepage's film, can be composed of multiple narratives that evolve in parallel, and that one of them is our own memory. As the personal and the collective memory, history is fragmented and partial. By pushing the concept further, ellipses in films may be compared to holes in history. Between each line of a history book, like between each cut in a film, may lay a forgotten event. The structure of the film, which uses multiple flashbacks, connects the concepts of memory and history, and suggests that holes in Quebec history are not necessarily empty and that fiction may contribute to recollecting those forgotten memories.

Le confessionnal[i] also offers historical, critical comments on the censorship of *I Confess*. A sequence of the film shows how furious Hitchcock was after the screening of the world premiere of his film in Quebec City, because the province of Quebec Censor Bureau had censored it, in spite of all his efforts to prevent this from happening (Marineau 18). On one level, this sequence comments on the power of the Church, even on the film industry, since the beginnings of cinema in Quebec.[ii] It also shows that during this era, even films had their own confessors. Fictitious characters were not allowed to say some truths on the big screen, but instead could only speak to the censor![iii] On another level, the reflexive allusion refers also to the influence of ideologies on the production process and the adaptation of a literary text to the screen. In this sense, the film comments on the constraints that must face filmmakers to meet the expectations of the film industry, and the Establishment, in regards to the form and the content of the story.

Hitchcock and Lepage not only use the filmic device to confess their method of creatively interpreting reality and expressing truth through fiction, they also use the medium for self-confession. The films reflect some biographical connections with their creator, while also seeming to convey a personal discourse on political events outside the realm of the films. For example, in the film on the making of *I Confess*, Hitchcock's Confession: A Look at "*I Confess*" (Laurent Bouzereau, 2004), the filmmaker Peter Bogdanovich considers I Confess as one of Hitchcock's most personal films because its subject relates to Hitchcock's Catholic background and his very strict Jesuit upbringing. Furthermore, Hitchcock's film may be interpreted as commentary upon "the dark moment in the history of Hollywood at which it was made: its story about

---

[i] *The Confessional*

[ii] According to Marineau, "no member of the clergy sat on the Censor Board at the time, though the notion of a convergence of views and interests between the two institutions seems generally accepted"(19).

[iii] Father La Couline, who saw the film on its release in 1953, says that the cuts were made where Anne Baxter explicitly says she had loved Father Michael before his acceptance into the priesthood (Marineau 19).

the courage and despair of a man scorned for his refusal to testify under interrogation is a thinly veiled allegory of McCarthyism and the blacklist" (Rothman 248). The danger of being considered anti-American during this period could have given Hitchcock personal reasons to shoot the film in a Catholic city outside of the United States.

Le confessionnal's[i] dedication to the memory of Lepage's father, a taxi driver like Pierre's father in the film, certainly gives the impression of a self-confession and forecasts other autobiographical references in the film[ii]. To know where one comes from is important for him, as he had mentioned in an interview about *Le confessionnal*: "What I hope comes out in the film is that the past haunts the present. And whether it's through our psychology, or whether it's ghosts, I think that the past always comes back at you if you haven't solved it." (Alioff 14). The discourse that metaphorically comes out of the film is that Québec needs to come to terms with its past, if it wants to move forward and progress. A society should be based on openness rather than hide behind secrets, whispers, gossips and remorse. In some ways, Lepage's own quest for his origins is mirrored in his characters' identity quest.

In conclusion, in *I Confess* and *Le confessionnal*, Lepage and Hitchcock use reflexivity, theatricality and transtextual strategies to manifest their authorial status, as well as to involve the spectators in the adaptation process. In attracting the spectator's attention to the discourse conveyed by the film, those strategies suggest that the viewer should look for meanings that may be hidden under false appearances. Also, by the complexity of its intertextual negotiations, *Le confessionnal*[iii] acknowledges the impossibility of faithfully representing a culture, problems of identity, historical facts or a socio-economical context. The film relies on the spectator's memory, or on their knowledge of the society depicted in the film, which also changes over time.

---

[i] *The Confessional*
[ii] Dundjerovic notices many other autobiographical elements in *Le confessionnal*'s narrative (55).
[iii] *The Confessional*

CHAPTER SEVEN

SOLITARY VISIONS ON THE CUTTING ROOM FLOOR: THE EFFECT OF COLLABORATION ON NARRATIVE IN HITCHCOCK'S FILM ADAPTATION OF *REBECCA*

by Karen R. Tolchin

The fiction writer enjoys virtual dominion over his or her narrative.[i] Barring the editorial influences of a small cadre of agents, editors, and publishers, the author's vision drives the literary product. Characters, plot, and setting all come into being through the function of one person's imagination at work, a single pair of eyes observing and a single pair of hands recording over a period of time. Post-structuralist theory has exposed the myth of the singular, essential, and impervious authorial voice. Yet the writer of short stories and novels has the luxury of making every narrative choice in solitude; by contrast, films—even independent films with modest budgets—are ensemble projects requiring the participation of many. The ensuing works reflect the contributions of screenwriter, director, producer, cinematographer, casting director, actors, composer, editor, grips, set designers, and others.

The adapted work of literature undergoes a significant transformation simply jumping from word to image. By necessity, it also changes when it shifts from the vision of one to the vision of many. Splicing solitude with mayhem, filmmakers produce narratives of an altogether different sort. In film adaptation, we see a shift from a work made by one crowd—the text driven by the cultural and linguistic zeitgeist embodied by the sole author—to a creation by crowds of crowds, multiplying exponentially with each member of the film crew. The Swedish filmmaker Ingmar Bergman considered it the height of folly to attempt a film adaptation of a literary work:

> Film has nothing to do with literature; the character and substance of the two art forms are usually in conflict. ... We should avoid making films out of books. The

---

[i] This is not to suggest that every fiction writer represents a proverbial island, resistant to the tides of linguistic, social, historical, political, and aesthetic influences, but that most writers work alone and enjoy a far greater measure of autonomy than most filmmakers.

irrational dimension of a literary work, the germ of its existence, is often untranslatable into visual terms—and it, in turn, destroys the special, irrational dimension of the film. If, despite this, we wish to translate something literary into film terms, we must make an infinite number of complicated adjustments which often bear little or no fruit in proportion to the effort expended. (Harrington 226)

The "complicated adjustments" to which Bergman refers could also be read more positively as a series of creative challenges and narrative choices. The hard-won "fruit" of the film adaptation may merit the expenditure of effort.

This essay will examine the effect of collaboration on a film narrative with literary origins, Alfred Hitchcock's first American film, 1940's *Rebecca*. Hitchcock took a decidedly different view of the marriage of literature and film than Bergman's: "You see, the nearest art form to the motion picture is, I think, the short story. It's the only art form where you ask the audience to sit down and read it in one sitting" (Harrington 117). Noting film's affinity with the short story was not merely an opportunity for a Hitchcockian witticism. The director was no stranger to the adaptation process. The majority of his films began as works of literature, adapted from stories, novelettes, novels, and plays: 1960's *Psycho* came from a Robert Bloch novel; 1943's *Lifeboat* originated from a John Steinbeck story; 1936's *The Secret Agent* came from a scenario by Charles Bennett from a play by Campbell Dixon which had been adapted from a novel by Somerset Maugham called *Ashenden*, and Alma Reville (Hitchcock's wife) is credited with the film adaptation. Hitchcock turned to Du Maurier material often. 1939's *Jamaica Inn* (1939) and *The Birds* (1963) came from a Du Maurier novel and short story, respectively (Truffault).

Adapted not from a short story but from a best-selling novel published in 1938—proof of its potential to yield high revenues at the box office—*Rebecca* proved to be a collaborative effort of monumental proportions. A hotly contested affair with the legendary producer David O. Selznick controlling the purse strings, *Rebecca* was the only Hitchcock film to win a Best Picture Oscar. Somewhat astonishingly, it is also the only film about which the director has said, "It is not a Hitchcock film." In *Creative Collaboration*, Vera John-Steiner argues that successful collaborations "require a prolonged period of committed activity. They thrive on dialogue, risk taking, and a shared vision" (203). *Rebecca* enjoyed none of these advantages as it was being crafted. Finances demanded speed, censors prevented risk-taking, no one shared a vision, and communication on the set was often poor. Yet the film emerged from the strife a coherent, compelling text all its own.

Rebecca's rapid journey to Hollywood could have been foretold by Du Maurier's theatrical family heritage. Like Hitchcock, Du Maurier also hailed from Britain, the daughter of the most famous theatrical actors' manager of the period, Gerald du Maurier, and the granddaughter of a caricaturist and writer,

George du Maurier. The Du Maurier clan was steeped in creative collaboration, and Daphne grew up in a house filled with such imaginative luminaries as J.M. Barrie. Yet Hitchcock's *Rebecca* differs from the novel that spawned it for a variety of reasons, beginning with the nature of the film collaboration. Unlike the lively and congenial sort of theatrical collaboration Daphne Du Maurier may have witnessed with some frequency in her successful family's circles in Britain—and the private, solitary, creative process she may have enjoyed in the writing of the book as an established author—the process by which the American film production of *Rebecca* came into being was characterized by discontent. Indeed, no one, not the director, producer, lead actor, lead actress, or anyone else, appears to have had a moment's happiness on the American set of *Rebecca*. In fact, the sadistic Hitchcock quickly noted the tenor of the set and decided to capitalize on its fractious nature in order to get a great performance out of his lead actress.

Recognizing the screen potential of *Rebecca* after adapting *Jamaica Inn*, Hitchcock first tried to purchase the film rights to it on his own in 1939, but quickly found himself out of his financial depth. When Selznick invited him to come to the United States to make films for him, also in 1939, Hitchcock agreed. Fresh from his success with *Gone with the Wind*, Selznick bought the rights to *Rebecca* that Hitchcock alone couldn't afford, and the two men discarded the project that had first brought Hitchcock across the ocean to focus on adapting Du Maurier's Gothic novel for the big screen. A bevy of Hollywood's best screenwriters was secured. *Rebecca*'s credits include five writers: "Scenario by Robert E. Sherwood and Joan Harrison from the Du Maurier novel; Adaptation by Philip Macdonald and Michael Hogan." As the project developed, everyone got involved in the rewriting of *Rebecca*.

Selznick had a clear picture of how he wanted Manderley to look, and scoured the American countryside for an appropriate location to depict the imposing estate that serves as the narrative's setting. Finding no location to match his private vision, he decided they would use a highly convincing miniature replica—a decision that must have rankled Hitchcock, who had just left a country with ancient, beautiful estates. Ironically, the toy estate and the invisible title character (Rebecca herself is never seen, having died before the action begins) both emerge as more tangible, potent characters than the actors who fill the screen for hours. As befits a *film noir*, (a genre characterized by paranoia, claustrophobia, and self-delusion), *Rebecca* turns on the insecurity of a young, lowborn second wife whose image of her high-born predecessor corrodes her marriage to a man with secrets. In Du Maurier's novel, the estate and the dead first wife occupy the same "real" space as any other setting or character. In an unexpected twist, (because most novels allow more room for the reader's imagination than most films), the film actually amplifies the novel's message about how far imagination can take the reader.

The next major changes to the novel came from the film industry's self-imposed censors, then in the heyday of their power. Chief among them was the Hays Office—run by Will Hays, a "Hoosier Presbyterian elder" (Maltby 81). In the early 1930's, Hays teamed with a Catholic layman and motion-picture trade publisher named Martin I. Quigley and a Jesuit priest named Daniel A. Lord, and sponsored the Quigley-Lord Code. As film historian Robert Sklar explains in *Movie-Made America: A Cultural History of American Film*, the code "attempted to establish once and for all a standard for moral values in a popular mass medium" (Sklar 173). Sklar alleges that the censors were responding to the American elite's growing concerns about the rapid rise of movie culture, in which the product was manufactured and owned by immigrants (often Russian Jews) who became moguls, and embraced by the working class. Their effects on American culture at large were not yet unknown.

Hugo Munsterberg, a Harvard psychology professor, was the first scholar to ask the following question: "What happens in our heads and our nervous systems when we go to the movies, and what are the social consequences?" (Sklar 125). Munsterberg found that films " 'obey the laws of the mind,' where a variety of spatial and temporal images can co-exist, 'rather than the laws of the outer world' " (Sklar 125). While this posed a distinct threat to the status quo, the censors were savvy enough to the realities of the film industry as an industry to recognize that "without sex and crime pictures, there wouldn't be enough patrons to sustain a movie business" (Sklar 174). Hence, as critic Richard Maltby explains, "The regulations [the censors] devised to render objectionable books or plays unobjectionable sought both to maximize commercial advantage and to distribute an affirmative cultural vision" (82). In the spirit of good will and commerce, they developed a "formula of 'compensating moral value': if 'bad' acts are committed, they must be counteracted by punishment and retribution, or reform and regeneration, of the sinful one. 'Evil and good are never to be confused throughout the presentation,' the code said" (Sklar 174). In essence, complying with the Quigley-Lord Code meant crafting a narrative that would spark no sympathy for wrongdoers.

It is difficult to imagine a filmmaker for whom it would be more distasteful to craft a narrative that would spark no sympathy for wrongdoers than Alfred Hitchcock. Hitchcock was a recent arrival to the United States, and was hardly a propagandist for moral clarity. On the contrary, he was a subtle architect of moral dilemmas, and a brave explorer of ambiguous moral terrain. Neither he nor Selznick wanted to alter *Rebecca* so that "evil and good would not be confused throughout the presentation." Yet *Rebecca* contained two major plot events that might still provoke angst in audiences today: an abortion, and the murder of a young, beautiful woman. Ultimately, the filmmakers were compelled to shroud the first act in innuendo; the murder metamorphosed outright into an accidental death. The distance between a murder and an accidental death seems vast, yet the film made that migration—one that made the male protagonist more sympathetic.

The changes to Du Maurier's original narrative multiplied as Hitchcock lost certain important artistic battles that directly influenced the finished product. Determined to make a fortune out of the picture, Selznick insisted that Hitchcock include a sweeping and obvious musical score that would cue the audience when danger lurked, etc. Hitchcock preferred to design the film for an audience savvy enough to discern such danger from the plot and the actors' facial expressions. Yet the finished, scored film reflects the will of the producer, not the director.

Discord and shaky collaboration marked the atmosphere of the set, some of it by the director's design. Hitchcock used Joan Fontaine's anxiety over being mistreated by the male lead, Laurence Olivier, (who had wanted her part to go to his wife in real life, Vivien Leigh), by telling the young actress that she was actively disliked by the entire cast and crew. He then instructed the cast and crew to snub her whenever possible to heighten her paranoia and dismay.

From 1955 through the mid-sixties, the French director Francois Truffault interviewed Hitchcock extensively for a book on his idol. Truffault called Hitchcock "grossly underrated" (14). In their talks, he asked him if he was satisfied with *Rebecca*. In his response, Hitchcock distances himself from the film, going so far as to deny paternity: "Well, it's not a Hitchcock picture; it's a novelette, really. The story is old-fashioned; there was a whole school of feminine literature at the period, and though I'm not against it, the fact is that the story is lacking in humor" (91-2). Ironically, although Hitchcock often went to literature for the stories of his films, what he objected to in *Rebecca*'s narrative was its very storied-ness. Asked if he was intimidated by the transition to the realm of American filmmaking, Hitchcock revealed more complex feelings about *Rebecca*:

> "Well, not exactly, because in fact it's a completely British picture: the story, the actors, and the director were all English. I've sometimes wondered what the picture would have been like had it been made in England with the same cast. I'm not sure I would have handled it the same way. The American influence on it is obvious. First, because of Selznick, and then because the screenplay was written by the playwright Robert Sherwood, who gave it a broader viewpoint than it would have had if made in Britain." (92)

Later, Hitchcock elaborates that if the film had been shot in England, they would have found a real house and not used a miniature. Then, "the house would not have been so isolated because we'd have been tempted to show the countryside and the lanes leading to the house. ... we would have lost the sense of isolation." When Truffault questions him about the film's highest award, a terse exchange ensues:

> FT "... the picture won an Oscar, didn't it?"
> AH "Yes, the Academy voted it the best picture of the year."
> FT "I believe that's the only Oscar you've ever won."
> AH. "I've never received an Oscar."
> FT "But you just said that Rebecca ...."
> AH "The award went to Selznick, the producer. The directing award that year was given to John Ford for *The Grapes of Wrath*."

Hitchcock's answers appear to cause Truffault some consternation, as though he detects that Hitchcock does not enjoy the subject of the making of *Rebecca* but feels compelled to query him on it just the same. The French director treads as lightly as possible when asking if *Rebecca* was a faithful adaptation, and receives the same sort of blunt, dismissive response:

AH "Yes, it follows the novel very faithfully because Selznick had just made *Gone with the Wind*. He had a theory that people who had read the novel would have been very upset if it had been changed on the screen, and he felt this dictum should also apply to *Rebecca*. ..." (91-95)

More than half a century later, filmmakers who adapt beloved books by a variety of authors take the same risk in diverging from the text: witness the pressures voiced by the directors of the *Harry Potter* series. Yet Hitchcock implies that he would not have felt as compelled as Selznick to follow the novel as faithfully as the censors would allow. It is difficult to imagine Hitchcock caring very much if viewers felt upset about changes to the novel, or anything else for that matter. After all, in most Hitchcock films, upsetting the audience appears to be the main goal. His critical and mass appeal as a filmmaker suggests that filmgoers appreciate his gift for stealing their sense of comfort. Furthermore, they appreciate the unique fingerprints he leaves, creatively speaking, on the texts he adapts.

In the case of *Rebecca*, the differences yielded by collaboration seem writ large upon the final product. Besieged by demands from his producer, American censors, lead actor, and others, Hitchcock himself seems not to have realized how brilliantly he imbued the Du Maurier novel with his own distinctive voice. Orson Welles once noted that before any filmmaker attempts an adaptation, "I believe you must say something new about a book, otherwise it is better not to touch it" (Harrington 3). In another director's hands, the film *Rebecca* might have been too pat, too sentimental a tale of woe. Under Hitchcock's direction, the heartlessness of the heroine's treatment—even, or especially by those who purport to care for her—coupled with the folly of her desperation to please, stand out in *bas relief*. The film seems quintessentially Hitchcockian in its unflinchingly *un*sentimental rendering of a sentimental story. Perhaps to offset the blunting and gentling of the plot necessitated by the censors, Hitchcock took great pains to emphasize moments of everyday cruelty, as well as the crispness of its wit. His creative direction lent a dimension to the narrative virtually as central to the success of the film as an artistic product as the original text. Despite all of the chaos—or perhaps because of it—the film emerged as an enduring success.

The case of *Rebecca* suggests the potential yield of even the most contentious collaborations. A multitude of filmic narratives have emerged as distinct entities from the literary narratives that spawned them, often out of processes that seem like fiascoes. Rather than lamenting the differences between texts, we may mine the shifting tectonic plates between the original text and the filmic product for meaning. We may counter Bergman's claim that filmmakers who adapt literary texts "must make an infinite number of complicated adjustments which often bear little or no fruit in proportion to the effort expended." We may insist that the harvest can be well worth the planting.

CHAPTER EIGHT

SPECTERS OF *PSYCHO*: FREUD, FEAR, AND FILM ADAPTATION

by Shannon Donaldson-McHugh and Don Moore

This chapter[i] interrogates the cultural significance of Gus Van Sant's 1998 near word-for-word, scene-for-scene adaptation of Alfred Hitchcock's 1960 classic horror film *Psycho* by reading it alongside Jacques Derrida's concept of hauntology. Approaching a film like Van Sant's *Psycho* outside of a psychoanalytic framework such as Slavoj Zizek's Lacanian readings of Hitchcock's films may seem almost counter-intuitive, particularly since our essay deals primarily with the ways in which Hitchcock's Freudian psychology haunts Van Sant's adaptation. Unlike Zizek, however, we do not seek to understand how the "Real" symbolic order is fundamentally distorted through the immanent (im)possibility of symbolic identification in both films. Instead, we interrogate the ways in which such a spectral, *infrastructural*[ii] symbolic order which so plausibly produces horror effects in Hitchcock's film seems to break down entirely as a supposed transcendental – if distorted– source of "terror" in Van Sant's version, particularly when viewed through the hauntological lens of historical distance. Unlike Zizek, who seems to be always already seduced by the very psychoanalytic "ground" of the Real that he critiques, Derrida's hauntological model, for us, is much more self-reflexive in its approach to infrastructural totalities like the symbolic order, or the illusion that we have historically "progressed" from an older, Freudian psychoanalytic model to a more "enlightened" Lacanian one that can "explain" Freud's hidden truths.

Like *différance*, hauntology is a classic Derridian "double" gesture and circumscribes the homonym (in French) between ontology and hauntology., figuring what Derrida sees as their aporetic (meaning fundamentally

---

[i] EDITORS NOTE: This article was also published in the *Journal of Popular Culture* (April 2006, 39:2) under the title: "Film Adaptation, Co-Authorship, and Hauntology: Gus Van Sant's *Psycho* (1998)" 225-233

[ii] Rodolphe Gasché's book *The Tain of the Mirror* (1986) contains perhaps the best discussion to date of Derrida's concept of infrastructure, which is a way of understanding the de-ontologizing effects of deconstructive "method" as exemplified in such terms as dangerous supplementarity, the trace, the hinge.

contradictory)—not reflective—relationship. In other words, where hauntology.allows for the possibility that an ontological specter *could* materialize, it nonetheless underlines the aporetic and/or impossibly complex conditions of possibility for that materialization to occur, as well as the impossibility of such a specter's having any trans-historical "essence" or ontological "presence" outside of its own infrastructural logic. Differently put, the concept of hauntology contrasts the "spirit" of a thing – its impossible "origin" or a-historical "essence" – with its multiple, heterogeneous *specters*, these, the non-material materializations, or *supplements* that stand in for the (im)possibility of a spiritual presence and thus paradoxically allow it to *live on* as a memory or quasi-messianic promise. It can never be repeated too often, Derrida asserts in *Specters of Marx,* that there is always *more than one* specter and/or spirit of a concept, and they are always heterogeneous. Not to recognize this hauntological quality of a concept, idea, or being, he suggests, is to do an injustice to what it was, is, or might become in the future.

Using this Derridian concept of hauntology to inform our analysis, we will probe the ways in which Hitchcock's film's ideological, historical, and moral "contexts" of late-1950's middle-America haunt Van Sant's 1998 version of *Psycho* as the "specters of Hitchcock" – specters that we argue represent nothing but the dangerously supplemental, heterogeneous translation of Hitchcock's (always deferred) spirit produced by and through Van Sant's particular historical lens. While Van Sant seems to trust in the continued psychoanalytic relevance and ideological power of the "Hitchcock effect" – our term for the status of Hitchcock's films as almost a-historical, iconographic cultural references for the essence of "terror" – what we are interested in are the ways in which Van Sant's remake illuminates the historical specificity, as opposed to the seeming "timelessness" of Hitchcock's "genius," and how Hitchcock's Freudian psychoanalysis still haunts the contemporary North American psyche through technologies of ideology and gender such as Hollywood cinema.

Yet another spectral level on which the hauntological process of adaptation between Van Sant's and Hitchcock's films is "reflected" in our paper is in our self-reflexive "co-authorial" format. This format is intended to make as explicit as possible our own collaborative process in order to probe its limitations and productive possibilities as a method for the hospitable mingling of heterogeneous "authorial archives" of knowledge, experience, and ideas. As Derrida provocatively suggests in *Archive Fever: a Freudian Impression*, the "archive"

is only a *notion*, an impression associated with a word and for which, together with Freud, we do not have a concept. We only have an impression, an insistent impression through the unstable feeling of a shifting figure, of a schema, or of an in-finite or indefinite process. [...] [T]here are essential reasons for which a concept in the process of being formed always remains inadequate relative to what it ought to be, divided, disjointed between two forces. And this disjointedness has a necessary relationship with the structure of archivization. (29)

In other words, the laws and formal structures of "archivization," Derrida explains, are always inadequate to the heterogeneous, expansive, and shifting nature of any particular archive. Later on in the book, he characterizes the archive as *spectral*, referring to its impossible yet insistent infrastructural coherence. This way of thinking about archivization informs our critique of the psychic "laws" of authorship as seeming ready archives of authentic authorial "voice" and "intent." Even the term "authorial voice" invokes a kind of originary phono-centric psychic archive for which language – and for Freud, culture in general – becomes the supplement that must (always inadequately) mediate the "truth" about what the author meant to "say." In the chapter on "Freud and the Scene of Writing" in *Writing and Difference*, Derrida pays special attention to Freud's conceptualization of a psychic language of memory as a kind of "mystic writing-pad" which the psychoanalyst must interpret by way of a "talking cure." This writing-pad, for Freud, is a kind of psychic archive with transcendental laws and rules that are only decipherable by the trained psychoanalyst who holds the magical key for unlocking and interpreting them correctly.

The paradoxes and inadequacies of such seemingly transcendental oedipal laws are, for us, made glaringly obvious in co-authorships (or film-adaptations) because the disparate authors, their genders, psyches, individualit(ies), and the different archives of knowledge that they bring to bear on their shared subject are, through their spectral intermingling as ostensibly one co-authorial voice, rendered indistinguishable from one another. In other words, the infrastructural coherence of so-called disparate authorial psychic-archives, in a co-authorship or co-*auteur*ship, disintegrates and becomes effectively one "collective" voice. Furthermore, such a disintegration of authentic authorial "voice" points to the certain ways in which all authorships are always already complex, multi-layered co-authorships haunted by the specters of many "authors," "archives," and influences.

In short, film adaptations, like co-authorships, viewed through the lens of a hauntologicalcritique, are without authentic "origins" – or precisely definable authors/auteurs – and thus cannot *properly* be called adaptations (though they may be), since they are merely supplemental adaptations of earlier adaptations. Differently put, in the same ways in which, as individual writers, our spectral "psychic-archives" intertwine and play off each other to produce new perspectives and ideas about our subject matter, so do we see Van Sant's historical archive colliding and intertwining with Hitchcock's to produce, not a "faithful" or "unfaithful" homage to a supposed authentic Hitchcockian "original," but rather a unique spectral reading of Norman Bates' schizophrenia, his "trans-sexuality," and the ways in which the audience is manipulated into a prescribed relationship to Norman's psychological "gaze" as a technology of ideological training.

Our "shared experience" of the hybridizing, dangerously supplemental effects of co-authorship lead us to question theories of co-authorship and collaboration that characterize it entirely in terms of the political unification of two (or more) ontologically coherent voices in a kind of identity politics of "shared experience." Our collaboration instead aims at a kind of "queering" of essentialist identity politics around authorship and the implied "insider archival knowledge" attached to such supposedly "pluralist," politicized identities. This is not to say, however, that the *event* of this co-authored labour and the material conditions of its being carried out cannot be legitimately examined for their particular methodological levers and unique productivities. Our deeper purpose here is to stipulate, like Heidegger, that the event-ness of this particular event should be given more careful scrutiny.

For example, one such product of our self-reflexive, co-authorial method is its performative queering of our joint-authorial "voice" as representative of our collective, and ostensibly cross-gendered, psychic "archives." Such a "queer" co-authorial voice stages a self-reflexive critique of Freudian concepts of gender and psychic identity as they are presented in Hitchcock's (1960) and Gus Van Sant's (1998) *Psycho*s as symbolically "Real" subjects to objective psychoanalytic diagnosis. The spectral logic of Van Sant's adaptation of Hitchcock in fact underlines the ways in which both of these films can be read as "queer" (in Judith Butler's paleonymic sense of that term) in spite of their anxious and excessive psychoanalytic supplementation of the Freudian gender norm in order to explain Norman's "illness" by way of the psychiatrist's speech at the end of both versions.

For us, Van Sant's almost word-for-word, scene-for-scene reconstruction of Hitchcock's "original" *Psycho* creates the effect of a hauntological "co-authorship" between these two directors that hinges upon the attempt to span each other's historical "moments" and thereby stay "true" to each other's authentic conceptual visions. Van Sant, in fact, calls his 1998 *Psycho* "a mirror to the original film: its sort of schizophrenic twin" (Van Sant qtd. in Schneider n.p.). It would seem, therefore, that on one level Van Sant attempts a kind of performative re-enactment of the Hitchcockian psychic "law" of *Psycho* with the intention of resurrecting its "spirit." On a more careful reading of Van Sant's description, however, he explicitly refers to the 1998 remake as "schizophrenic. " This intriguing word choice both invokes its psychoanalytic remainder, and at the same time infers that his version is not meant merely to be a reflective "copy" but something *radically other* than Hitchcock's film: a more complex mutation of *Psycho* in spite of the proclaimed "shot-for-shot, scene-for-scene" duplication. This schizophrenic mirroring, for us, problematizes notions of direct reflection of an "original" or its "spirit" and instead points to the ways in which the specters of such a supposed original are always multiple and heterogeneous, and without direct access to origins. Van Sant's film, instead, enacts a kind of performative resurrection of a lifeless (implying something in the past, and therefore dead) ideal of Hitchcock's – and Freud's – geniuses. Such performative resurrections, however, as Judith Butler has convincingly argued, always result in a "queer," or imperfect copy of the ideal law. Butler's concept of performativity thus illuminates the impossibility that the ideal might ever have existed as an authentic origin, and instead demonstrates that it was always only a series of multiple, heterogeneous supplements to itself. At the same time, performativity also proves to be the very condition of possibility for keeping the spirit of the ideal *alive* as a normative concept. In other words, even if the ideal concept never existed except as an originary supplement, a metaphor without a referent, that founding supplementarity is nonetheless *something*, even if its lack of origins means that it is always in reference to nothing, and therefore is always already becoming something else.

Butler's insights would suggest that Van Sant's attempt to a-historically transfer the "essence" of Hitchcock's film, both the underlying Oedipal law grounding the diagnosis of Norman Bates' psychosis, as well as a word-for-word, scene-for-scene rendering of the original, with the exception that the time-frame of the action is transferred from 1960 to 1998, was bound to "fail." But the questions and unforeseen consequences produced by this so-called failure – *e.g., how and why* it "failed," as well as the "erroneous" details and excesses produced by this failure – for us, are much more interesting than Van Sant's originally stated aim, and indeed throw into question his film's oft-repeated critical status as a "failure." Indeed, we see the critical and box-office "failures" of Van Sant's version as symptoms of the historical and epistemological limitations of such an attempted a-historical transfer of "artistic genius" that Van Sant's film undertakes. In fact, the very mimetic structure of his film – with the important exception of the date – underscores these hauntological issues of temporality, archival transferability, and the impossible structural "unity" of a so-called "authentic" text.

Derrida argues in *Archive Fever* that "the structure of the archive is *spectral*. It is spectral *a priori*: neither present nor absent 'in the flesh,' neither visible nor invisible, a trace always referring to another whose eyes can never be met" (*Archive Fever* 84 original emphasis). As a hauntological effect, the archive materially exists, but represents an impossible, idealized unity of its archive, an organization of the past with a definite beginning and end that is contradicted by the very mode of material production and laws governing such an archive. The spectral archive that Van Sant draws upon for his remake of *Psycho* is Hitchcock, or what we characterize as the "Hitchcock effect." This effect, for us, is related to Hitchcock's massive cultural reproduction in multiple, heterogeneous spectral forms and as an icon and ready archive of cinematic "terror." The Hitchcock effect represents the very possibility of the spectral "return" of *Psycho* for "a new generation," in spite of its impossible unity as the authentic "spirit" of the original. For example, it should not be forgotten that there are at least four versions of *Psycho* at work here: Robert Bloch's novel of the same name, Van Sant and Hitchcock's movie versions, and the "real life" story of 1950s serial killer Ed Gein. If these different adaptations of Gein's story amount to a negotiation of the "moral climate" around which murder is judged in the particular historical contexts in which these adaptations present themselves, the historical "events" of the cinematic and literary versions of Gein's story have become at least as, if not far more, important than the "original" historical event of his killing spree as vectors through which North American audiences conceptualize their moral outrage around murder, as well as their diagnosis of the "symptoms" of mental illness and the supposed "origins" of the desire to commit mass murder.

There is also the so-called "affair" between Marion and her boyfriend Sam which is framed as the central motivation for the action that follows. While both Sam and Marion are unattached, consenting adults in both Hitchcock's and Van Sant's versions, Marion's deviance from normative American cultural values around heteronormative marital sex, it is implied in both films, leads her into moral corruption which manifests in her embezzlement of money belonging to her boss. This chain of events effectively positions Marion not as an innocent "victim" preyed upon by a mass murderer, but rather as somehow justly punished for her own social deviance at the hands of Norman Bates, who is himself depicted as a victim of deviant, Oedipal desires which have supposedly manifested as his psychopathic, schizophrenic, trans-sexual inhabiting (or entering) of the "body" of his mother.

These Freudian readings of Marion's and Norman's gendered transgressions implicit in both films, however, no longer ring true in Van Sant's version due to the "unheimlich" (Freud's word meaning unhomely, or out of place) transfer of the story to the context of 1998 middle-America. Furthermore, Van Sant's near mimetic copy allows us to revisit the Freudian psychoanalysis of Norman and Marion in Hitchcock's version, revealing that Freud's theories are as out of place in the "original" 1960 context as they are in 1998. Van Sant's version, we argue, trans-historically haunts its source, providing us with a different perspective – literally a "*reframing*" – of Hitchcock's film with which to view

Norman's "condition" in a more "queer" register than the doctor's analysis at the end of both films would suggest. This anxious, excessive reframing of the Freudian subtext in the remake (for example, all the hyperbolic talk of "respectability" in the opening), we argue, self-consciously points to the phallocentric logic implied in Hitchcock's film and thereby renders these repressive "norm"(s) ridiculous. In these ways, Van Sant's version haunts Hitchcock as much as Hitchcock's "original" haunts Van Sant.

For example, in Hitchcock's version of the shower scene, Norman gazes at Marion through the peephole and the viewer is made to share Norman's perspectival gaze.

This eroticized, androcentric gaze upon the sexually objectified Marion is thereby encoded as the viewer's default position. Theresa De Lauretis explains in *Technologies of Gender* (1987) how this kind of male-centered directorial gaze often couches itself in the guise of "realism" but ostensibly works as a "technology of gender," or a kind of subtle training of the viewer in the normativization of phallocentric gender roles. The effect of this gaze in Hitchcock's shower scene, however, plays upon the normative assumptions of the audience, but forces them into identification with Norman who is ostensibly depicted as a disturbed cross-dresser with homicidal tendencies. These presuppositions are in fact the source of the "horror" in the film: Norman's phallocentric gaze is ideologically framed as the gaze of the audience itself, interpellating them into "Norman's" perspective, or the "*Norm.*" The psychotic "disease" that has infected the serial killer and driven him to murder can be located, Hitchcock seems to suggest, in the very disordered psyche of the society that produced such a killer. Van Sant's restaging of this scene, however, encourages the audience of Hitchcock's film to rethink their original presupposed phallocentric gaze, an ideological technology that is belatedly brought in to focus through the spectral lens of Van Sant's adaptation.

Van Sant achieves his reframing of *Psycho*'s shower scene in two ways: First, the audience not only gazes through the phallocentric perspective of Norman into the peephole at the sexualized body of Marion, but we also gaze upon Norman, who is obviously masturbating. Stephen J. Schneider, in his article "A Tale of Two Psychos," proposes that Van Sant has thus effectively "queered" the scene (Schneider n.p.). The audience, instead of exclusively inhabiting Norman's gaze (though we are allowed to look through the peephole) instead witnesses Norman looking and masturbating. Norman is thereby also rendered a sexualized object of the audience's gaze. Secondly, while there was doubt left in Hitchcock's version as to whether or not Norman derived any sexual satisfaction out of watching Marion's nude body in the shower (and hence maintaining the possibility that it could also be his "mother" watching at any given time), there is no doubt in Van Sant's version that Norman, the male gazer, eroticizes Marion in an "inappropriate" and, as Stephen J. Schneider points out, "(male) unisexual way" (Schneider n.p.). Therefore, the audience members, now in the position of metacritics, are faced with the clear phallocentrism of Norman's gaze, as opposed to merely being conspicuously interpolated into that very perspectival gaze, or invited to contain and dismiss Norman's "dis-order" by diagnosing it as a heteronormative concept of homosexuality. Schneider suggests that Van Sant's Norman's "multi-sexuality" doesn't really privilege one side of Norman's personality over the other, but allows him to be unisexual at any given time (Schneider n.p.). Likewise, the audience is given many options from which to choose Norman's possible gender orientation which creates an ambivalence that both encourages a wider range of audience identification with Norman's sexuality, and at the same time derails the ideological interpellation of the audience into *one* privileged normative sexual default position (heteronormative monogamy) by which to judge Norman's "deviance."

In fact, instead of making a clear separation between Norman's two distinctly binarized male-female subjectivities and putting them in a kind of Hegelian death-struggle for gendered self-identification, Schneider's analysis seems to point to a more "monstrous" conceptualization of Norman's sexuality in Van Sant's version. For, Van Sant's Norman is not a-sexual, and perhaps not even unisexual, since that would imply a kind of universalizing stability to any one of Norman's sexualities that is still very much cast within an *un*stable, performative male-female binary. That binary, however, in Norman, has turned in on itself, as his onanistic display during the shower scene indicates. Our best evidence in both films, in fact, leads us to conclude that he has sex *only* with himself. Norman's auto-erotic sexual energy, however, seems to feed off of an intensified and murderous death-drive, which Freud sees as a kind of uncanny compulsion to repeat traumatic incidents and thus links Norman's matricide with a sexualized desire to inhabit his mother. Van Sant's Norman's imperfect performances of male and female gender – performances that, during the peep-hole/masturbation scene, are on many levels simultaneous – *in their close adherence* to the Oedipal laws implicit in Hitchcock's original script, thus seems to performatively short-circuit and/or cancel out male-female binarized sexuality, replacing it with onanistic violence. What Van Sant thus manages to illuminate, if unconsciously, by shifting the viewer's perspective in this scene is a revelation of the impossibly confused and dangerously supplemental condition of the gendered "Norm"-an in both Van Sant's and Hitchcock's versions of *Psycho,* and the violence of the Oedipal law itself in its exclusion of all forms of radically other sexuality that cannot be accounted for within its own rigid epistemological framework.

Tellingly, it is at the very end of both movies in a scene that is not part of the action "proper" but more of a supplement or postscript where we encounter the psychoanalyst. Like a stand-in or spectral supplement for Freud himself, the psychoanalyst walks in to the waiting room of the County Court House (the symbol of justice and public ethical arbitration par excellence) which is set up like an impromptu lecture hall. Outside the County Court House, onlookers gather, signaling a wider public significance to the psychoanalytic trial underway within, and also over, Norman's private psyche; a trial mediated and interpreted both by the psychoanalyst and the justice system. The psychoanalyst then proceeds to calmly, authoritatively–and in the Hitchcock version even with a hint of dark, world-weary laughter–provide a scientific explanation of the Freudian "truth" about Norman's psychosis. In doing so, *he* effectively provides the overarching moral message uniting the action of the whole film, or the transcendental ethical truth that will supposedly ground the law in moral certitude. As the Sheriff, a representative of the force-of-law over private citizens par excellence, deferringly quips just before the psychiatrist's entrance, "If anybody can get any answers, it'll be the psychiatrist. Even I couldn't get to Norman, and he knows me." (*Psycho* 1960).

Everything about both versions of the scene implies distanced, scientific rationality and a much wider trial over the ethical limits and juridicial boundaries that the public sphere imposes upon and/or tolerates for its "private" citizens. Scientific rationality is indicated, for example, by Marion's sister's wearing a coat in the chilly anti-room of the Court House, signaling an atmosphere of cold, scientific calculation that will inform blind justice notwithstanding her warm (read womanly/soft/homely) feelings for her transgressive sister. The (Freudian) danger that we are being alerted to is that these very virtuous feminine qualities that Marion strayed from, a digression that leads her to sexual and moral corruption and eventually to her death, are the same "weak" feminine qualities that might lead her sister to unjustly forgive Marion's role in the tragedy and thus lead to the further corruption of American society. Indeed, asserts the psychiatrist in both versions, it was Norman's "clinging, demanding" mother who was largely responsible for Norman's sexual perversion and murderous pathology. The psychiatrist's ominous, phallocentric diagnosis at the end of both films is, in fact, that "mother killed the girl."

The differences between Hitchcock's version of the last scene and Van Sant's, however, are instructive. Unlike any other scene, nearly a third of the original psychoanalyst's speech from Hitchcock's *Psycho* is cut in Van Sant's version, which represents a drastic editing of the very central Freudian moral core of Hitchcock's film. Van Sant's psychiatrist seems less arrogantly self-assured than Hitchcock's. His truncated speech seems to indicate an almost apologetic need to just get the message out, as opposed to Hitchcock's psychoanalyst's drawn-out, moral proselytizing. There is also less of an indication in Van Sant's version that Norman was merely an overly-doting son whose psychotic, murderous behaviour was solely the fault of his mother. In fact, there is less emphasis in Van Sant's version that Norman and his mother might be "pathologically jealous" of each other. This revision opens the possibility of there being a less-than-rigid gender binary at work in Norman's sexual role-playing and more of a gender simultaneity whose monstrous, performative imperfection is short-circuiting the logical unity of the Oedipal law, and destroying it from within its very "Norm."

Another important difference between the two versions is that in Hitchcock's film the psychiatrist offers a description of his job to the police chief: "PSYCHIATRIST: (laughing) A psychiatrist doesn't lay the groundwork, he merely tries to explain it" (Hitchcock's *Psycho*). His derisive laughter denotes an almost arrogant detachment from the inferred politics of the legal system. He is a man of cold, hard reason and scientific facts, and is therefore above question or reproach, at least outside of his own scientific community. The word "ground" here also connotes a kind of transcendental, universalized symbolic order–or Oedipal truth–upon which Freudian psychoanalytic judgments are almost phenomenologically rooted. In other words, the psychiatrist doesn't see psychoanalysis as a creation and recreation of its own laws and frameworks, but as the scientific illumination of itself as a "Reality" that was already there.

The occlusion of this line in Van Sant's film, however, seems to signal a more contemporary shift away from Freudian psychology and its categorizations of sexual "disorder." Jacques Lacan, for example, critiqued Freud on the basis that the symbolic order, for Lacan, can only ever represent an obscured, hopelessly flawed linguistic impression of the nonetheless "Real" symbolic structures of the psyche. But even this Lacanian critique of the Freudian Oedipal law ends up privileging the seeming immanence of the Symbolic order, to the point where Lacan assumes that even if always imperfect, it is still deeply embedded within *every* human psyche. This Lacanian impression, therefore, is still haunted by Freud's Oedipal law which still acts as Lacan's more obscured, yet still firm psychoanalytic groundwork. Likewise, the omission of that crucial line about the "grounding" of psychoanalysis in the "Real" haunts even the substantially edited psychoanalyst's speech in Van Sant's version of the movie, and imbues it with the missing Freudian content that remains the psychoanalytic moral foundation upon which Van Sant's film is built. This spectral Freudian remainder, and the particular *ways* in which it haunts Van Sant's film, however, reveal more of a fundamental disjuncture – what Derrida calls a constitutive "out-of-joint-ness" – from within that very psychoanalytic law of sexuality. For Norman, the Oedipal law, instead of acting as a grounding "norm-alcy," turns symptomatically and onanistically inward, rendering Norman, much like the law itself, both its own sexual subject and object to the violent, murderous exclusion of any others.

Although our focus thus far has been on how Van Sant's film is itself haunted by and haunts Hitchcock's original, and more generally how in particular ways all film adaptations are *hauntological*, we have also considered the ways in which the "unified" voice of our paper is itself haunted by the spectral "presences" of its co-authors who speak in and through one another as a method for self-reflexively engaging with our topic. Van Sant describes his collaborative process in adapting Hitchcock's film to be "like staging a contemporary production of a classic play while remaining true to the original" (Van Sant qtd. in Schneider n.p.). What we contend, and moreover *demonstrate* by way of our co-authorship, is that the processes of adaptation are not so transparent or simple as they may appear. In fact, co-authorships, we argue, are always subject to the hauntological character of their own event-ness, which occurs not only between two or more co-authors at a particular originary historical place and time, but as a multiple and shifting constellation of archives and readers, times and places, all of which contribute toward such an attempted unification of authorial "meaning."

At the same time, however, our co-authorship also opens up the possibility for what Derrida terms an "objectivizable storage called the archive" (*Archive Fever* 26). In the sense that our paper becomes a sort of repository for collected ideas and theories that we strive to systematically store in a "finished" product (which, of course, is always already a produc*tion* without a definable beginning or proper ending, and will therefore never be "finished"), we continue to write together to reach an ultimately unattainable "truth," or, rather, the promise of such a truth. The tasks of co-authorship and adaptation then become examples of *consignation* – what Derrida calls a "gathering together [of seemingly disparate] signs" *aimed* at coordinating a vision in which "all the elements articulate the unity of an ideal configuration" (3), even if the point is to show how such an ideal configuration is never possible. We thus use the verb *aim* to imply that this act is itself problematic, for this ideal single corpus is itself only an *impression*, a *specter* that can never fully manifest but that which inevitably haunts the activity. This quality of haunting, nonetheless, is the very condition of possibility for bringing such productive activity to life.

CHAPTER NINE

UNREQUITED ADAPTATION: CHARLIE KAUFMAN AND *THE ORCHID THIEF*

by Lars Söderlund

The book, *The Orchid Thief,* by Susan Orlean is a non-linear memoir that chiefly reflects on the themes of rarity and love through the subject matter of orchid collecting. The film, *Adaptation,* directed by Spike Jonze and written by Charles Kaufman, is a film that chronicles not only Orlean's investigation of the orchid thief, John Laroche, as well as her process of writing, *The Orchid Thief,* but also Kaufman's attempts to write *The Orchid Thief* screenplay. This chapter will identify the film's subtle but malignant misogyny by analyzing the film character of Charlie Kaufman and his interactions with the women in his life including his manipulation of *The Orchid Thief* text. Put simply, Orlean's unique and feminine authorial voice is subverted by the dominance of Charlie's misogynistic storytelling.

Charlie subverts Susan Orlean's voice in *The Orchid Thief* by making its film adaptation about his own romantic life. The film becomes a story about Charlie's journey from powerlessness to powerfulness, from failure with women to success. In addition to making *Adaptation* about his own romantic life, he reduces the subject matter of *The Orchid Thief* to Orlean's romantic life, changing her text by creating an illicit affair and an orchid drug abuse problem for Orlean. In portraying her in this way, Charlie destroys Orlean's credibility, both as a journalist and as a storytelling voice in the film, and even asserts a sexual power over her by placing her in one of his sexual fantasies. As the author-turned-drug-adulteress, Orlean is the female most roughly used by Charlie in the film, but she is not the only female manipulated by him. Charlie also asserts the sexual power of fantasy over Valerie the studio executive and Alice the waitress. Though less obvious, I would even hold that Charlie uses Emilia, his love interest, to further his plot: since Charlie writes himself into his screenplay, a happy ending with Emilia is necessary if the movie is to come to a close.

I will begin my analysis with an important side note:

As I mentioned above, Charlie Kaufman wrote the screenplay for the film *Adaptation,* a film that contains a character also named Charlie Kaufman. I will hereafter refer to the character in the film as "Charlie" and the screenwriter as "Kaufman," to avoid confusion.

Confusion, in fact, is a good place to begin with a discussion of *Adaptation*, as many elements in the film seem to conspire to prevent the viewer's full comprehension of the events that transpire. The movie exhibits postmodern film features such as the multiple meanings of the word "Adaptation," and eccentric mix of real and fictional events: for instance, the film contains a character named "Donald Kaufman, " Charlie's brother, for whom no real-life antecedent exists. Similarly, the film realistically presents a love affair between John Laroche and Susan Orlean (fictional) but portrays Laroche's action of launching a pornography website (real) as goofy and larger than life. Also, the latter portion of the film often confuses viewers of the movie, because it is then that the film completely departs from the book and shows Donald and Charlie tracking Orlean and Laroche to Florida to spy on them.

Unfortunately, the plot of the film is not easier to comprehend if a viewer is ignorant of its semi-fictional nature. Scenes from *The Orchid Thief* intertwine with scenes from Charlie's life, and often the onscreen images are difficult to trace to a particular author. For example, one scene in the film shows a series of orchid hunters who died on their respective orchid hunts. Orlean narrates the scene, but as she speaks the film shows each hunter in turn:

> Orchid hunting is a mortal occupation. Victorian-era orchid hunter William Arnold drowned on a collecting expedition. Osmerse vanished without a trace in Asia. Augustus Margary survived toothache, rheumatism, pleurisy and dysentery only to be murdered when he completed his mission and traveled beyond Bhamo.

However, later in the movie we are shown a page of Charlie's draft of the screenplay. He reads in voice-over form:

> We see orchid hunter Augustus Margary. He wears a filthy, spittle-soaked rag around his head to quell the excruciating pain. The back of his trousers are stained, greasy, black from an anal leakage due to dysentery. He moans with each tentative step through the sickeningly overgrown jungle.

Who, then, has written the scene that Orlean reads? Even if the scene is collaborative (Orlean writes the words, Charlie writes the visual direction) it is difficult to recognize who has the dominant voice.

This scene also illustrates the problem of interpretation within the film: even when the film shows action occurring onscreen, it is often difficult for the viewer to understand what is taking place. There are no fewer than twenty-five voice-overs by five different characters throughout the movie, and each voice provides a different perspective on the film's events.

Certain critics and commentators have further muddied the waters by insisting that the film can be understood only if the viewer knows "the secret." This makes an analysis of the film difficult, because the secret is different depending on the critic. Some have insisted that Charlie wrote the first half of the film and Donald, though fictional, wrote the second half. Proponents of this idea believe that when Charlie's ponderous and experimental plot about himself trying to write *The Orchid Thief* screenplay loses steam, his brother Donald (whose screenwriting genre of choice, he informs us, is "Thriller") steps in to make the second half of the movie about Orlean and Laroche's torrid, drug-ridden affair and Charlie and Donald's adventure in Florida investigating it. This theory claims to explain the random appearance of guns and crocodiles in the latter half of the film as well as the reason why Donald gains physical strength and audience admiration as the movie progresses.

For Henry Bean, the secret is that Kaufman created a film in which "everyone in it is there simply as a neural configuration in Charlie's mind." (20). *Adaptation,* then, would exist entirely within Charlie's psyche, and so when Charlie emerges at the end of the film, clear-headed and calm, it is a happy ending that illustrates Charlie's new ability to love himself and be mentally at peace.

The common element in all interpretations of *Adaptation* is indeterminacy. Taking all of the considerations listed above into account, it seems impossible to have a coherent understanding of author, plot, or even the cast of characters. I will read the film in a way that simplifies these matters: I will prove that Charlie holds the power of storyteller in the film, and since he assumes this power it follows that he is the author of all elements of the film that are not derived from *The Orchid Thief.*

Susan Orlean is the author of *The Orchid Thief,* and Charlie attempts to adapt the book. In order for Charlie to be the main storyteller of the film, he must somehow dominate Orlean, which he does repeatedly throughout the film. The most obvious way that Charlie gains storytelling control is by destroying Orlean's credibility. Charlie makes Orlean into a "Popcorn Venus." Popcorn Venus is a term coined by the feminist critic Marjorie Rosen in her novel of the same name. A "Popcorn Venus," is "a delectable but insubstantial hybrid of cultural distractions" (19). Rosen cites the "Popcorn Venus" as a misogynist trope that recurs throughout male-dominated classical cinema. Like Venus, the Popcorn Venus is full of beauty and grace. Like popcorn, the Popcorn Venus is easily digested and delicious enough to casually savor. When a Popcorn Venus is made of a female author, she ceases being a storyteller and becomes merely an object to be examined.

Susan Orlean maintains her intelligence and credibility for much of the film, but her integrity is overturned by the movie's conclusion. Near the end of the film, Orlean admits to journalistic fraud, cheats on her husband, and generally becomes, as Charlie calls her, "a lonely, old, desperate, pathetic drug addict." At the beginning of her downward spiral, Orlean delivers a voice-over monologue that is not included in *The Orchid Thief*:

> What I came to understand is that change is not a choice. Not for a species of plant, not for me. It happens, and you are different. Maybe the only difference between the plant and me is that afterward I lied about my change: I lied in my book I pretended with my husband that everything was the same but something happened in the swamp that day.

Orlean's affair with Laroche also involves her addiction to a drug made by orchids. After taking the drug, Orlean becomes a silly giggling jumble of simplistic observations and random impulses. In a scene following her initial affair with Laroche and her first time taking the drug, Orlean lies in the grass near Laroche's home and looks at an ant crawling on a tree leaf. She says, "I wish I was an ant. They're so shiny!" With these words, Orlean is fully recognizable as a Popcorn Venus. The woman who once appreciated nature in a way so complicated that it had to be chronicled in a two-hundred page book has now been reduced to an adulterous, drugged-out floozy that makes ditzy comments about the shininess of ants.

Despite all the artistic artifice, *Adaptation* contains misogyny so classical that it can be identified and interpreted using methods that have been used by feminist film critics since as early as 1973. Rosen's book was published in that year, but the film also perpetrates the crimes against women that Laura Mulvey rallied against in her essay, "Visual Pleasure and Narrative Cinema." What does it mean that these decades old feminist articles about classical cinema still have bearing on contemporary films? It is too great a topic to fully address in this essay, but such a fact probably means that we should question Hollywood's development from the overt sexism of classical cinema to the current film world that sees itself as culturally progressive.

Under the guise of innocent unrequited love, Charlie imagines sexual fantasies with three of the central women in his life. I will argue that Charlie abuses his power as storyteller in doing so, manipulating the female characters and forcing the audience to be complicit in such a manipulation. As I explore the misogynistic implications of Charlie's fantasies, I will be assisted by Mulvey's now classical film theory. Mulvey rightly said, "... the look, pleasurable in form, can be threatening in content, and it is woman as representation/image that crystallizes the paradox." (68).

Charlie's power as main storyteller in the film is illustrated by his frequent voice-overs and the fact that his narration determines the images that the film shows onscreen. For example, at one point in the film Charlie races through a series of false starts on his screenplay:

> Okay- we open with Laroche. He's funny. Okay he says- Okay he says, "I love to mutate plants. He says, "Mutation is fun." Okay, we show flower and- okay we have to have the court case. Okay we show Laroche. He says, "I was mutated as a baby. That's why I'm so smart." That's funny. Okay, we open at the beginning of time. No. Okay we open with Laroche driving into the swamp.

As Charlie says these words, the film uses a montage of frantic images to illustrate his ideas and show his confusion. The scene makes it clear: Charlie controls the film.

Simultaneously, Charlie is intimidated by the strong women in his life. Valerie is the studio executive from whom he desperately seeks approval. Susan Orlean, too, has the power to affirm or deny the validity of the work that he is doing on her book. Even Alice, the waitress who serves him at a diner, has the ability to affirm or reject his social life with her response when Charlie asks her for a date. These three women of power appear in Charlie's masturbatory fantasies. Why? Laura Mulvey's essay "Visual Pleasure and Narrative Cinema" posits that in film, when a man fears the power of a woman, he will frequently respond by making her a fetish object. The woman comes to "signify male desire" instead of signifying the power that she wields over him (65). This scopophilia, or pleasure in looking, is utilized by Charlie to exert his control over the women in his life.

Laura Mulvey identifies three manifestations of "the gaze" in cinema: the gaze of the camera, the gaze of the audience, and the gaze of the male protagonist in the film, in this case Charlie. *Adaptation* unifies these three perspectives. This means that everything that Charlie sees, or imagines, the audience sees. The film does not immediately identify, however, when Charlie is fantasizing and when he is not. The audience is thus forced to participate in 's fantasies and is wrenched from them before the audience has a chance to consider their theoretical significance. Charlie seems less pathetic when viewers of the film are initially unaware of the fantastic nature of his sexual encounters. The audience is initially manipulated into viewing these fabrications as real, viewing the sex as consensual and real, when it is not. As Charlie objectifies these women, the audience is kept from reacting to it by their limited perspective.

In one particularly telling scene, Charlie is again having trouble writing the screenplay. He reads Orlean's book and says, "Such sweet, sad insights." He then sets the book down on his bed, and looks at the book jacket photograph of Susan Orlean and says, "I like looking at you." Charlie imagines Orlean whispering, "I like looking at you, too, Charlie." He then lies back and Orlean's hands appear on top of his chest. Briefly, a sex scene takes place, and the camera cuts between shots of Charlie and shots of Orlean on top of him. Orlean starts to moan, and as he whimpers with decreasing volume, it is obvious that Orlean has disappeared. Charlie rolls over to again stare at Orlean's picture, and the audience becomes fully aware that Charlie and Susan's intercourse was a fantasy. In this scene, Charlie defensively asserts sexual control over Orlean, conjuring her to satisfy his amorous desire because his professional life is under her control. This is confirmed by the words that he says to the dust jacket photograph after his fantasy. He whines, "I don't know how to do this. I'm afraid I'll disappoint you. You've written a beautiful book." In his words, he seeks her professional approval, but in his behavior he forces her to give him her sexual approval.

Earlier in the film, Charlie fantasizes about Valerie the studio executive in a similar way. He creates a fantasy in which he finally finishes the script. First, the film shows his title page, and then a blurred view of the many pages that the script has. The scene then cuts to Charlie and Valerie in bed together. Valerie whispers, "You're a genius. You're a genius, you're a genius," in a very impressed tone. Quickly, the camera cuts to a view of her on top of him, their bodies thrusting together. Just as suddenly, the scene cuts again and shows Charlie's legs on the end of his bed twitching and the sound of his voice moaning is audible. He then utters a muffled groan, and his legs lay still. Charlie chooses to fantasize about Valerie for the same reason that he fantasizes about Orlean: to assert sexual control, albeit imaginary, onto a woman who has control over his writing career. Also like the scene with Orlean, the audience only realizes the fictional nature of the scene after the scene is over. Because of this, the audience been has manipulated into participating in Charlie's fantasy. In these ways, Charlie foregrounds the gender of the female characters and exerts control over them in an effort to make the women less threatening to him.

Alice the waitress does not have professional control over Charlie, but does have social control over him. She waits on him at an upscale diner in Los Angeles and she mentions that she "loves" orchids. Charlie's nervousness is apparent, as he repeats the word "please" when ordering his slice of key lime pie and coffee. After Charlie orders, there is a scene in which Alice joins Charlie at an orchid show. She says, "I'm so excited! I've always wanted to come to an orchid show. I think these flowers are so sexy!" She then touches Charlie's hand with hers and says, "Let's see what's around back." They then walk through a wooded area, and when Alice stops walking she giggles and awkwardly kisses Charlie. Then she promptly takes her top off, at which point there is the sound of a door knocking and Charlie is yanked out of his fantasy. The audience then sees that he has been in bed touching himself. The next day, Charlie returns to the diner and shows why the fantasy was significant to

Charlie: Charlie uncomfortably asks Alice to an orchid show, and she acts afraid and alerts another waitress to Charlie's behavior. Charlie is disappointed, his social impotency reaffirmed, and it is obvious that Charlie created his fantasy to convince himself, and perhaps the audience too, that he can be sexually successful with a woman. However, by having Alice fill his fantasy role, Charlie asserts his power over her in a devious manipulation.

Just as Charlie manipulates the women in his life, he also manipulates the audience on the subject of his apparent quality of innocence. Robert McKee notes, in his commentary on the screenplay, "When Charlie berates himself as a pathetic loser, it prompts us to think: 'No, you're not. You only imagine you are. You're really rather lovable'" (134). Because the audience views the film in this way, it sees Charlie's failings and insecurities as benign and pleasantly fallible. Charlie's self-loathing, then, is but a device to cause the audience to further empathize with him. Charlie is not a naïve character bemoaning his lot in life, but a deceitful manipulator attempting to assert control over the women in his life over whom he has no real control. The appearance of innocence and frustration is finely crafted. Charlie's objectification of Valerie, Susan and Alice is therefore even more malignant and much more likely to be overlooked by an audience that acutely identifies with him. Charlie engages in scopophilia and fetishistic objectification in an effort to destabilize the integrity of the women in his life but the audience merely views these things as symptoms of how Charlie is a victim of low self-esteem and an unfair world.

The audience understandably takes Charlie's romantic failings as a signal that Charlie is the character with whom they should sympathize. However, it is Charlie's loser status that causes his objectification of women and forces the audience to overlook and even be complicit in the acts of objectification. For a full understanding of Charlie's deviousness, it is necessary to note the ways in which Charlie shows his social ineptitude and wins over the audience.

In details both obvious and subtle, Charlie is a loser. The film begins as a black screen with small white words that serve as the credits. Over this darkness, Charlie delivers the following soliloquy, the first of several exhibitions of self-doubt:

Do I have an original thought in my head? My bald head? Maybe if I were happier my hair wouldn't be falling out. Life is short, I need to make the most of it. Today is the first day of the rest of my life. (sigh) I'm a walking cliché. I really need to go to the doctor to have my leg checked. There's something wrong. A bump. The dentist called again. I'm way overdue. If I stopped putting things off I would be happy. All I do is sit on my fat ass. If my ass wasn't fat I would be happy. I wouldn't have to wear these shirts with the tails out all the time. Like that's fooling anyone. Fat ass! I should start jogging again. Five miles a day, really do it this time. Maybe rock climbing. I need to turn my life around. What do I need to do? I need to fall in love. I need to have a girl friend. I need to read more. Improve myself. What if I learned Russian or something? Or took up an instrument? I could speak Chinese. I would be the screenwriter who speaks Chinese. And plays the oboe. That would be cool. I should get my hair cut short. Stop trying to fool myself and everyone else into thinking that I have a full head of hair. How pathetic is that? Just be real. Confident. Isn't that what women are attracted to? Men don't have to be attractive. But that's not true. Especially these days. Almost as much pressure on men as there is on women these days. Why should I be made to feel that I have to apologize for my existence? Maybe it's my brain chemistry. Maybe that's what's wrong with me: bad chemistry. All my problems and anxiety can be reduced to a chemical imbalance or some kind of misfiring synapses. I need to get help for that. But I'll still be ugly, though. Nothing's going to change that.

The fact that the film starts with a blank screen and the thoughts of the screenwriter means that the audience's perspective is united with Charlie's perspective from the beginning of the film. As Charlie's words indicate, everything in Charlie's life seems to be ultimately uncertain. He doubts his ability to create artistically original work, his looks, his personal charm, and his eating habits. Charlie exposes himself to the audience, and the scene that follows the monologue above exacerbates Charlie's exposure: Charlie is kicked off of the *Being John Malkovich* movie set, even though he wrote the screenplay for the film. Standing alone outside the soundstage, Kaufman muses aloud, "Why did I bother to come here today? Nobody even seems to know my name." These situations do involve Kaufman exposing himself, but in doing so he draws the audience nearer, eliciting their sympathy and empathy, rather than pushing them away.

As the film progresses, Charlie's inner monologues show the audience his nervousness around women. This is especially clear during a brief scene in which he has lunch with Valerie, the studio executive, in order to get the job of writing the adaptation of *The Orchid Thief.* It is an important scene, because it conflates Charlie's insecurities about romance and about writing. As he sweats profusely and stares at Valerie, we hear the following voice-over:

My leg hurts. I wonder if its cancer. There's a bump. I'm starting to sweat. Stop sweating! I've got to stop sweating! Can she see it dripping down my forehead? Oh- she looked at my hairline. She thinks I'm bald.

Though the interview should be based on his writing ability, Charlie can't stop worrying about his personal appearance. Charlie's sweat is, in fact, unattractive to the audience, but being exposed to Charlie's thoughts and observing the coldly statuesque and androgynous beauty of Valerie ensures that the audience will identify with Kaufman as the scene progresses. Again, Kaufman's social awkwardness wins him the esteem of the audience.

The most compelling scene that shows Charlie's romantic helplessness and pleads for the audience's sympathy occurs when Charlie takes his friend Emilia home from a classical music concert. Charlie keeps a picture of Emilia under his pillow at home, and his conviction in the film's opening soliloquy that he should "have a girlfriend" alerts us to the fact that he is romantically interested in her. Charlie drives her to her home, where despite his interest Charlie is unable to make any type of romantic advance toward Emilia. She even tells him, "Well, here we are. So what are you up to now, then?" Charlie responds by saying, "I should probably get to bed. I have a lot of work to do tomorrow." It is painful to watch, but the audience still understands that Charlie's romantic hesitancy is based on his lack of self-confidence. The ambiance of the scene makes it clear that Charlie deserves sympathy. The song playing faintly in the background is "Dead Melodies" by Beck, which has the following lyrics:

Where will you go
When this day is over
A gambler's purse
Lays on the road
Straight to your door
Snakes have gone crazy tonight
Winding their way out of sight
A laugh, a joke
A sentiment wasted
Seasons of strangers
They come and go
Doldrums are pounding
Cheapskates are clowning this town
Who could disown themselves now
Engineer, slow down this old train
Cinders and chaff
Laugh at the moon
Night birds will cackle
Rotting like apples on trees
Sending their dead melodies to me

Loneliness and melancholy are the main themes in the lyrics. Snakes "wind their way out of sight," fleeing from the speaker's point of view. The "gambler's purse lays on the road" abandoned and separated from its owner. Like Charlie's inner monologues and best of intentions, the song refers to a "sentiment wasted," which also echoes the miscommunication that occurs between Charlie and most of the people that he encounters. In fact, Charlie's life is comprised of "seasons of strangers," meeting people with whom he does not make an emotional or psychological connection whom then "go." As Emilia walks toward her door (no doubt another reason for the song's appropriateness), Charlie thinks:

> Why didn't I go in? I'm such a chicken. I'm such an idiot! I should have kissed her! I've blown it! I should just go and knock on her door right now and kiss her. It would be romantic. Something we could someday tell our kids. I'm going to do that right now.

After this final thought, he promptly drives off. Because of his timidity and shyness, though, the audience remains on his side.

There is one remaining element in Charlie's character that marks him as a loser that bears discussion. Throughout the film, Charlie masturbates. Charlie's masturbation in the film is frequently cited as an embarrassing act that brings attention to his social ineptitude and self-loathing. This is the reason that most viewers feel more embarrassed for Charlie than for the women in his fantasies. That view is an exaggeration. As Robert McKee contends, "Jerking off in movies is no more embarrassing than smoking" (132). What's more, this false stigma of masturbation as the ultimate in shame enables the far more odious shaming of the women in *Adaptation* to take place. In an interview, Susan Orlean recalls that upon reading the *Adaptation* screenplay she was embarrassed about the treatment of her character and slow to lend her name to the project. She agreed to grant her name to the film only after she was convinced (by her male producer) that Charlie's masturbation was far more embarrassing than the transformations that her character undergoes. The film makes clear, however, that being a masturbator is not as embarrassing as being in a fantasy created by him.

I have addressed how Charlie abuses his power as storyteller in creating sexual fantasies that at first appear real, thus manipulating both the female characters in the film and the audience. I now turn to a more general discussion of how Charlie's storytelling style is itself gendered.

Many would hold that any story told from the perspective of one who has a gender will necessarily be gendered. A woman tells a story from the perspective of a woman and a man tells a story from the perspective of a man. This may be true, but Charlie's way of telling the story of *Adaptation* is gendered in a very particular way. Though Charlie continually asserts that he wants to be true to *The Orchid Thief*, and by extension true to Orlean's delicate feminine style, Charlie causes *Adaptation* to revolve around his own masculine carnality. His sexuality is not just his point of reference; it is his way of manipulating and telling his story. Charlie's link to the text of *The Orchid Thief* is primarily illustrated through sexual means. Charlie turns Orlean into a Popcorn Venus, but by telling the story in this way, Charlie even usurps Orlean's power to tell her own story and reaffirms his ability to make the film exclusively his own.

At several points in the film, Charlie reads *The Orchid Thief* and hears the voice of Susan Orlean. Several times, he then talks back to her, as if they were having a conversation. The most acute example of this is the passage cited above, in which he imagines Orlean talking back to him ("I like looking at you, too, Charlie ..."). These instances illustrate the process of reading that everyone has: reading is a conversation, one way or another, between the reader and the author of a book. However, at certain times in the film, Charlie stops Orlean's voice-over, or changes it in mid-sentence. At these times, Charlie exercises control over Orlean's female authorial voice, changing the story that she is telling into the story that he is telling.

At one point, he is reading her book on the airplane, and hears her say, "Life seemed to be filled with things that were just like the ghost orchid. Wonderful to imagine, easy to fall in love with, but a little fantastic, and fleeting, and out of reach." Charlie then repeats her words in his own voice-over, "but a little fantastic, and fleeting, and out of reach." He then closes his book, having apparently read the final page. The problem, though, is that Orlean's book does not end with those lines. The book's final page narrates how Orlean and Laroche make it out of the Fakahatchee swamp, without finding the ghost orchid, and the last image in the book is the light shining off of Laroche's van, creating a beacon for Laroche and Orlean to follow out of the swamp. Orlean ends *The Orchid Thief* being grateful for her survival, not lamenting fate's caprice at not allowing her to see the ghost orchid. Charlie tells Orlean's story, but tells it slant so that he can tie it to his own sexual struggle.

This is made more apparent in another instance of Charlie's manipulation of the text. After his offer to take Alice to an orchid show is rejected, Orlean's voice-over begins and Charlie appears alone at the orchid show. Orlean narrates, "There are more than thirty-thousand known orchid species. One looks like a turtle. One looks like a monkey. One looks like an onion." Charlie then breaks in with a voice-over of his own concerns:

One looks like a schoolteacher. One looks like a gymnast. One looks like that girl in high school with creamy skin. One looks like a New York intellectual, with whom you do the Sunday Times crossword puzzle in bed. One looks like a Midwestern beauty queen. One looks like Emilia. One has eyes that dance. One has eyes that contain the sadness of the world.

When Charlie mentions the one whose eyes contain the sadness of the world, Orlean is shown on-screen, insinuating that she is disappointed with her passionless life. From his truncation of her book's ending to his judgment about the sadness of her eyes, it is obvious that Charlie is judging Orlean's existence to be full of disappointment. Also, Charlie's link from flowers to women, juxtaposed with his rejection from the ditzy but attractive Alice, uses Orlean's reflection as a way to sum up his chauvinism.

Perhaps this chauvinism should not come as a surprise. Since I have previously discussed how Charlie exerts his imaginary sexual power over Orlean and Valerie, his two "bosses" on the adaptation writing job, it is clear that Charlie has sexualized his occupational link to the writing of *The Orchid Thief* screenplay. Charlie cannot make progress in writing the screenplay, but it seems more important to his story that he cannot get laid.

As soon as Charlie puts himself into his screenplay, he ensures that this was to be the case. In the film, after several false starts, Charlie decides that he can only relate to himself. Because of this, he decides to write about himself writing the script. Charlie does this so that he can better relate to the material, but this also means that until he comes to some sort of ending for himself, his script cannot be finished. Since Charlie thematizes his relationships within the film, I believe that this explains not only Charlie's imposition of the relationship between Orlean and Laroche, but also his inclusion of his relationship with Emilia. Due to the conventions of Hollywood, the film must end with the flowering of a romance.

In the conclusion of the film, Charlie again favors his own story over Orlean's. Her romance with Laroche ends with Laroche dying while Charlie's romance with Emilia ends with Emilia confessing her love for him.

Laroche dies in the portion of film in which Charlie and Donald follow Orlean to Florida. After arriving in Miami, Charlie and Donald tail Laroche and Orlean to Laroche's house. Charlie exits the car to get a closer look at the couple. Orlean and Laroche catch Charlie and decide that they must kill him since he has discovered their secret affair and drug running operation. Orlean forces Charlie at gunpoint to drive to the Fakahatchee state preserve. Once there, Donald helps Charlie escape into the swamp, and Charlie and Donald share a heartfelt moment in which Donald teaches Charlie the lesson, "You are what you love, not what loves you." The following morning, Charlie and Donald nearly escape, but in the melee Donald is killed and Laroche and Orlean chase Charlie back into the swamp. Laroche and Orlean corner Charlie, but before Laroche can shoot Charlie an alligator attacks Laroche. Charlie escapes, but not before trading insults with Orlean. She calls him a "fat piece of shit," and he calls her "a lonely, old, desperate, pathetic drug addict." She holds Laroche's lifeless body and cries onto it, wishing to be born again, to have her life back "before it all got fucked up." Orlean appears demented by the loss of Laroche. Orlean's romance, that Charlie created, ends violently, and Orlean's character is once again demeaned.

Charlie's ending is happier. Just before the film ends, Charlie has lunch with Emilia, who now has a boyfriend. Charlie and Emilia are discussing her recent trip to Europe when he kisses her. She protests, reminding him that she is in a relationship with someone else, and Charlie says, "I love you." Emilia leaves, but before walking away she says, "I love you too, you know?"

Charlie leaves lunch with another voice-over:

> I have to go right home. I know how to finish the script now. It ends with Kaufman driving home after his lunch with Emilia thinking he knows how to finish the script .... I wonder who's gonna play me? Someone not too fat .... Anyway, it's done, and that's something. So. Kaufman drives off from his encounter with Emilia, filled for the first time with hope. I like this. This is good.

Romantically, the ending of the film is satisfying. Since the audience has been commiserating with Charlie for almost two hours, it is cathartic to see him come to a happy end. However, the ending, from the death of Laroche to Charlie's last monologue, is symptomatic of Charlie's manipulation of the women in his life and *The Orchid Thief*. As the scriptwriter, it is Charlie's burden to give the film an ending. Emilia, then, is being used to bring the story to a close. Likewise, Orlean's romance with Laroche must flame-out so that Charlie can learn the life lesson from Donald that he needs to succeed with Emilia. Orlean is again used by Charlie to tell his own story. After she has helped Charlie learn his lesson, he cuts her from the story. Just as Orlean earlier evaporates after fulfilling Charlie's sexual fantasy, at the end of the film Charlie leaves her a puerile simpering mass of confusion.

I will now briefly turn to a comparison of misogynist themes in the film that is a prequel to *Adaptation* in many ways, the previous collaboration of Spike Jonze and Charlie Kaufman, *Being John Malkovich*. *Being John Malkovich* is the story of Craig, an out-of-work puppeteer who finds work in a filing agency that contains a portal into the head of John Malkovich. Craig and his wife, Lottie, fall in love with Craig's co-worker Maxine. Maxine comes to love Lottie, but only when Lottie inhabits Malkovich's head. In the end, through a misuse of the portal, Craig is trapped in the head of Maxine and Lottie's daughter with no hope of control or escape.

Like *Adaptation*, *Being John Malkovich* contains the strong theme of unrequited love, but the difference is that in *Malkovich* unrequited love is stripped of its innocence. Craig's love for Maxine is not returned, and so Craig must resort to desperate measures. In order to seduce Maxine, Craig abandons his own body and controls the mind of John Malkovich for an extended period of time, since Maxine cannot love Craig as he is. He also locks his wife in a chimpanzee cage to prevent her from entering Malkovich's head. These methods are clearly devious. The difference, then, between *Adaptation* and *Being John Malkovich*, in addition to the false innocence that is lacking in *Malkovich* and present in *Adaptation* is that in *Malkovich* Craig is punished for his crimes of love. The film makes it clear that Craig goes too far in his adoration of Maxine. No such problem befalls Charlie, despite his scopophilia and manipulation of the females in his life. It seems that Charlie's innocence differs from Craig's guilt in that the audience does not detect Charlie's transgressions.

To conclude, *Adaptation* is one of the most brilliant works of film in recent history. The decision made by Kaufman to put a version of himself into his screenplay is daring in concept and stunning in execution. I can say this confidently, having now studied the film closely for thirteen months. However, the film makes Charlie's decision to implant himself into his screenplay seem self-effacing and haphazard, which it is not. It is instead a method that increases his power as storyteller and a means to destroying the integrity and potency of the female characters in his life. Upon casually viewing *Adaptation*, the viewer will likely be impressed by the synergistic relationship between *The Orchid Thief* and the film. However, once the façade of Charlie's respectful treatment of Orlean's work is stripped away, his misogynistic manipulation of the text becomes apparent. The irony that a contemporary film could harbor such archaic chauvinism is staggering. It is a testament to Laura Mulvey and Marjorie Rosen that their respective 1973 works on the misogyny of classical cinema could identify not only cultural sins of the past, but iniquities that would persist into the future.

CHAPTER TEN

MUTANT AUTHORS AND CROSS-POLLINATED TEXTS IN CHARLIE KAUFMAN'S *ADAPTATION*

by Cecilia Sayad

In his introductions to both *Literature and Film: A Guide to the Theory and Practice of Film Adaptation* and *Literature Through Film: Realism, Magic and the Art of Adaptation*, Robert Stam offers an approach to the transposition of literary works into moving images that dispute judgments about fidelity to the original in favor of a dialogical understanding of such a practice. Commonly described in terms of "violation," "betrayal," and "vulgarization" of the literary source, the adaptation of novels into films, Stam suggests, may instead constitute a fertile dialogue. Recalling the anecdote in which a writer and a filmmaker traveling on the same boat share a desire to throw the other overboard, Stam notes that, quite often, "The inter-art relation is seen as a Darwinian struggle to the death rather than a dialogue offering mutual benefit and cross-fertilization" (*Literature and Film*, 4). The associations between Darwin's evolutionist theories and filmic adaptations of books displayed in director Spike Jonze's and screenwriter Charlie Kaufman's *Adaptation* (2002) thus constitute, to Stam, a refreshing and enriching take on the issue. Where critics normally lament the loss of elements from the literary source, supposedly deformed in its cinematic version, *Adaptation* meditates on the translation of the literary into the filmic through metaphors of cross-fertilization, mutation, and even parasitism, "evoking adaptation as a means of evolution and survival" (*Literature and Film*, 2-3).

In line with Stam's dialogical approach, this chapter proposes that filmic adaptations of literary works be read as an ongoing dialogue involving different authors—a perpetual exchange that is sometimes fruitful, sometimes predatory. Drawing also on Mikhail Bakhtin's theories of polyphony, Roland Barthes's challenges to authorial control, and post-structuralist, decentralizing conceptions of authors as constructs, this essay observes issues such as originality, faithfulness, and translation through the lenses of film authorship. The approach to adaptation suggested here bypasses reflections about pre-determined relations between different media, film's putative inability to convey interiority, and comparisons between "original" and "imitation." The purpose of this essay is to tackle the practice of adaptation as a dialogue where appropriation, collaboration, compromise, and susceptibility give body to the figure of the author while at the same time challenging traditional conceptions of authorship grounded in ideas of originality, individuality, independence, and control.

Film authorship is often seen as either untraceable or accidental: untraceable insofar as the auteur's expression dissolves among the contributions of producers, directors, screenwriters, actors, or cinematographers; and accidental when film becomes the product of uncontrollable economic, social, and political forces. The analysis of film authorship involves deciding whether film's collaborative and multimedia aspects allow for the subjective expression of one individual artist. It involves the problem of deciding whose is the prevalent expressing voice: whether that of the director, that of the screenwriter, or that of the actor. The discussion of authorship in film also entails deliberations over artistic compromises resulting from commercial demands; considerations that, though by no means exclusive to cinema, acquire greater significance in a medium whose modes of production are markedly industrial.

In order to avoid supposedly naïve or inaccurate attributions of authorship, film theorists sometimes employ an abstract terminology in which disincarnated "instances," "agencies" and "functions" stand in for the author's name. Echoing debates taking place in the domains of literature, this terminology calls to mind Wayne Booth's "implied author," a figure that at once unified and disembodied the authorial voice in novels. The implied author restored unity to what Russian formalists and structuralist theorists had transformed into a dispersed, untraceable authorial voice; a voice that to these theorists disappeared behind an autonomous text, the meaning of which was defined by language itself, independently of authorial intention. However, if on the one hand the idea behind the implied author was to attribute the organization of textual meaning to a unified entity rather than to abstract, ungraspable systems, on the other it rendered this author intangible, for it differentiated the perspective adopted in the text from that of the real, biographical writer.

According to Booth, the implied author is an artificial version of the writer himself, who constructs a "second self" as a means to detach his own standpoint from the views communicated in the text (Booth 1983, 71). "This implied author," says Booth, "is always distinct from the 'real man'—whatever we may take him to be—who creates a superior version of himself, a 'second self,' as he creates his work" (151). This fabricated entity embodies the work's artistic designs, which includes decisions concerning narrative structure, plot, characters, and the very narrator—the omniscient, partial or multiple perspective this narrator assumes in relation to the narrative, whether this perspective is neutral or committed to a certain viewpoint, and so on. In Booth's words,

Our sense of the implied author includes not only the extractable meanings but also the moral and emotional content of each bit of action and suffering of all of the characters. It includes, in short, the intuitive apprehension of a completed artistic whole; the chief value to which *this* implied author is committed, regardless of what party his creator belongs to in real life, is that which is expressed by the total form (73-4).[i]

The implied author recuperates a supposedly undermined authorial voice, he "chooses, consciously or unconsciously, what we read; we infer him as an ideal, literary, created version of the real man; he is the sum of his own choices" (75). By incarnating the text's artistic designs, the implied author restores the idea of a thinking artist behind a supposedly self-sufficient text, calling attention to that work "as the product of a choosing, evaluating person rather than a self-existing thing" (74).

Yet another, less explored aspect of the implied author is the abstract quality it ascribes to the text's authorial voice. By distinguishing implied author from real writer, Booth correctly calls attention to the possibility that the text may not always reveal the writer's real dispositions, emotions, and ideology. To be sure, the role of the implied author goes beyond the distinction between author and narrator; the implied author is different from, and more encompassing than the text's narrator. The implied author therefore stands between writer and narrator, creating one more degree of separation between writer and reader. In the end, with the implied author the text may become the basis for the construction not only of meaning, but also of an author that is not identical to the real writer.

Of all attempts to reconfigure the concept of authorship, to revise dreams of self-expression and authorial control, Barthes's "The Death of the Author" (1968) is the one that finally gave this agonizing figure its coup de grâce. In this seminal essay, Barthes unmasks the myth of originality, asserts the inevitability of intertextuality, and transfers from author to reader the construction of textual meaning (Barthes 1968, 213). Barthes tells us that it is the text's structural relations, or language, that speak (210). He announces the death of the author also in the empowering of the reader, now ascribed the construction of meaning (213), all the while an immanent grid of intertexts posit the writer too as reader. Nonetheless, Barthes articulated not so much the demise, but a new conception of authorship, which a year after the publication of his essay was already being envisioned as function by Michel Foucault and as structure by auteur structuralists. While Foucault claimed that "the subject (and its substitutes) must be stripped of its creative role and analyzed as a complex and variable function of " (137-8), auteur structuralists saw the author itself as defined by recurring elements that would in turn constitute structures. Situating this new author

---

[i] Booth's emphasis.

within the domains of cinema studies, Peter Wollen suggested that, recognizing that films were "network[s] of different statements, crossing and contradicting each other," auteur analysis aimed not at "retracing a film to its origins, to its creative source. It consists of tracing a structure (not a message) within the work, which can then *post factum* be assigned to an individual, the *director*, on empirical grounds" (1972, 167-8). It is ultimately in the articulation between agency and structures that "The Death of the Author" inaugurates post-structuralism, defining authorship as the orchestration of symbolic and textual systems.

The author as orchestrator incidentally recuperates a concept articulated in the late-1920's writings of Mikhail Bakhtin, whose conception of the text as the polyphonic encounter of different voices, define him as an avant-la-lettre post-structuralist. In the end, Booth's theory dialogues with Bakhtin's *Problems of Dostoevsky's Poetics,* which accounts for the author as conduit for voices other than his, charged with historical, social, and cultural perspectives. Bakhtin's author, just as Booth's, extrapolates from self-expression, acting out, or "absorbing," voices that are exterior to him or her. Just as subjected to readers' dispositions and backgrounds as textual meaning was for Barthes, the previously conceived implied author (Booth's book was first published in 1961) also generates from the text—rather than preceding the literary work, this author springs from it. Implied authors might therefore be just as unstable and variable as the possible interpretations of the works that originate them, concurring with Barthes's claim that the writer is not the origin of textual meaning, and that the true place of writing is reading (212).

Adapting Authors

By self-reflexively examining the problems of assigning authorship to specific artists, film's expressive potentials, and authorial control in the light of dialogism, *Adaptation* constitutes a privileged example of the ways that the issues of film authorship and adaptation might illuminate each other. A transposition of Susan Orlean's *The Orchid Thief*[i] onto the screen, the film supplements the debate about filmic adaptation of books with Darwinian metaphors of evolution and mutation, suggesting a dynamics among authors that can be defined simultaneously in terms of cross-fertilization and parasitism. In addition, *Adaptation* touches upon authorship by presenting an ambivalent take on the centrality of the biographical or real-life artist and, consequently, on authorial intention. The film's protagonist is a fictional screenwriter bearing the name of Charlie Kaufman. *Adaptation* therefore stresses the figure of one of its

---

[i] See Orlean, Susan. The Orchid Thief (New York: Random House, 1998).

own creators, and Kaufman indirectly recuperates to the medium the possibility of making manifest a personifiable author by obliquely inscribing himself into his own script; to be sure, in the guise of a fictional screenwriter played by Nicolas Cage.

Adaptation exposes its own genesis in the form of a fictional plot, transmuting real-life writers into fictional characters played by renowned actors, and centering its principal drama in the relations between these several writers. Orlean's screen version is incarnated by Meryl Streep; Robert McKee, author of scriptwriter's guide *Story*,[i] and Charles Darwin, whose theories influence Kaufman's depiction of artistic processes, are also characters in the film, played, respectively, by Brian Cox and Bob Yerkes. Finally, Kaufman invents a fictional twin brother, Donald (also played by Cage), who, conceived as an aspiring screenwriter, functions as the protagonist's alter ego. Through this net of authorial agencies, *Adaptation* reveals the collective nature of scriptwriting as much as it exposes the individual journey of an artist. It portrays the writing of *The Orchid Thief* by Orlean, the struggle of fictional Kaufman to adapt her book into a movie, and the process through which his work becomes a film that turns out very similar to *Adaptation* itself; just like the actual Kaufman writes himself into his script as a fictional writer working on the adaptation of *The Orchid Thief*, fictional Charlie Kaufman writes a script that is identical to the film we are watching—one in which the screenwriter writes himself into his script as someone adapting Orlean's book. When Charlie finally decides what to do of *The Orchid Thief*, he paces around his room and talks into his handheld tape recorder, describing a sequence seen in the film's first minutes: "We open with Charlie Kaufman, fat, old, bald, repulsive, sitting in a Hollywood restaurant across from Valerie Thomas." The film then cuts to the image of Charlie talking into his handheld tape recorder again, saying: "Fat, repulsive Kaufman paces furiously in his bedroom. He speaks into his handheld tape recorder, and says 'Charlie Kaufman, fat, bald, repulsive, old, sits at a Hollywood restaurant with Valerie Thomas ....'" With these lines the protagonist multiplies the levels of narration, generating a film within the film within the film.

Despite the fictional qualities of both the artist and his creative process, *Adaptation* places its own writer at the center of its narrative, thus presenting itself as a personal movie insofar as it depicts the personal struggle of an author. The film evidently sides with auteur-oriented approaches, which underline the artist's self-expression and, by arguing for distinctiveness, value artistic originality. However, in the movie's plot the central artist is not the director, but

---

[i] See McKee, Robert. Story: Substance, Structure, Style and the Principles of Screenwriting (New York: Regan Books, c.1997).

the screenwriter. By focusing on Kaufman, *Adaptation* recuperates the writer as the key artist in film—an idea contested by both Alexandre Astruc's concept of writing with a camera (Astruc 1968) and the politique des auteurs' empowering of the director to the detriment of the writer. The film ultimately ignores all the stages of filmmaking subsequent to the writing of the script. The centering on the writing of the film thus places the question of who is the film's author at a stage anterior to the incorporation of other artistic activities embodied by cinematographers, editors, actors, art directors, or composers. The problem of the collaborative quality of film authorship is transferred from the realm of the collective enterprise that is the making of films to the realm of the intertextual endeavor that constitutes the writing of any text. Rather than the belief that film authorship is always multiple,[i] the film echoes Barthes's idea that "the writer can only imitate a gesture that is always anterior, never original" (Barthes 1968, 211). Finally, while contradicting auteur theorists in its privileging of the writer over the director, *Adaptation* nonetheless indulges in the French theorists' love for the very literary analogies that eventually led them to ascribe to film directors the role of auteurs.

Though in *Adaptation* collaboration concerns mainly the transforming of a book into a film, restricting the issue of control to the pre-production stage, the discussion proposed by Kaufman greatly emphasizes the pressures of the industry. The hero's conflicts consist mainly in avoiding both conventional narrative formulas and the demands of Hollywood-oriented modes of filmmaking. The book he is supposed to adapt is a plotless, contemplative work about flowers centered in the figure of orchid collector John Laroche. The conflict between the self-reflexive approach to a film topic as unusual as flowers and the commercial demands of the film industry are portrayed in the form of dialogues with characters representing the two sides of the question. On the protagonist's side is Orlean, to whose book he honestly wishes to remain true. The hero's interchanges with Orlean are many, albeit for the most part indirect or imagined: he obsessively comments on the beauty of her writing, endlessly flips the pages of her book, fantasizes having sex with her, and finds inspiration in imaginary conversations. On the side of commercial demands are McKee, the scriptwriters' guru, and, most importantly, fictional twin brother Donald, who is also working on a screenplay: a thriller involving a serial killer suffering from multiple-personality disorder. While Charlie intends to write himself into his self-reflexive script, which does not easily fit into any cinematic genre, Donald is applying McKee's scriptwriters' guidelines to a movie entitled *The 3:*

---

[i] Berys Gaut and Paisley Livingston discuss this idea in, respectively, "Film Authorship and Collaboration" and "Cinematic Authorship," both in Richard Allen and Murray Smith, eds., Film Theory and Philosophy (Oxford and New York: Oxford University Press, 2003), 149-172; 132-148.

the story of a serial killer who is at the same time both the cop who chases him and his own victim.

If within auteur-oriented approaches artistic control defines the extent to which a film is personal, *Adaptation* is ambivalent in relation to the writer's power—and also in relation to the extent to which the concepts of "exclusive control" and "personal" are interchangeable. The emphasis on the artist in the film does not give him absolute power over his work. On the contrary, the protagonist's scriptwriting is portrayed as the result of an extensive (although incidental) collaboration with many of the film's characters. Though entailing solitude, writing is portrayed as collaborative from the start, when a studio executive suggests to the hero that in his script Orlean and Laroche could fall in love, which is exactly what happens in the movie we see. In addition, in his writer's-block despair fictional Kaufman surprisingly resorts to Donald, whose contribution twists both the script the protagonist is writing (the film within the film) and *Adaptation* itself (which mirrors the protagonist's script). The brothers follow Orlean only to find out that, in addition to the subject for a book, Laroche provides her with drugs and love. This discovery is followed by a series of sensationalist events: car chases, the shooting of Donald, his death in a car accident, Laroche's attempt to kill Kaufman, and an alligator emerging from a swamp to kill Laroche. At last, Kaufman survives and finds an ending for his script, which nevertheless develops into an orchid heist with car chases, embodying everything the protagonist wished to avoid. Finally, *Adaptation* incorporates McKee's guidelines—like the classic demands for conflict and character transformation—while also disobeying the guru by abusing of the voice-over narration McKee so emphatically condemns during the screenwriting workshop that Charlie reluctantly attends.

The aggregation of the elements coming from the many authors who in the film dialogue with the hero result in a hybrid script blending action ingredients with the protagonist's confabulations about the hardships of adapting a book. The script written by fictional Kaufman subverts *The Orchid Thief* by transposing its evolutionist metaphors of mutation and adaptation into an investigation of creative processes. Suggestions of parasitism (which is how Laroche defines Orlean's interest in him), cross-fertilization (in recurring images of insects pollinating flowers), and mutation (of Orlean's work into Kaufman's) abound in the film's self-reflexive meditations. The very script written by the hero (like *Adaptation* itself) turns out to be a hybrid of Kaufman's ideas with, on the one hand, those of Orlean, and on the other, those of Donald and McKee. Such hybridity is translated into images during a sequence in which the protagonist's voice blends with that of Orlean's. As Kaufman visits an orchid show, Orlean's voice-over wonders about the flowers ("one species looks like a monkey, one looks like an onion"), orienting the protagonist's perception of the orchids. Her narration then fades as the hero's attention drifts from orchids to women ("one looks like a schoolteacher, one looks like a gymnast"). The hero's voice-over narration overshadows Orlean's, constituting a dynamics in which Kaufman steals Orlean's discourse, transforming it into something else.

The appropriation of one's words is, in the end, a key element in *Adaptation*. When Charlie Kaufman fictionalizes Orlean and McKee, he attributes to himself the power to create (or recreate) their words, literally extracted from their respective books (whose pages are actually seen on screen). However, on a metalinguistic level, instead of leading to the parasitic consumption of one of the parts involved, this appropriation results in the mutation of Orlean's speech in the mouth of the protagonist, of McKee's in the mouth of Donald, and so forth. In the end, it is Kaufman as a character who mutates into a different human being after assimilating the many voices that inhabit his conflicted writing. When the real Kaufman writes himself into his script he is not only mutating his real self into this fictional character, but also duplicating his fictionalized version through the figure of Donald and, furthermore, multiplying his own voice through the many voices he incorporates. The result is an amalgam of voices coming from different authors and orchestrated by the protagonist, whose script is as polyphonic as it is hybrid.

While the film borrows a Darwinian terminology to offer a positive take on the issue of adaptation, it equally envisions creative processes through a darker evolutionist image: the idea of parasitism, which defines the relations between the screen versions of Kaufman and Orlean and the characters that inspire them. Donald, who in addition to being Kaufman's brother is also a character in the protagonist's script, colors Kaufman's life when he drags him to the very adventures that will enable the protagonist to finish his screenplay. Likewise, Laroche's passion for flowers seduces Orlean: it is through the orchid collector that she rediscovers passion and the intensity of her feelings, enhanced by the drugs provided to her by Laroche. The ways in which authors live through their characters in the film reflect the book's discussion of parasitism among flowers and host trees, which involves the harming of the host by the parasite. No wonder both Donald and Laroche have to die in the end, while Kaufman and Orlean survive.

The dialogical structure of the film and the resulting multivoiced script whose genesis we witness recall Bakhtin's concept of the polyphonic novel, in which abstract ideas are presented as consciousness, voice, and point of view, all embodied by characters (Bakhtin 1984, 93). In *Problems of Dostoevsky's Poetics,* Bakhtin says:

> "An authorial idea or thought must not perform in the work the function of totally illuminating the represented world, but must rather enter into that world *as an*

image of a human being, as one orientation among other orientations, as one word among many words" (98). [i]

Bakhtin detected these dynamics in Dostoevsky's *Notes from Underground,* which follows the Dostoevskyan pattern where other voices rejoin in the hero's internal dialogue (265). In that novel, the protagonist anticipates the reader's responses to his self-definitions. "Condemning himself," Bakhtin says, "[the hero] demands that the other person dispute this self-definition, and he leaves himself a loophole in case the other person should suddenly in fact agree with … his self-condemnation" (233). The protagonist's conversations with other characters in *Adaptation* epitomize this process; when he gazes at Orlean's picture and fantasizes talking to her, telling her that he is "fat and repulsive," she protests, saying, "you're not, you're not." While Kaufman claims that writing himself into his own script is "self-indulgent, pathetic," Donald often calls him a genius. In other moments, however, Donald is challenging, finding deficiencies in Kaufman's screenplay, forcing the hero to defend it. In short, Donald gives flesh to a voice existing inside Kaufman's conflicts, dramatizing the protagonist's shifting impressions about himself in the form of a rather comic dialogue between brothers. [ii]

While recuperating the centrality of the scriptwriter and stressing the importance of personal expression, *Adaptation* simultaneously aligns itself with the literary critics who overthrew the author as a figure of authority. Following Barthes's lessons, the film refuses closure—the status of the adventures experienced by Kaufman is never clarified; we are left wondering whether they happen in his life or in his scrip, and whether life and script are to be divorced. *Adaptation* also undermines the author's control over his own work when the protagonist asks for help to finish his screenplay, which leads him to reluctantly embark in Donald's adventures and ultimately incorporate them into the film. Finally, *Adaptation*'s portrayal of authorship privileges intertextuality through the borrowing of ideas from Orlean, Donald, McKee, and even the protagonist's agents.

Rather than threatening the author, the elements challenging his exclusive control redeem this figure by rendering it human—creativity crisis and intertextual borrowings become part of a personal drama, calling attention to the personal dimension of writing for cinema. As a consequence, the writer's personal journey gives a body, a face, and a voice to an entity that has been long relegated to abstraction in theoretical writings. Conversely, by portraying the writing of his own film as a fictional event and depicting his surrogate author as

---

[i] Emphasis mine.

[ii] Stam calls attention to the similarities between Charlie and Dostoevsky's Underground Man in Literature and Film (2).

a fictional character, the actual Kaufman also sets himself apart from the character played by Cage. The personal quality of Kaufman's statement about creative processes is undermined by the fictitiousness of the protagonist, despite his bearing of the author's name. While the hero manages to blend his personal choices with commercial demands, conciliating self-reflexive ruminations with action-plot elements, the degree to which the film manifests the anxieties of the real Kaufman is rendered ambivalent by the work's fictional status.

What is certain is that the evolutionist metaphors of mutation and hybridity offer a positive take on authorship by defining adaptation in terms of conscious borrowing in an intertextual dialogue that is more fruitful than threatening. The film thus provides a model for adaptation in which authors gain from their capacity to mutate and incorporate other voices into the tumultuous orchestration of pre-existing and newborn elements that constitute all creative practices. The focus on the author offers a prism through which to understand adaptation as a process where, rather than compete with, the adapted text dialogues with the original work, in an approach that envisions intertextuality as the locus not for the death, but for a new conception of authorship.

CHAPTER ELEVEN

AFRICAN TALES AND AMERICAN HERITAGE IN *DAUGHTERS OF THE DUST:* A COMPLEX TALE OF ADAPTATIONS

by Alina Patriche

The proliferation over the past few decades of critically acclaimed and commercially successful films based mainly on canonic Anglo-American literature (*e.g.,* by Shakespeare, Jane Austen, E. M. Forster, Henry James, Edith Wharton) has given rise to a film genre called "heritage," a term originally employed derisively by British film scholars. Tana Wollen and Cairns Craig, for instance, argue that films like *Chariots of Fire, A Room with a View* and *Brideshead Revisited* express reactionary and racist Thatcherite politics through their celebrating a colonialist, pre-world war English society as the historical basis for a narrow British national identity. On the other side of the Atlantic, however, the colorful, detailed rendition of English landscape and architecture, subtly depicted character relations, rich classical soundtracks, even the literary scriptwriting (with its social class dilemmas and country manor intrigues) offered a fresh cinematic palette and perspective to filmgoers bored by drab conventional literary adaptations, but exhausted by contemporary Hollywood action spectaculars. Able to enjoy the British heritage films' outstanding rendition of history guilt-free, the Americans could find in them a critique rather than a validation of conservative values.

In 1991, at the height of the critical controversy surrounding the role of heritage movies in expressing and promoting nostalgic views of colonialism, African American filmmaker Julie Dash employed all the visual and textual elements of this film genre to shape a chronicle of African heritage in her celebrated *Daughters of the Dust.* Set in 1902 on the Sea Islands off the coasts of Georgia and South Carolina, Dash's film is a cinematically beautifully rendered, richly detailed and historically accurate drama about an extended African American family on the eve of Northern migration. Like Anglo-American heritage, *Daughters of the Dust* adapts a treasured narrative tradition: West African storytelling. Writer-director Julie Dash models most characters in her film on Yoruba deities and discursively narrates the complex family history griot-style, thus bringing "African American experience into the very white frame of costume drama" (Pidduck 112). This essay reads *Daughters of the Dust* as a trans-Atlantic answer to heritage film (used now in a more neutral descriptive manner even in Britain). Dash's film shares with its British counterparts a stunning visual style in its recreation of the past, a preoccupation with class/ethnic representation and the aesthetic arsenal of postmodernism, including intertextuality and self-reflexiveness. Balancing well the blend of heritage formulas and specific African American themes, *Daughters of the Dust* makes a case for the idea that a cinematically expressed fascination with social history need not impede, but rather can help account for and preserve the popular memory of a complex cultural legacy.

Daughters tells the story of the Peazants, an African American family on the verge of leaving the islands where their ancestors had been brought as slaves, to move to the mainland in pursuit of more successful lives. This sets the stage for the central theme of the movie: the conflict between the importance of preserving West African traditions, which have survived almost intact in that isolated area, and the need to reach the mainland as a necessary step toward social and cultural integration into the mainstream ethos. The family's matriarch, Nana Peazant, stands for the African inheritance, whereas Hagaar Peazant, who "married into the family," is the most aggressive advocate of the northern migration as the only path to social, cultural and financial progress for the descendants of African slaves. Representatives of the integrated mainlanders are also present at the farewell picnic held on the island the day before crossing: Viola Peazant, a Baptist missionary, has come there with a photographer, Mr. Snead, to document her family's departure. Viola's cousin, Yellow Mary, who the film implies has worked as a prostitute in Cuba, is also visiting with her colleague and apparently lesbian lover Trula. By the end of the movie, after heated debates about tradition and progress, Hagaar leaves the island with her son and daughter Myown (her other daughter Iona remains there to marry her Native American lover), while Nana stays behind with her grandson Eli and his wife Eula, pregnant with the couple's first child. The visitors also take different paths: Viola, Mr. Snead and Trula return to the mainland, while Yellow Mary remains behind.

The screenplay for *Daughters of the Dust* and the final cinematic product are the result of Julie Dash's ten-year academic research into the Gullah traditions and rituals, a culture specific to a group of African Americans who maintained the purest forms of West African mores in the US. Dash employs African storytelling practices in the ways she conceives her characters and the narrative structure of the movie. Like most African peoples, West Africans are primarily oral peoples, and their art forms are oral rather than literary. In contrast to written literature, African "orature" is orally composed and transmitted, and often created to be verbally and communally performed by griots as integral part of dance and music rituals. Furthermore, in the ancient beliefs of the Yoruba tribes, the worlds of the Unborn and the Dead are connected and both can communicate with and influence the world of the Living. The primary meaning of this belief refers perhaps to the fluidity of time, which runs uniformly, without clear separation among future, past and present. The cinematic narration in *Daughters* is circular, rather than linear, in a way an African griot would recount a family history: the present intertwines with the past and the future through flashforwards and flashbacks. Significant for the film's roots in West African oral traditions, two narrators, Nana Peazant, the great grandmother of the family, and Eula's and Eli's Unborn Child (whose spirit materializes in an attempt to reconcile her parents) guide the viewer through the intricate family history of the Peazants.

Taking the Afro-centrism of this "adaptation" a step further, Dash models the main characters in *Daughters of the Dust* on major Yoruba deities. In her audio commentary on the DVD alternative soundtrack, the director elaborates on the film's ability to relate to and at the same time depart from Western narrative traditions: "Most characters in American narrative films are grounded in parameters dictated by the archetypal gods and goddesses of classical Western literature. The crucial underlying references for the family in *Daughters of the Dust*, the Peazants, are the deities of classical West African cosmologies." The mythical model for Nana Peazant, the family matriarch, is Obatala, the sculptor god who shapes human bodies and practices witchcraft. Nana views the Peazant women, those leaving home, as daughters of Oshun, a Yoruba goddess, the young daughter who leaves home to seek her fortune in the city. Nana's grandson Eli is the family blacksmith, inspired by Ogun, the deity of iron and war (whose Western equivalent is the Greek god Hephaestus). Eli's pregnant wife Eula represents the continuation of the Peazant family. Her character adapts well in both the sacred and the secular worlds and is modeled on the West African deity Oya Yansa, the spirit of the winds of change. Eula's Unborn Child occupies the very space between the sacred and the secular and is symbolically connected with Eshu Elegba, the guardian of the crossroads, messenger of the gods and master of potentiality. According to the film's official website, "Yellow Mary's name is derived from the name of the Yoruba goddess, Yemonja (Mami Wata-Ghana). She is the Mother of the Sea, the Mother of Dreams, the Mother of Secrets and often referred to as the Veiled Isis." Her return home is depicted as a universal rite of transition: she seems isolated in an intermediate position in life, on a boat traveling to Ibo Landing.

Drawing on her own inheritance as a Gullah-descended New Yorker, Dash tries to avoid biases in the film's debate surrounding the Peazants' choice between the old and the new ways. Despite its obvious Afro-centrism, the film also elaborates on the other side of the argument. The integration of the people of African descent into Western culture is presented as a necessary turn of events. Preserving one's cultural identity does not mean isolation, but a way to integrate into a world marked more and more by diversity; it is at the same time a way to preserve a sense of self, and to bring a contribution to the world's culture. In keeping with the film's emphasis on symbolism and cultural allusion, the family member that represents the will of the Peazants to move north and start a new life, Hagaar, is associated with a character in the Bible, a text emblematic for Western culture. According to the film's official website:

> Hagaar's name may refer to the biblical character of Hagar, the Egyptian serving maid of Abraham's wife, Sarai. When Sarai was unable to have children, she permitted Abraham to have a child, Ishmael, with Hagar. However, Hagar became proud and began to be disobedient to Sarai. As a result of her behavior, she was expelled from Abraham's house and community. She eventually returned to Egypt, where she found a wife for her son and became the mother of another race. According to *Bible Bulletin Board*, Hagaar's name translates from Egyptian as 'fugitive' or 'immigrant.'

Although the film seems to construct Hagaar as the antagonist, her character matches all of Nana's arguments against Northern migration with valid claims supporting integration into the mainstream culture.

Dash later expands on her point about the compatibility between social change and the preservation of African values in her 1997 novel *Daughters of the Dust*, the sequel to her 1991 film, which follows the destinies of Eli's and Hagaar's families twenty 22 years after the family's crossing to the mainland. Here, Amelia, Myown's daughter by her New York undertaker husband (and Hagaar's granddaughter), is a promising anthropology student (perhaps modeled in part on Zohreh Neale Hurston) who travels to the Sea Islands to research her dissertation project on Gullah culture and to meet her extended family. There she befriends her older cousin Elizabeth, Eli's and Eula's unborn child in the movie, a free-spirited schoolteacher, who has chosen to live by herself in her great-grandmother Nana's old house. The different paths the two cousins take at the end of the novel bespeak Dash's views of the relation between tradition and progress. Amelia, Hagaar's descendant, renounces her academic perspectives on the mainland and decides to go back and live on the Islands, taking her ill and unhappily married mother with her; instead of researching the cultural past of her ancestors, she decides to live it. On the other hand, Elizabeth, clearly depicted as Nana's spiritual successor, leaves her native land to go not to New York, but to Paris, where she plans to open a shop with "the charms, scarves and jewelry" (Dash 1999, 275) she was designing based on Nana's teachings about African artifacts.

Thus, *Daughters* challenges the conventional perception of the colonial subject as a homogenous entity; "the subaltern," as Gayatri Spivak famously put it, "can speak" and voice divergent opinions on the very topic of cultural identity. In its notion that upholding tradition is not only the subaltern's own choice, but it can also become the means of communicating with other cultures from an equal standpoint, Dash's film questions the mainstream assumption of collective ethic representation. It is also what *Daughter of the Dust* achieves as a movie: finding nuances in Afro-centrism and propelling it to an international cultural level. As Greg Tate observes in his foreword to Dash's screenplay, "The idea that black art can be cosmopolitan and Afri-centric bursts from every frame of *Daughters*, as does the idea that the truly Afri-centric is the very essence of cosmopolitan universality" (Dash 1992, 71).

Indeed, *Daughters* puts a revitalizing ethnic twist on the quintessential aesthetic elements of this film genre. Despite their undeniably progressive stances on social issues (*e.g., The Jewel in the Crown, A Passage to India, Howards End* and *The Remains of the Day*), heritage movies have been panned in Britain mostly for their visually stunning and historically accurate mise-en-scene. Tana and Stella Bruzzi criticize the "antiquarianism" and "museum aesthetics" embedded in a set of films clearly preoccupied with the visual recreation of the past and often quoting classical paintings in their mise-en-scene. More to the point, Andrew Higson argues that, "the past is displayed as visually spectacular pastiche, inviting a nostalgic gaze that resists the ironies and social critiques so often suggested narratively by these films" (109).

Displaying arrestingly beautiful visuals, "reminiscent of Impressionist painting" (Pidduck 113)–the kind of images which many critics of this genre would call "nostalgic"–Dash's movie can undoubtedly be described as a feast for the senses. Arthur Jafa's spellbinding, award-winning cinematography, brilliantly supported by John Barnes's African-inspired rhythms, render the Sea Islands at the turn of the century a lush and sensuous paradise. According to Dash's comments on the DVD soundtrack, the costumes and hairdos are accurately based on artifacts and period photographs (which she found at an ethnic museum on St. Helen Island) representing African Americans living on the Islands at the turn of the century. The same "antiquarianism" is discernable in the film's dialogue: *Daughters* is spoken almost entirely in the Gullah dialect, an idiom developed by the enslaved Africans brought to the coastal islands as a communication system effective enough to make themselves understood in a foreign land. About ninety percent of the Gullah vocabulary is English, but the grammatical and intonational features are largely West African, and the director had a dialect coach on the set to insure the accuracy of the actors' speech.

Although now regarded as a milestone of African American (as well as feminist) cinema, *Daughters* had received, at the time of its release, criticism similar to the British critics' complaints against the Anglo-American productions. Some African American critics charged Dash's film with being "'too beautiful,' as if 'black aesthetic' mustn't be too aesthetic" (Alexander 21). In fact, *Daughters of the Dust* has proven very important especially for the black aesthetic, as a movie which generated a new way of looking at black people on screen. Through its visual splendors, including its visual symbolism, *Daughters of the Dust* manages to challenge the traditional representation of African American history.

Perhaps the most significant example of the director's employment of heritage artistic strategies to challenge racial stereotypes is her presentation of slavery, an issue generally treated in two conventional ways in Hollywood films. One is, of course, the idealized pre-Civil War tableau from *Gone with the Wind* (1939), where slaves and masters seemed to live in perfect harmony. The other vividly depicts the experience of being enslaved, with all the iconography of violence involved: chains, flogging, beating and raping, as in the hit TV drama *Roots* (1977) or the recent adaptation of Toni Morrison's *Beloved* (1998). Set a few decades after the Civil War, *Daughters of the Dust* does not realistically document, but poetically suggests slavery through visual symbols. Dash uses the color indigo instead of the usual brutal iconography to signify slavery: one of the slaves' tasks on island plantations was to make indigo dye, and a couple of flashbacks show several black men and women mixing the dye accompanied by enthralling African incantations–with no chains or white masters in sight. The character closest to slavery, Nana Peazant, whose mother was sold away while she was a child, is always wearing an indigo dress; the color also appears on other characters' garments, including the Unborn Child's ribbon. Moreover, defying the conventions of realism, according to which the dye would have faded or disappeared from everyone's skin within a few years, the film symbolically draws attention to the black people's legacy of slavery by having the actors' hands covered with indigo dye in all scenes, including the ones set in the present. Far from detracting from its social themes, the film's stunning visuals contribute to the general message Dash is getting across as a heritage filmmaker. While her stylish narrative shows African American people in a new light, "resisting victimization" (Franke 44), the film also skillfully avoids melodrama and opportunistic "sentimentality." As Toni Cade Bambara phrases it in her preface to the published screenplay, through addressing slavery differently than the mainstream cinema does, Dash "intends to heal our imperialized eyes" (Dash 1992, xii).

Along the same lines, the film has been celebrated not only for its refreshing look at African traditions, but also for its emphasis on femininity: the published version of Dash's screenplay is suggestively subtitled "The Making of an African American Woman's Film." In an article entitled "Revolutionary

Brilliance," Zain A. Muse praises the movie's "Afrofemcentric aesthetic": "Dash's womanist consciousness is expressed most eloquently through the heartstopping portrayal Nana Peazant, [who] embodies the power, the gentleness, and the glory of maternal authority" (245). Not only are women at the center of the narrative, but the diversity and ambiguity of the female characters also mark a definite break with the stereotypes and "identity enclosures of the patriarchal discourse" (Muse 246-247).

In the chapter dedicated to "The Oppositional Gaze" in her study of *Black Looks: Race and Representation*, feminist critic Bell Hooks acknowledges the effect of Dash's groundbreaking representation of femininity on spectatorship. Hooks favorably compares Dash's focus on woman's subjectivity in a way that defies the male gaze, with Spike Lee's objectification of the black female body in *She's Gotta Have It* (1986). The critic contests "Lee's replication of mainstream patriarchal cinematic practices that explicitly represents woman (in this instance black woman) as the object of a phallocentric gaze" (126). On the other hand, Dash's emphasizing the female point of view "invites the audience to look differently": *Daughters of the Dust* employs "a deconstructive filmic practice to undermine existing grand cinematic narratives even as [it] retheorizes subjectivity in the realm of the visual" (130). In her interview with Julie Dash published as a preface to the screenplay, bell hooks takes this point further by quoting black female spectators who found that the movie finally offered them alternative black female images to which they can relate, as opposed to the stereotypical "prostitute, mammy, or slut":

> I interviewed a black woman yesterday who summed [it] up: 'All my life I have experienced my absence on the screen [...]'. So I think that physically, a lot of black women viewers were prepared for the radical visual and aesthetic intervention that *Daughters* makes. Because so many of them said to me again and again, in almost the same words, 'I was so starved for those images.' (Dash 41)

Although initially dismissed by potential sponsors and exhibitors as "too literary" for commercial entertainment (Alexander 22), this low-budget, independent, art-house production exceeded many distributors' expectations when it made $1 million in tickets sales upon its release in 1992. As a filmmaker who, according to her own testimony, has "a lot more respect for the general audience than the people who distribute films" (Brouwer 5), Dash not only challenges patriarchal on-screen representations of black women, but also entrusts the postmodern spectator with intellectual games ranging from intertextuality and cultural allusion to self-reflexiveness.

Like most heritage films, *Daughters of the Dust* is not only literary, but also literate: its intertextuality is both textual, as Dash's highly literary, almost poetical screenplay quotes other literary sources, and visual, as the mise-en-scene frequently quotes other films or film styles. Dash claims as her literary inspiration her heritage from African American women authors: "... after reading Toni Cade Bambara, Alice Walker, Toni Morrison, I wanted to tell those kind of stories. I see myself as a disciple of black women writers. They made me a whole" (Alexander 22). Moreover, Dash had Paule Marshall's permission to use an entire passage from her 1983 novel *Praisesong for the Widow* in the screenplay: Eula's monologue in which she tells her Unborn Child the story of the Ibo Landing is a quotation of Marshall's own treatment of the legend.

As far as her visual inspiration is concerned, Dash reveals in her audio commentary that she screened several 1920s and 1930s movies for texture. She was mostly inspired by Spencer Williams's works, especially his 1941 *Blood of Jesus*, and quotes this and other Southern rural religious film in the baptism scene of *Daughters*. (The movie also hints at the mainstream film legend Charlie Chaplin and his silent comedies in the scene in which Mr. Snead's taking pictures of the children on the beach is shot in fast motion.) In the film's mise-en-scene, Dash pays homage not only to such African American films as Bill Gunn's *Ganja and Hess* (1973) and Charles Lane's *Sidewalk Stories* (1989), but also to the works of renowned Harlem photographer James Van Der Zee. In her audio commentary, the director mentions Van Der Zee's portraits of African Americans in the 1920s as a source of inspiration (along with African icons, Egyptian reliefs and Ethiopian magic scrolls) for her structuring the film as a series of visual tableaus. Van Der Zee's use of props, including backdrops and costumes, to achieve stylized *tableaux vivants* in keeping with late Victorian and Edwardian visual traditions, is vividly reflected in *Daughters'* glamorizing look at African Americans at the turn of the twentieth century.

Finally, like many Anglo-American heritage films (such as *A Room with a View*, *Orlando* or *The Portrait of a Lady*), *Daughters* often mirrors its own cinematic devices. The director documenting her ancestors' history and culture has an on-screen alter ego in the character of Mr. Snead, who is always accompanied by his photographic camera when he wanders around the beach in search of local stories or images to record. As Joel Brouwer observes, the presence of optical devices designed to offer selective views of reality – like the photographic camera, the kaleidoscope or the stereoscope – serve as visual reminders that our perceptions of reality are limited. Dash's emphasis on those devices signals her awareness that the telling of the past involves privileging some stories and ignoring others. Therefore, "she both chooses to tell one of the stories never before told in a feature film, and refuses to claim that it is definitive" (Brouwer 11). By underscoring the inability of the movie camera, or any other means of representation, to capture "the truth" about the past,

Daughters seems to teach us that the "history lesson" heritage films propose "is inextricable from the history of representation" (Pidduck 113).

Like Anglo-American heritage films, which explore the past through the literary tradition of Western literature, *Daughters of the Dust* chronicles African American history in the manner an African griot would "recount, remember and recollect" a family history. Employing the artistic means of expression generally associated with heritage filmmaking, Julie Dash proposes an innovative way of re-presenting race and ethnicity on screen in a film which debates the issue of tradition vs. integration in connection to the descendants of African slaves. The position of *Daughters of the Dust* on the transnational map of heritage genre reflects the main point of the movie itself: gaining an understanding of one's own ethnicity and origins does not mean nostalgic nationalism or discriminatory isolation from other cultures, but common ground for intercultural communication.

CHAPTER TWELVE

CROSS-CULTURAL NOSTALGIA AND VISUAL CONSUMPTION: ON THE ADAPTATION AND JAPANESE RECEPTION OF HUO JIANQI'S 2003 FILM *NUAN*

by Hui Xiao

Although a classmate of "Fifth Generation" filmmakers like Zhang Yimou, the only recently established director Huo Jianqi initially worked in set decoration. Frustrated by the tepid response to his first Hollywood-style commercial films like *Yingjia* (*The Winner*, 1995)[i] and *Geshou* (*The Singer*, 1996), he turned to small-budget art films and began only lately to gain an international reputation, particularly in Japan, with his nostalgic melodramas *Nashan naren nagou* (*Postman in the Mountains*, 1998) and *Nuan* (2003). While *Postman in the Mountains* draws a beautiful picture of father-son postmen's journey to deliver the mail in forested mountainous areas, *Nuan* focuses on a Chinese peasant girl (played by Li Jia) who must abandon her dreams of migrating to a city.

In addition to its representation of picturesque landscapes, in keeping with the visual aesthetics of Huo's earlier film, *Nuan* also impresses its audience with the radiance of the actress's feminine beauty and its romantic love story. Structurally the film unfolds around the homecoming journey of Lin Jinghe, the first-person narrator (played by Guo Xiaodong) who ten years earlier had left his hometown. Jinghe is now a college graduate working in a big city and enjoys authority equal to that of a village chief on his return to help his former elementary school teacher get his monopoly of the village's lucrative duck-herding business. On the day he is leaving after successfully accomplishing his mission, he unexpectedly runs into Nuan, his first love, which brings the flashback of a story buried in the past. Ten years previously, Nuan was the prettiest girl in the village and also had brilliant talents in singing, dancing and acting. Infatuated with a handsome Peking opera singer who makes an itinerant tour to the village, Nuan dreams of going to the city to start a new life with him.

---

[i] Translations by author, unless otherwise noted.

After waiting hopelessly for two years, she gives up on the performer's promise in favor of Jinghe's assurance that he will take her to the city if he is admitted into college. However, an accident that cripples Nuan makes this promise empty too. She has no choice but to marry the village's mute duck-herdsman (played by Teruyuki Kagawa, a Japanese actor). Learning of all the sufferings that Nuan went through over the years, Jinghe feels so sorry for her that he promises to take her little daughter to the city in the future to receive a better education. Having made peace with the past that he regrets through this new promise, Jinghe sets out on his way back to the city where he has already got a happy family of a well-educated wife and a newborn son.

Although not at all warmly welcomed by the audience in China, *Nuan* as well as *Postman in the Mountains* has proven hugely popular and been critically acclaimed particularly in thoroughly modernized Japan. Although both films won the Best Picture award at China's government-sponsored Golden Rooster film awards, *Postman in the Mountains* gained no distributor at all in the domestic market, while the release of *Nuan* was limited to small-scale exhibition in six theaters in Beijing beginning on February 27, 2004. On April 18, a journalistic report described the director's bitterness at the disappointingly low box office income of the film (Wang Xuemei). Apart from the lack of effective copyright laws or a well-developed art theater exhibition circuit, another reason for the film's failure is that it represents not a popular imaginary but an elitist nostalgia rhetoric, which fails to resonate for the majority of the Chinese population as peasants in the rural areas.

In stark contrast to its obscurity at home in China, *Postman in the Mountains* became Japan's top box office grossing film and the talk of the town in 2001. The Japanese Ministry of Education even officially recommended it as a must-see educational film to Japanese middle-school students. So far the film has raked in at least 800 million yen (7.3 million U. S. dollars) in Japan. Following the success of *Postman in the Mountains*, the film *Nuan* won both the top award and the award for best supporting actor (Teruyuki Kagawa) in the 2003 Tokyo International Film Festival. At the film's mid-week premiere in Tokyo on November 4, eager viewers waited in a line longer than one hundred meters in front of the theater (Wang Yin, "To Gain Tears"). Encouraged by the enthusiasm of Japanese audiences for Huo's works, a Japanese distributor decided to release this film nationwide to regular theaters rather than to art theaters only. What's more, apparently confident about creating another box office miracle under an auteurist brand, the distributor is also negotiating the purchase of Huo's earlier films for Japanese release ("*Nuan* Will Shine in Japanese Nationwide Theaters").

This reception invites investigation into the basis for the popularity of Huo Jianqi's rural films in Japan. Clearly we should situate Japanese reception of

Huo's films in social and discursive conditions. In the face of problems caused by modernization, a cultural discourse of imaginary nostalgia can create an idyllic past of Japan that provides psychological refuge for the anxiety-stricken Japanese. Due to Japan's narrow territory and high degree of urbanization, housing is a grave problem in crowded towns and cities. For those city dwellers who have no strong sense of a rooted home, an imagined nostalgia for Japanese *furusato* (old village) can offer a feeling of returning home. Thus, *furusato* has arisen as the embodiment of the eternal "Japanese hometown" in response to Japanese national anxiety over the insufficiency of the natural and social resources. It does not refer to any particular place, "but rather the generalized nature of such a place and the nostalgic feelings aroused by its mention" (Robertson 113). With a strong familial and maternal aura, *furusato* is metonymic of Japanese vanishing agrarian traditions as well as intimate family relationships within a naturally formed community: the unitary national identity of Japan is built in part on this concept.

A popular trend in Chinese filmmaking is to follow the Japanese melodramatic mode to invent an idealized "natural community" to cover up the peasants' violent resistance and social upheavals as well as other class and gender conflicts in the process of modernization. Like the Miss Furusato Contests, an integral part of the state-sponsored native place-making campaign which functions to construct the image of "good wife, wise mother," nostalgic Chinese films also connect the feminine, the maternal, the familial with the lost virtues and innocence of a traditional agrarian China. In other words, a similar *furusato* construction exits in popular Chinese cultural forms, although it takes a Chinese name and face. Drawing on Linda Williams's theories of melodrama, I intend to underline the melodramatic structure of both Japanese *furusato* movement and the Chinese film *Nuan* to argue that the melodramatic adaptation from the original story into the current film plays a central role in assuring a smooth assimilation of the cinematic representation of Chinese ethnicity into current Japanese discourses of nostalgia. Moreover, Japanese visual consumption of cross-cultural nostalgia in the form of Chinese film melodrama further echoes the trends of internationalizing and feminizing *furusato* tradition evident in Japan.

Adaptation from Mo Yan's Story to Huo Jianqi's Film

At the start of *Nuan*, immediately following the title, a line reading "adapted from Mo Yan's short story 'White dog swing' [sic]" gives credit to the original literary text. However, a close look at the film compared to the story reveals the filmmaker's drastic changes in the process of adaptation. To discover how these changes function we should take into consideration the film's marketing orientation. Writing about how the investment in the film *Nuan* can pay off, Huo Jianqi asserts that the investing firm Beijing Aureate Ocean Ark Co. Ltd. had a very clear profit-promising pattern in mind, *i.e.,* "Mo Yan's story + Huo Jianqi's art film = Chinese art theater goers + Japanese market" (*This Time, This Place* 79). Due to the scarcity of art theaters and the flourishing digital video disc pirating business in China, the Japanese were clearly the film's primary target audience. Guided by such a market orientation, the adaptation from the original story integrally produced consumable images that well matched Japanese trends of internationalizing and feminizing the *furusato* tradition. This strategy encourages a potential assimilation of a Chinese film into Japanese *furusato* discourse, and consequently promotes the reception of this film in Japan.

Mo Yan, the story's author, first gained fame with *Hong gaoliang jiazu* (*Red sorghum family*), a novel covering the period of the war of resistance against the Japanese (1937-1945). The novel is marked with a very strong inter-ethnic antagonism. Zhang Yimou produced *Hong gaoliang* (Red sorghum), based on the first two chapters of the novel, as his debut film in 1987, which won the Golden Bear Prize at the Berlin International Film Festival and began to bring Chinese cinema to the world. Although *Baigou qiuqianjia* (*The white dog and the swing*), first published in 1985, does not express anti-Japanese sentiments, the story does bear some signature marks of the saga writer of the Chinese resistance.

First, the location of the original story is Gaomi dongbei xiang, or the Gaomi County of Shandong Province. Like William Faulkner's Yoknapatawpha County, Gaomi is Mo's imaginary fatherland in all of his important literary works including *Red Sorghum*. In Mo's fictional world, peasants living on this imagined land of North China are as vital and wild as the stout sorghum plants everywhere. Embodying the free spirit of "the untamed nature," Gaomi goes beyond merely serving as the setting of Mo Yan's stories and novels (Zhong 120). Standing firmly together with the peasants to resist violently against the Japanese invasion, Gaomi itself is a central character playing a role in Mo's anti-Japanese dramas.

In *Nuan*, this blood-soaked homeland of anti-Japanese nationalists disappears. Instead, the geographical setting of *The White Dog and the Swing* shifts to the Xiao taoyuan village located at the Wuyuan County of Jiangxi Province, which is famous for its picturesque landscape and stylized ancient architecture. Located south of the Yangtze River and characterized by warm humid weather, Wuyuan County cannot grow sorghum, the symbol of Mo's resistant peasant heroes. Compared to Gaomi dongbei xiang, this area of the pastoral peace and economic self-sufficiency has little historical memory of Japanese invasion and atrocities, and consequently, I would argue, is easier than

the original setting for a Japanese audience to accept as a visual embodiment of
an agrarian utopia.   Wuyuan County indeed appears as a Chinese *furusato*
perfect for nostalgic tourists. Interviewed about his filming experience in China,
Teruyuki Kagawa at Tokyo Film Festival said he had felt "the great power of
the earth" at his first step on Chinese land.   Gesturing to the bustling
automobiles crowding Tokyo's streets, he said his life in Wuyuan is
unimaginable for today's Japan. The Chinese peasants he saw keep traditional
customs and live a self-sufficient life. Compared to modernized Japan, Wuyuan
is another world that does not exist in Japan's present, but in its idyllic past
(Wang Yin, "Teruyuki Kagawa").

   The irony about Teruyuki Kagawa's fantasy about a Chinese *furusato* is that
the filmmaker chose Wuyuan, an already highly developed tourist spot, to paint
a nostalgic picture of a Chinese Shangri-la untainted by the forces of modernity.
The filmic scenery presented in the style of tourism photography adds another
touch from the rising consumerism in post-Mao China. Carefully framed, softly
lit still long shots of the landscape readily support auxiliary marketing as
postcards of the film. They also can easily sell as top-quality Japanese *furusato*
postcards due to the aesthetic resemblance of the two. In other words, this old
village of Wuyuan can be viewed as a Chinese extension of the internationalized
image of Japanese *furusato*. Because this pastoral national home of the natural
community is long lost on Japanese land, the popularization and consumption of
the tradition have to go beyond the national boundaries to find its new
incarnations.

   Supporting the trans-spatial nostalgia displayed by almost the identical
composition of some *Nuan* postcards and *furusato* photographs, the film also
modifies the story's setting in time. The original story was published in 1985, a
year still burdened with traumatic memories of the just-ended Cultural
Revolution. However, the adapted film is set in the 1990s, when the Chinese
economic reform had gathered more impetus after Deng Xiaoping's inspection
trip to the Free Trade Zone of the South China in 1992. The 1990s are the
momentous period when Chinese people began to witness a more and more
radical urban/rural divide and rich/poor polarization along with the ever-
quickening development of the capitalist free market economy. This temporal
adjustment makes the problems addressed in the film more relevant to Japanese
society, which has always taken the lead in the modernization of Asia. On the
other hand, the moving forward of the clock suppresses the memories of a
communist Other, which surfaces in Mo Yan's allusions to revolutionary songs,
his pungent political parody of Maoist rhetoric and the identity of Nuan's first
beloved in the story, a Chinese People's Liberation Army soldier whom the film
replaces with a Peking opera performer. This change of the time setting ascribes
the nostalgia to a trans-temporal idyllic village free of any sociopolitical

constraints instead of a communal golden age of a Red China. Thus, the dialectic of nostalgia and modernity transcends all historical specificities to become purified and universal, and consequently relevant to either China or Japan: in other words, to a wider international context.

Apart from the setting in Gaomi dongbei xiang and the collective memories of the communist era of China, another element that disappears is the story's title character. The importance of the white dog is evident from the opening lines of the original story:

> Gaomi Dongbei Xiangonce produced a species of large gentle white dogs, but now after several generations it's very difficult to find a pure breed. Today everybody raises mongrels, and even if a white one is occasionally seen, somewhere on its body will be patch of colored fur betraying its mixed blood. But if the patch of colored fur doesn't cover too much of the dog's body and isn't located in too prominent a place, everybody will habitually refer to it as a "white dog" without being too critical about the discrepancy between the name and the reality. (Mo, *The White Dog and the Swing* 45)

Beginning with comparing the mongrels and the pure breed of the white dog, the first-person narrator in the following sections of the story repeatedly expresses regret about the extinction of the breed and the loss of the purity—and thus more general nostalgic longing. Those familiar with Mo Yan's other work will likely connect this image of the white dog of mixed blood (zazhong) to hybrid/bastard sorghum (zazhong gaoliang), another ethnicity metaphor Mo frequently uses in *Red Sorghum* and other novels set in Gaomi dongbei xiang. This *zazhong* (hybrid/bastard/mongrel) condition of the white dog and the red sorghum is highly symbolic of the cultural hybridity of a rural China in post-Mao era. The disappearance of the white dog from the film tacitly evades the problem of the loss of the purity.

The erasure of the white dog goes hand in hand with the most radical change in the adaptation, the ending. In the original text, Nuan and her mute husband have given birth to three deaf boys. So toward the ending of the story, Nuan has the white dog lead the first-person narrator into a sorghum field where she boldly asks the first-person narrator to make love to her in the hope of being impregnated with a healthy child. This unexpected turn echoes the *zazhong* (hybrid/bastard/mongrel) idea reified by the white dog and the red sorghum in Mo's verbal texts. In other words, the purity of Chinese ethnicity, represented by Mo's peasant figures, cannot be maintained any more when confronted with the urbanizing forces of Chinese modernization personified by the first-person narrator, a college graduate returning home after ten years' absence.

What is even more challenging about the story's ending is the woman's taking the initiative in this sexual act to be performed in the wild. While waiting for the narrator to arrive, Nuan "had matted down some sorghum to clear an open space around which the sorghum stood like a tall four-sided screen. As I peered in she took the yellow cloth [to make clothes for her sons] out of her bundle and spread it out on the matted-down sorghum" (Mo, The *White Dog and the Swing* 60-61). The description of this erotic scene forms an intertextual dynamic with a similar field scene in *Red Sorghum*. . The difference between the two is that in the *Red Sorghum*, . the man is in control in the sexual consummation while in *The White Dog and the Swing*, it is the woman that plays the active role. In the story, the sexual free spirit and untamed nature of the woman threaten the masculinity of the first-person narrator.

Compared to this rebellious closure of the story, the film ends upon a far more sentimental and reconciled note. In the film, Nuan is lucky to have a healthy and pretty daughter who shares an intimate relationship with both her parents. Toward the end of the film, Nuan's family of three has gone to see off Jinghe, the first-person narrator, as he departs for the city. Knowing fully well the hardships of peasant life and Nuan's haunting dream of going to the city, the mute husband makes a self-sacrificing gesture by asking Jinghe to take his wife and daughter with him. Seeing this, Nuan drags her husband away and leaves Jinghe to look back at the reunited couple supporting each other. Gradually fading into the natural background of the vast grassland, the film's Nuan sublimates her desires to morality, as she voluntarily maintains the unity of her family at the cost of her dreams. Although physically crippled—an evident punishment for her once unchained desires—Nuan becomes spiritually complete by choosing the feminine virtues of loyalty and endurance. The image of a shameless lascivious woman in the story is thus transformed in the film into a standard Miss Furusato conforming to the traditional criteria of "good wife, wise mother." The reconstructed maternal image redeems her transgressions and retrieves the lost rural utopia based on pure domesticity and traditional ethics.

Being touched by the tears that the daughter, the mother/wife and the father/husband have shed, Jinghe holds the little girl tightly and promises her that he will take her to the city later. Then he turns around, embarking on his way back to the city. Accompanied with the melodious music played on traditional Chinese musical instruments, the first-person narrator concludes in voice-over that each of the three of them is lucky and fulfilled, although in a different sense. His final soliloquy goes this way:

> My promise is my confession. People always make mistakes, but not everyone can get the chance to make up for them. Therefore, I am lucky. My forgetting is my reminiscence. Even if one never returns to his hometown, he cannot escape the haunting memories of his first love. Therefore, the mute is

lucky. My worries are my consolations. What the mute can give Nuan, I cannot give to her. Therefore, Nuan is lucky.[i]

The final remarks of reconciliation make up for everyone's loss, and smooth out the "discrepancy between the name and the reality" (Mo, *The White Dog and the Swing* 45). With this highly melodramatic ending that re-establishes the normative order of social relationships, the film neatly solves all the unsolvable class and gender conflicts exposed by the original story. While the story undercuts any imagined nostalgia for an idealized hometown with a merciless picture of the cruel realities, the film allays all the anger and resistance of the oppressed by promising a bright ending that retrieves the irretrievable for everyone.

Cross-Cultural Melodrama, Cross-Cultural Nostalgia

In her article "Melodrama Revised," Linda Williams defines the melodramatic mode as "a peculiarly democratic and American form that seeks dramatic revelation of moral and emotional truths through a dialectic of pathos and action" (42). Without concerning herself whether melodrama is an exclusively American form or not, E. Ann Kaplan reads recent Chinese films in light of European and American melodrama theories. Kaplan's cross-cultural analysis of the melodramatic narrative affirms the view that "woman's films" in China tend to make comments on social issues through representing the frustrated sexuality and subjectivity of Chinese women.

Bringing to the fore both "the direct impact of American melodrama on Chinese cinema" and the historical rationale behind the melodramatic mode, Paul G. Pickowicz argues that the melodramatic narrative is the means Chinese films has adopted to address "the crisis of twentieth-century Chinese culture and society" (303). He quotes Peter Brooks to argue:

> [M]elodrama is popular in places where "the traditional imperatives of truth and ethics have been violently thrown into question, yet where the promulgation of truth and ethics, their insaturation as a way of life, is of immediate, daily, political concern." "Melodrama," [Brooks] reminds us, "starts from and expresses the anxiety brought by a frightening new world in which the traditional patterns of moral order no longer provide the necessary social glue." (303)

Kaplan and Pickowicz both persuasively demonstrate the relevance of the melodramatic narrative to Chinese cinema. Brooks's view that melodramas address cultural crisis is particularly pertinent to the interpretation of *Nuan*.

---

[i] First published in *Dangdai* (Contemporary literature bimonthly) in 2003, and later released as monograph by Beijing People's Literature Press in 2004.

Placing the reading of the film into the intertextual conditions of cross-cultural melodramas, I would argue that the structure of the film *Nuan* well fits the melodramatic pattern, proposed by Williams, of retrieving the lost innocence "through a dialectic of pathos and action." In this film, when Nuan is attracted to the Peking opera performer, her desires for the man and the urban lifestyle he represents erodes the virginal innocence that she and the pure land represent. A series of highly erotic swing scenes visually displays the dangerous pleasure of losing the virtuous innocence. When the swing reaches its highest point, Nuan stares forward as far as possible, even seeing the capital Beijing in her imagination. Her yearnings for the performer and for the city life transgress the idealized purity and innocence of a Chinese *furusato*. As a result, she must be punished. Because the rope has worn out, Nuan and the male narrator both fall from the swing. But only Nuan is injured. While the man later gets the chance to fulfill his aspirations of getting a college education and residing legally in a city, the crippled woman has to abandon her own dream of moving to the city. Left with no choice, she marries the mute in the village and gives birth to a daughter. The melodramatic narrative of the film redeems her innocence through this harsh punishment and her virtuous suffering thereafter as a good wife and a loving mother. This virtuous suffering of an oppressed woman echoes the *feminisuto* tradition in Japanese melodramas:

> The image of a woman suffering uncomplainingly can imbue us with admiration for a virtuous existence almost beyond our reach, rich in endurance and courage. One can idealized her rather than merely pity her, and this can lead to what I call the worship of womanhood, a special Japanese brand of feminism. (Russell 146)

What's more, "the *feminisuto* tradition is indicative of the fundamental role of the mother in Japanese culture and psychoanalysis" (Russell 147). Connecting the Japanese cultural identity with a suffering maternal image, the tradition in Japanese cinema now finds its follower in contemporary Chinese films.

However, this close connection to Japanese melodramas can hardly be found in the literary text. The presence of the melodramatic "dialectic of pathos and action" materialized by a maternal figure's silent but virtuous suffering in the filmic adaptation stands out for its absence in the original story. The style and narrative mode of the film radically change the verbal text. In the story, Nuan's maternal experience of giving birth and nurturing children is compared to animals' breeding. When the first-person narrator wonders why Nuan has three boys despite the "one-child only" policy put into practice in post-1978 China, Nuan "explained coldly, 'I had three at once, plunk, plunk, plunk, just like having pups'" (Mo, *The White Dog and the Swing* 52). Another intertextual link can be made here through the canine metaphor. Like Xiao Hong's *The*

Field of Death and Life (*Shengsi chang*, 1935), a novel interweaving national trauma and embittered motherhood during the anti-Japanese war period, Mo Yan's literary representation of Chinese women's bodily experiences is stripped of any sentimental touch of a romanticized aesthetics. The peasant women's life-and-death cycle in an old Chinese village, after the invasion of the Japanese in Xiao Hong's novel and of modernity in Mo Yan's story, is presented as tormented and animal-like.

Psychologically traumatized, the rural women's bodies are also severely injured and deformed in both writers' works. In the story *The White Dog and the Swing*, when Nuan falls from the swing, her right eye is pierced by a spike of locust tree needles. With a "deeply sunken eye socket," she becomes known as "One-Eyed Nuan" (Mo, *The White Dog and the Swing* 50). When the first-person narrator returns to the village after ten years, he can hardly recognize Nuan. At the first sight of her, he "wouldn't have been able to tell it was a woman" (Mo, *The White Dog and the Swing* 47). Then standing on the river bank, seeing Nuan's "large drooping breasts," the narrator thought dryly to himself, "Just like the song the village kids sing: 'Unmarried she's got golden breasts, married she's got silver breasts, having children she's got bitch's teats'" (Mo, *The White Dog and the Swing* 52). Rather than redeeming the lost innocence through being a "good wife, wise mother" in the *feminisuto* tradition, the story shows family life as a burdening institution that deprives the rural woman of her free spirit and untamed nature. What's even more unfeminine about Nuan is her brutal manners and down-to-earth language. Using vulgar language, even cursing freely from time to time, Nuan relentlessly ridicules the intellectual narrator's nostalgic speech. When he claims to feel homesick for the old village, Nuan says: "What's there to miss in this beat-up place? You missed this broken-down bridge? It's like a goddamn rice steamer in the sorghum fields, about to steam me to death" (Mo, *The White Dog and the Swing* 52). With its objective observations and gruesome style, Mo Yan crushes the utopian myth with his dystopian writing. His story is a parody of the texts about the imagined nostalgia for a pure old village that is always associated with the sublimated maternal image.

The melodramatic adaptation much dilutes, and in part overwrites, the sarcasm and bitterness in Mo's story. In the film Nuan's feminine image occupies center stage. To preserve the radiance of her feminine beauty, the outcome of the accident that changes Nuan's fate becomes the crippling of her right leg. In this way, her radiant maternal image, in the place of a grotesque one-eyed slut, can be seamlessly integrated into the glamorized natural landscape, which is quintessential for constructing a melodramatic "nostalgia for rural and maternal origins" (Williams 65).

When talking about using the name Nuan as the film title, director Huo Jianqi said it was not only because she is the protagonist of the film but also because "nuan" in Chinese means warmth, or heart-warming affections (Wang Yin, "To Gain Tears"). Indeed, sentiments and pathos play a central role in the filmic narrative. In audiences' comments on the film *Nuan*, the word most frequently used is "tears." After witnessing a preview showing of *Nuan*, the head of the Beijing branch of *Asahi Shimbun* (Asahi newspaper), one of the biggest Japanese newspapers, said: "This film will create a new miracle [in Japan]!" while wiping away tears from his face (Shen). Confessing to the director what he felt after viewing the film, even Mo Yan said it had touched the softest spot in his heart and he had shed tears silently. Wang Yin, the correspondent sent to Tokyo to give a series of special reports on the film festival, provided a vivid description of some middle-aged Japanese women's insuppressible sobbing at the film's premiere (Wang Yin, "To Gain Tears").

This tearjerking effect of the film was frequently mentioned around the film's premiere in Tokyo in 2003. For example, the headline of a film report in the Guangdong-based *South Weekend*, the most influential weekly newspaper with the largest circulation in China, reads "The film *Nuan* goes to Tokyo to gain tears shed by the Japanese" (Wang Yin, "To Gain Tears"). After *Nuan* won the Best Picture Award on November 9, the report headline was "Tears won over the Tokyo Film Festival. " When interviewed about his expectation for the film's reception in Japanese market, Huo Jianqi said this film would make Japanese audiences cry out their eyes (Wang Yin, "Tears Won over"). This self-conscious move of categorizing the film as a "weepy," or "family melodrama" shows the filmmaker's awareness about what can sell well in the Japanese market. His prediction is not groundless for at least two reasons. First, his previous family melodrama *Postman in the Mountains* had enjoyed a huge success in Japan. Second, the melodramatic mode is structured in Japanese national identity, as Catherine Russell argues:

> Melodrama, unlike modernism, has deep roots in Japanese cultural history and might even be said to dominate Japanese cinema as a kind of metagenre to the same extent that it informs North American narrative film. In fact, emotional intensity is a key attribute of the so-called Japanese "character." (143)

Interestingly enough, while defending himself against some Chinese film critics' charge that *Nuan* catered to the Japanese market, Huo simultaneously acknowledged that he produced this sentimental melodrama with a recognition of "emotional intensity" as the Japanese national character. Talking about Teruyuki Kagawa's happy tears at receiving the Best Supporting Actor Award, Huo generalized that Japanese people love crying. (Huo and Yi 87) The above cross-cultural analysis on melodramatized nostalgia reveals the Chinese director's awareness of his film's resonance with a Japanese cultural tradition, even with a presumed Japanese national character. Huo's attitude begs the question: is the narrative convergence of cross-cultural nostalgia in Chinese and Japanese melodramas just a historical coincidence? In the following two sections, I will deal with the "inter-textual" (both Japanese and Chinese) conditions of reading and producing Chinese melodramas.

"Inter-textual" Dynamics: Nostalgia for *Furusato*

When investigating the reception of Bond novels and films in England, Tony Bennett and Janet Woollacott investigate "inter-textuality" in distinction from Julia Kristeva's concept of intertextuality:

> [W]hereas Kristeva's concept of intertextuality refers to the system of references to other texts which can be discerned within the internal composition of a specific text, we intend the concept of inter-textuality to refer to the social organization of the relations between texts within specific conditions of reading." (44-45)

Just as the reading of Bond films cannot be separated from the "inter-textual" politics of cold-war ideology, to better understand the popularity of Huo Jianqi's *Nuan* in a cross-cultural context, we must look first into the "inter-textual" dynamics, or the social and discursive conditions of Japanese reading of the film. In view of its filmic representation of an agrarian utopia lost in modernizing China, I would connect Japanese audiences' viewing and appreciating the film *Nuan* with a central "inter-textual" condition, *i.e.,* the discourses around nostalgia for the *furusato* tradition.

Since the advent of Japanese modernization beginning in the nineteenth century, the state has taken strategic moves to regulate and invent traditions for the sake of maintaining a "highly disciplined national community and a unified and totalizing culture" (Robertson 11). Native place making is one such state-sponsored program to stage the so-called *furusato* tradition. According to Robertson,

> [a]lthough furusato literally means "old village," the word is used most often in an affective capacity to signify not a particular place—that is, an actual old village—but rather the generalized nature of such a place and the nostalgic feelings aroused by its mention. "Furusato Japan" thus imbues the state with a warm, fuzzy, familial, and ultimately maternal aura. (113)

To materialize this family-state ideology, Japanese government has invested in a national-scale movement to develop *furusato*-centered tourism. In 1985 the Furusato Information Center was established with an annual operating budget of

4 million U. S. dollars (Robertson 116). *Furusato* parks, museums, theaters were established in a number of counties. In some towns, such as Kurino, a "*furusato* bus" service is provided for tourists to travel around. Different counties have designed different *furusato* sightseeing packages to welcome "homecoming" tourists from the city who have suffered from housing problems and thus have a strong sense of uprootedness in the face of Japan's fast-paced urbanization.

In addition to being a cultural icon and a tourist industry regulated by the state, *furusato* has also taken specific popular cultural forms. The *fursato* music compact disc series (including *Furusato, Furusato Reborn, Furusato Encore* and *Furusato* 2) have been marketed under the name of "homeland melody" ("Furusato Encore"). *Juurokuya Renka: Kami Furusato* is an adventure game for PlayStation 2, which enacts a painter's return to his small home village. Bored with his career for profit and fame in the city, he abandons the city life and chooses to come back to the *furusato* to re-experience romantic relationships ("Juurokuya Renka"). As early as 1983, both a feature film *Furusato* and an animated film *The Little Ninja—The Chapter of ·the Great Clash in His Native Country* (*Ninja Hattori-kun NinxNin Furusato Daisakusen no Maki*) were released.

Nostalgia for *furusato* is also visible in the anime master Hayao Miyazaki's works. While *My Neighbor Totoro* (*Tonari no Totoro*, 1988) creates the legendary supernatural being "Totoro" to depict a harmonious relationship between human and nature in 1950s Japanese countryside, the 2002 Oscar winner *Spirited Away* (*Sen to Chihiro no Kamikakushi*, 2001) gives "an insight into the troubled present and a sense of what we have lost in our neglected past" (Richie 8). The term *furusato* is even explicitly mentioned in *Only Yesterday* (*Omohide Poroporo*, 1991), which is about the childhood memories and the "old village" return journey of a thirty-year-old office lady residing in Tokyo.

Compared with these films, an even more direct anti-modernization declaration made by Miyazaki is his 1994 feature anime *Pom Poko* (*Heisei tanuki gassen pompoko*). This film draws on Japanese Shinto mythology to tell a story about how a group of raccoons (*tanukis*) use "*Tanuki* transforming science*" to fight against humans' urbanization plan. Of all the amazing spectacles their battles create, the most intriguing is the raccoons' last desperate strike to change the "damaged land," the already developed suburban city of Tokyo, back into their original natural habitat. The raccoons strive to recuperate with their supernatural powers an agrarian past featuring intimate and harmonious interpersonal relationships of a traditional agrarian community, which is reminiscent of the quintessential *furusato* landscape: "forested mountains, fields cut by a meandering river, and a cluster of thatched-roof farmhouses" (Robertson 116). However, that beautiful scenery does not endure;

it disappears in a flash. The audiences, along with the raccoons in the film, may be disappointed to realize that the beautiful *furusato* landscape is just an illusion, whether created by raccoons' legendary magic or by the cinematic apparatus. Ironically enough, the raccoons' nostalgia for the vanished *furusato* brings back only ephemeral fantasies that can be visualized and circulated for audiences' visual consumption only through the technology of modern media. This paradoxical intertwining of nostalgia and consumption is endemic in the *furusato* construct, a point that proves to be highly relevant to my analysis of the film *Nuan*.

As the above-mentioned texts show, the state and popular forms produce *furusato* as a Japanese trope for traditional agricultural community that, in contrast with problematic life in modernized cities, presumably enjoyed cultural and economic self-sufficiency. Two trends stand out in the simultaneous movement to promote *furusato* as both the embodiment of Japanese family-state ideology and as a consumable product marking "Japaneseness." The first trend is the rising internationalization of the cultural icon of *furusato*. In advertisements, the Japanese post office claims: "International Furusato Parcels help you deliver your sentiments to your family member(s) or friend(s) abroad" ("International Furusato Parcels"). In the global market, *furusato* is not only deliverable but also edible: a Google search readily identifies numerous *furusato* sushi bars and restaurants in Honolulu, Los Angeles, Toronto, Berlin, Manila, Macao, and Sydney. The second trend is the feminization intrinsic to the *furusato* tradition. Robertson points out that "the groups employing the *furusato* image in their campaigns invariably link that concept with 'mother.' The association of mother and *furusato* is so tenacious that some Japanese social critics have insisted that the two words are synonymous" (124). What makes the association even more appealing and sensational are the Miss Furusato contests that started as early as 1908 all over Japan. In 1989 about 3,400 contests were registered. Analyzing the Miss Furusato contests, Robertson says that "the thousands of Miss *Furusato* represent collectively a type of femininity, in the service of both nostalgic males and the dominant gender ideology, summed up by the expression 'good wife, wise mother' (*ryosai kenbo*) coined in the Meiji period" (125-26). Notably, this Meiji Japan term is identical to the familiar Chinese expression *Xianqi liangmu* (good wife, wise mother). In view of the strong cultural legacy Japan inherited from ancient China, it is very likely that the Japanese term is a loan word from traditional Confucian ethics.

The contemporary role that Chinese resources are playing in the internationalization of feminized *furusato* nostalgia extends the strong cultural connection between China and Japan that yields the two dominant trends of *furusato* traditions noted above. Since the actual *furusato* villages in Japan are vanishing due to the process of urbanization, the images of old Chinese villages visualized by the cinematic apparatus offer the most readily available redemptive means to fill the huge gap between a modernized and an idyllic Japan. In conclusion, I will further address how Huo and other Chinese filmmakers have responded to such an international market for Chinese-inscribed melodramatic nostalgia.

Conclusion

Comparing the film *Nuan* and his own story, Mo Yan said: "The director re-tells this tragic story with *wenqing* [heart-warming affections]. This style is very different from my original story, which is much more cruel and gruesome" (Mo and Ding 83). Responding later, Huo Jianqi said: "Personally I prefer the original ending in the story. However, the helplessness and despair in it are too much and too heavy for film audiences to bear. So we made some adjustments there mainly for the sake of the audiences' reception" (Chen and Ding 100). Qiu Shi, Huo's wife and also the scriptwriter of *Nuan*, added that they just wanted to picture a normal everyday life in which *wenqing* normalizes interpersonal relationships (Chen and Ding 101). As a result of this market-oriented adaptation strategy, the prevailing *wenqing*, which sharply contrasts to the absence of sentimentality in the original story, transforms the film into a woman's weepie. All the tears shed on and off the screen are reminiscent of the icy river in *Way Down East*, the film Williams addresses as an exemplar of film melodrama. As the chilly water in this 1920 D. W. Griffith film cleanses Anna's sexual guilt, the tears in Huo's film restore Nuan's innocence and purity that has been sullied by her strong desires (Williams 77). The pathos aroused by the virtuous suffering of a motherly figure assures the continuity of the melodramatic narrative and makes it possible for the happy ending to "reconcile the irreconcilable" (Williams 75).

Huo has attested that in making films with rural settings, he wants to express his nostalgia for a vanishing pastoral era and his warm feelings toward Chinese peasants in the transitional period of China. Though virtually inaccessible to the majority of Chinese peasantry, the film *Nuan* is believed to be able to bring spiritual warmth to console those who live in the countryside struggling in poverty (Shen). But what does this *wenqing*-ism connote if read in the "inter-textual" conditions of a modernizing China? In 2003, the same year when the film was produced, a best-selling book in China was *An Investigation of the Problems of Chinese Farmers* (*Zhongguo nongmin wenti diaocha*).[i] It exposed

---

[i] For a more detailed discussion of nostalgia in Zhang Yimou's film *The Road Home*, please see Hui Xiao's article "Visualizing Cultural Hybridity and Problematic of Chinese 'National Cinema'", *Orientations: Transcultural Perspectives on Asia*, 2004: 6.

the increasing urban-rural divide in the growing economy of China. For its honest revelation of the biggest social problems in modernizing China, *i.e.,* the exploitation in the countryside, Chinese peasants' stark poverty, and the growing social inequality in post-Mao China, the Chinese Communist Party banned the book. However, what cannot be so easily banned are a series of peasant riots and social unrests. On December 8, 2004, *The New York Times* reported that Chinese farmers were waging a sustained fight against the real estate boom to gain back their lost land, or at least more compensation (Yardley). The Japanese anime *Pom Poko* is thus staged in Chinese reality a decade later, although this time the battle is less hilarious or spectacular but more earthy and cruel, ending up on the Chinese peasants' doomed failure in their face-to-face confrontation with the state apparatus.

In contrast with (or in compensation for) the grave social reality, a prevalent trend of nostalgia and *wenqing*-ism characterizes Chinese cinema at the end of last century and at the beginning of the new millennium. For example, "a nostalgia for the simplicity of life and youthful idealism" permeates *Hei junma* (*A Mongolian tale*) directed by Xie Fei in 1995 (Zhang and Xiao 254). In 2000, the same director demonstrated his nostalgia again, this time for the "primitive" Tibetan culture, with *Yixi zhuoma* (*A song of Tibet*), a Tibetan woman's triangular romance. Even films depicting an urban China such as Zhang Yang's *Xizao* (*Shower*, 2000) show a very strong tendency of rejecting the impending modernity while reconstructing the ideal family relationship and traditions like Chinese-style "bathhouse" culture. Apart from *Nuan*, two other films *Nuan chun* (*Warm Spring*) and *Nuan qing* (*Warm Feelings*) produced in 2003 and 2004 also feature the Chinese character "Nuan" in their title and both have been advertised for the formula of social problems (*e.g.,* laid-off single parent, homeless orphan girl) + heart-throbbing family melodramas.

Suggesting that *wenqing* has already been a dominant feature of the Chinese cinema at the threshold of the new century, Zhang Yingjin quotes an allegorical scene from Zhang Yuan's *Huijia Guonian* (*Seventeen Years*, 2000). Compared with his earlier work *Beijing Zazhong* (*Beijing Bastards*, 1992) and *Donggong, Xigong* (*East Palace, West Palace*, 1996), that later film offers less sound and fury from those marginalized rock-and-roll youngsters, gay men, and jobless drifters who once occupied the center stage of the films made by some Fifth-Generation and most Sixth-Generation directors. Although the central character, a woman prisoner, still represents those who suffer and struggle for a living at the margin of Chinese society, in Zhang Yuan's 2000 film she begins to show gratitude for the *wenqing* offered by the woman police officer in uniform, a personification of the state apparatus. Toward the ending of the film, the mother and daughter, who are reunited after a seventeen-year separation, both kneel down in front of the aging father to ask for his forgiveness. Considering that this is the first of Zhang Yuan's films to be allowed to be shown in China, Zhang Yingjin interprets this scene as a gesture of reconciliation from the once resistant Fifth- and Sixth-Generation who had made rebellious underground films (Zhang, "Observations Made on Mainland Chinese Films" 259).

Building on what Zhang says, I would argue that the prevalent *wenqing* in contemporary Chinese cinema represents the filmmakers' compromise not only with the institutionalizing forces of the state, but also with those of the market. Due to the strict government censorship and the steep decline of the domestic film market dominated by imported Hollywood and Hong Kong films as well as pirated digital video discs, many Fifth- and Sixth-Generation directors must build their careers by winning awards in international film festivals to attract foreign investment. Under such harsh conditions for the survival of Chinese cinema, they must be doubly reconciled in order to orient their films toward an international as well as a shrinking domestic market.

Targeting mainly Japanese audiences, Huo has succeeded in establishing himself within this trend of appealing to an international market, particularly with what *Nuan* has achieved in the Tokyo International Film Festival. His hope of popularizing other Chinese films in Japan through his own success is also quite likely to be fulfilled in the light of Japan's increasing import of Chinese films and the rising number of Sino-Japanese co-productions. But as optimistic as one might be about this quantitative change in Chinese cinematic exports, the reverse direction of the impact of Japanese pop culture in China is not such a new or distinctive development. It is worth noting that *Nuan* was produced with the financial support of the Movie Television Inc. of Kenichi Morohashi and Japanese post-production facilities, suggesting that even nostalgia for an idyllic China can be materially realized only when the Chinese *furusato* becomes an active factor in the circulation of global capital. The problems that Japan experienced in the midst of modernization that engendered a movement of searching for cultural roots now appear—within the inter-Asian context of the consumption of the "technologized visuality" in Rey Chow's terms—and also have begun to dominate Chinese literature and cinema. Nostalgia for traditions is the dominant mood in the cultural scene of post-Mao China and Chinese cinema not surprisingly now visualizes a romantic view of old village life to represent the past idyllic era. In this melodramatic narrative of the national subjectivity, it is still the sublimated maternal figure that is assigned the task of shouldering the historical burden of Chinese past and present. Her "primitive" body—as represented through her everyday manual labor in a communal utopia—stands as the site of competing with institutionalizing forces of the state and the globalization.

I have argued that we can understand the nostalgia inscribed in the form of cross-cultural melodramas as contemporary Chinese directors' direct address to the tough conditions of reality, be it national or cinematic-industrial. In the case of Huo Jianqi and his film *Nuan*, it is clear that the highly self-conscious melodramatic narrative and setting are central elements that have led to the film's success in Japan. Of course the factors contributing to *Nuan*'s reception in Japan can be multiple: the star image of the female lead who resembles Gong Li, a Chinese superstar with an international appeal; the use of a Japanese actor; the "Oriental" music composed by San Bao, who also wrote music for *Wo de Fuqin Muqin* (*The Road Home*), another nostalgic rural film produced by Zhang Yimou in 1999; and Huo's highly stylized set design and camerawork, cinematic techniques which have been compared to the work of some Japanese master directors and are favored by Japanese audiences. [3] However, considering that the construction of the *furusato* tradition itself is a national melodramatic narrative about retrieving lost innocence, I suggest that the melodramatic adaptation of the film *Nuan* turns the empty but mobile signifier of an idyllic China into reified memories and images about a utopian past. That vision of the past can transcend temporal and spatial boundaries to fulfill Japanese audiences' needs for *furusato* fantasy with an internationalized, consumable Asian nostalgia.

CHAPTER THIRTEEN

FROM FRENCH CHINESE NOVEL TO CHINESE FRENCH FILM: RESHAPING THE ADDRESS OF DAI SIJIE'S *BALZAC AND THE LITTLE CHINESE SEAMSTRESS* ACROSS NARRATIVE FORMS

by E. K. Tan

In 2000, émigré filmmaker Dai Sijie published his first novel *Balzac et La tailleuse Chinoise* (*Balzac and the Little Chinese Seamstress*) in the French language. The novel, a semi-autobiography of Dai's teenage experience as a send-down youth during the Chinese Cultural Revolution, achieved immediate success, attracting international attention and translation into approximately twenty-five languages and winning five literary awards. In 2002, Dai himself adapted his novel to a film with the same title, which was circulated internationally as a French film even though it was made in the Chinese Szechuan dialect. The film has been actively circulated at international film festivals. In Asia, the film has been screened in Taiwan, Hong Kong and Singapore. Even though China has banned the film from official distribution in the country, a pirated version of the DVD is easily accessible in the mainland. This essay attempts to trace how the shift in focus from the French-addressed novel to the more widely targeted film complicates the text's identity and changes the meaning of the written text through the use of vocal and visual language.

Author Dai Sijie was one of the youths from the city who were relocated to rural sites for reeducation during the Cultural Revolution. After spending four years laboring in the mountains, Dai returned home to complete his high school education. When Chinese universities began to enroll college students after the Cultural Revolution in 1977, Dai attended college and obtained a degree in Art History. In 1984, Dai left China for France to study Western Art and Cinema at the French Film Institute.

As a filmmaker, Dai produced his first film in 1989 titled *China, My Sorrow*, a film that tells the tale of a thirteen-year old boy who is arrested by Mao Zedong's cultural police for listening to popular music. Due to the content of the film, Dai was banned from entering China by the Communist government until

1995 when the restriction was removed. Before his latest film to date *Balzac and the Little Chinese Seamstress*, Dai made two other films: Canadian film, *Le mangeur de Lune* (1994) and *Nguol Thùa* (1998), which is a French, Vietnamese. and Canadian co-production. Today Dai resides in France, although he still maintains his Chinese citizenship.

Dai's first novel *Balzac and the Little Chinese Seamstress* draws a love story surrounding two send-down teenage boys who are dispatched to Phoenix Mountain to practice labor in the rural outpost. The youths accidentally come across a suitcase of forbidden European novels, which they end up indulging in. To share the joy of reading, they both take turns reading novels to the Little Chinese Seamstress, the young lady they love. The stories end up transforming the Little Chinese Seamstress from a naïve young girl into a sophisticated young lady who chooses to leave Phoenix Mountain for a life she desires.

The Novel as Culture Ambassador

The novel *Balzac and the Little Chinese Seamstress* begins with the arrival of Luo and the narrator at Phoenix Mountain, the place where they have been assigned to for re-education during Cultural Revolution in China. [i] The story is told with a traditional narrative structure through a first person point-of-view. The novel begins with Luo describing his first encounter with the villagers are Phoenix Mountain. He depicts:

> The village headman, a man of about fifty, sat cross-legged in the centre of the room, close to the coals burning in a hearth that was hollowed out of the floor; he was inspecting my violin. Among the possessions brought to this mountain village by the two "city youths"—which was how they saw Luo and me—it was

---

[i] In 1966, Mao Zedong, Chairman of the Communist Party launched the Great Proletarian Cultural Revolution in China. The declaration functioned as a political tool to secure Maoism in China as the state ideology and to counter oppositional political parties. The political event greatly affected both the political and social realms. One of the outcomes of the event was the "send-down" policy, which involved the dissemination of approximately 17 million urban youth to work in order to be "re-educated" in the countryside. The policy began as an immediate effect of the revolution and ended two years after the official denouement of the revolution in 1976. To justify the necessity of the policy, Mao pronounces in 1968 "It is necessary for the educated youth to go to the countryside, and be re-educated by the poor peasants. We need to persuade cadres and others in urban areas to send their children who graduated from junior high, senior high, and college to rural areas. Let us have a mobilization. Comrades in rural areas should welcome them." The above statistic figure and Mao's quote comes from Xueguang Zhou and Liren Hou's essay titled "Children of the Cultural Revolution: The State and the Life Course in the People's Republic of China."

the sole item that exuded an air of foreignness, of civilization, and therefore
aroused suspicion. (3)

From the very beginning, the novel hints at the fact that the narrator is not
merely telling a story about his reeducation but engaging the reader in a journey
to "spiritually conquer" Phoenix mountainby proclaiming a sense of superiority
over the villagers in his use of words such as "foreignness" and "civilization."
The amount of control the narrator has over his story grows as the narrative of
the novel develops. Even though the second half of the novel offers individual
confessions by three other characters, namely Luo, the little Chinese Seamstress
and the miller, the narrator is still the one who controls the story by
incorporating the three individual narratives into his reminiscence of the past.
The novel progresses in a linear storytelling fashion to retell the reeducation
experience of Luo and the narrator.

What is troubling in the novel's narrative is the language in which the story
is told through the recount of the narrator, or on the structural level, the author.
Even though the novel is set in China and is exclusively about the time of the
Cultural Revolution, Dai Sijie wrote the novel in French, a language that is not
even close in structure to any Chinese languages. As a semi-autobiography,
Dai's intention can be seen as an innocent desire to capture an important
personal memory. However, the fact that *Balzac and the Little Chinese
Seamstress* is initially a novel written for European readers, mainly the French,
certainly raises the question of its textual integrity as reflected through its
targeted audience. As a literary work, the function of identification gets elided
due to the inevitable distancing caused by the language of narration between the
subject matter (the narrator's past) and the French reader. Nevertheless, the
distancing is not necessarily a pitfall in textual representation of the send-down
experience. This rupture in representation between experience and reception
alternatively produces agency for the author, whose task is none other than that
of a translator. For Walter Benjamin, the task of a translator is directed at the
totality of language to uncover the intention hidden in the original, which can
only be brought into light through translation.[i] The original language and its

---

[i] Benjamin explains in the following quote on how the main objective of translation is on
transporting meanings from one language to another. To him, "the task of the translator
consists in finding that intended effect [Intention] upon the language into which he is
translating which produces in it the echo of the original. This is a feature of translation
which basically differentiates it from the poet's work, because the effort of the latter is
never directed at the language as such, at its totality, but solely and immediately at
specific linguistic contextual aspects" (76). The passage is from "The Task of a
Translator" collected in the collected works of Walter Benjamin titled *Illuminations:
Essays and Reflections*.

intention re-emerge through the act of translation. By differentiating the task of a translator from that of a poet, Benjamin argues that translation is not specifically about transmitting information. Instead, translation serves the purpose of revealing the mutual relationship between languages. In this sense, the very space of translation is the place of contact zone where cultures converge and negotiate for a better mutual understanding that transcends language. The dominant power introduced to the novel through the French language is almost immediately reconfigured once the audience recognizes the role of the narrator as a cultural informant. Dai's task as a cultural translator in his writing of *Balzac and the Little Chinese Seamstress* is to depict an experience without falling into the trapped of self-orientalizating the Chinese culture under the influence of a Western framework. In other words, by avoiding the act of literally translating the unique experience, Dai, the author of *Balzac and the Little Chinese Seamstress* delineates a space of contact and exchange for the native narrator and the foreign reader. The question, however, is what risks does a "cultural ambassador" like Dai Sijie face in writing a novel using a second language? How can he free himself from criticisms such as that of self-orientalization through literary aesthetics?

The hypocritical nature of multiculturalism does not necessarily hinder us from drawing any advantages from its discourse. The loose categorization of *Balzac and the Little Chinese Seamstress* as a French novel based on the fact that it was written in the French language not only expresses the openness of the French literary environment but provides a text the liberty to not transmit a unique and specific Chinese experience that is haunted by the danger of self-orientalization. This assumption is no doubt suggested default of any political implications of the generous attitude of the French culture. If the unique representation of experience in *Balzac and the Little Chinese Seamstress* is a literary one, the manifestation of cultural specificity in the French novel is unconsciously exuded from the author's inevitable depiction of the historical and geographical setting of the story. Nevertheless, the novel focuses on illuminating the greatness of a literary experience that has evolved for the characters through the act of reading.

Both Luo and the narrator understand that their actual reeducation comes from their reading of the forbidden books, which according to the nation's ideologies are bad for the minds of the young. Throughout the novel, the two read Chinese translations of Russian, English and French novels by prominent Modern Chinese writers. Secluded from the lives in the city they used to live, they feel a strong connection with the characters in the books they read because the modern heroes also experience displacement in their societies. Secretly running through another sent-down youth, Four Eyes' suitcase, the narrator describes his thrill:

a company of great Western writers welcomed us with open arms. On top
was our old friend Balzac, with five or six novels, then came Victor Hugo,
Stendhal, Dumas, Flaubert, Baudelaire, Romain Rolland, Rousseau, Tolstoy,
Gogol, Dostoyevsky, and some English writers, too: Dickens, Kipling, Emily
Bronte. (99)

On another occasion, the narrator mentions *Don Quixote* a Spanish novel
that was read to him by his aunt when he was little (51). The mentioning of *Don
Quixote* at the beginning of the novel foreshadows the transformation of the
characters in the novel. A lover of chivalry tales, Don Quixote gives in to his
fantasy and takes up a knight's expedition. Even though Don Quixote suffers
greatly from his hallucination, he embraces his dreams and happiness before he
returns home to die. Both Luo and the narrator's lives undergo a transformation
that they have not expected and this transformation is way more rewarding than
the reeducation that they have been assigned to. Not truly conscious of their life
evolution, Luo talks about his reading of Balzac to the little Chinese Seamstress
in order to educated her. Books, in the case of the little Chinese Seamstress,
indirectly initiate her transformation. As a total surprise for both Luo and the
narrator, the little Chinese Seamstress experiences the biggest transformation
among the characters. The little Chinese Seamstress eventually learns, through
the female protagonist in Dumas' *The Count of Monte Cristo*, about her
sexuality and self-importance as a gendered individual. She is able to make her
own decision for the first time at the end of the novel to leave Phoenix Mountain
for her own dream and desire. By telling us a story that emphasizes the power of
a written text, the novel invites us to join the journey of a possible
transformation through the act of reading.

From Novel to Film

In the year 2002 Dai Sijie adapted the novel *Balzac and the Little Chinese
Seamstress* into a film of the same title. This attempt seems natural since Dai
Sijie is after all a filmmaker. However, adaptation is usually tedious as it
involves different levels of negotiation. It triggers questions such as: What is
sacrificed in a written text when the text undergoes the transformation into
visual images? What kind of filmic motifs should the film adopt in order to
maintain the balance of visual creativity and textual originality? Does the film
have to be a faithful visual manifestation of the novel? What kind of audience
should the film address?

The first scene of the film marks a clear distinction between the text in its
cinematic form and it written form. The film opens with Luo and the narrator
walking in the mountains on the way to Phoenix Mountain. The camera pans
across the beautiful scenery to create a cinematic aesthetic that points to one

characteristic of the film as a "cinema of attraction"[i] in Tom Gunning's terms. For Gunning, the cinema is not merely about constructing linear and conventional narratives; instead, it involves the employment of various forms of visual representations to complement the theme or objective of a film. These forms, such as visual images as spectacle, introduce novel viewing experiences of time and space to the audience apart from the traditional narrative of storytelling in the modern age. This not only expands perspectivism but contributes to the emergence of modern visual culture.

In this sense, storytelling no longer holds the central role in the film adaptation of *Balzac and the Little Chinese Seamstress*. Narrativity in the film is constructed not through tradition but visual stimulations created by modern technology and cinematic language. Instead of the singular narrative that carries a restrictive and homogenous point of view; we, the audience adopts the role of an onlooker of the story through the eye of the camera. In this sense, we seemingly have a better control over his or her evaluation of the story, which is default of manipulation from any narrator. The unrestricted narrative provides the audience self-agency throughout the viewing experience. Even though we know that the story is still told by a narrator, we no longer feel totally obligated to resign our loyalty to the narrator's voiceover. We identify with the camera, adopting a voyeuristic position that caters to our desire for information and knowledge. This point of view is always problematic because we are never free subjects in front of the cinema screen; in addition, what the cinema screen offers is a perspective reality that interpellates us into the illusional world of the big screen. This fantastical position of a voyeur is best exemplified in *Balzac and the Little Chinese Seamstress* by the scene when the camera leaves the room to survey the surrounding while the villagers gather to inspect the belongings of Luo and the narrator. Beautiful scenery decorated the film from beginning to the end. Aesthetic visualization of the rural is not necessarily politically unethical even though some might argue that such an approach contains the danger of portraying China as backward and exotic, even in an unconscious sense. Literary and cultural critic Rey Chow in her book, *Primitive Passions*, argues

---

[i] Tom Gunning defines the "cinema of attraction" as an art of exhibiting images as objects of visual aesthetics and stimulations. Giving a specific definition to the term, Gunning explains, "[w]hat precisely is the cinema of attraction? First it is a cinema that bases itself on the quality that Léger celebrated: its ability to show something. Constrasted to the voyeuristic aspect of narrative cinema analyzed by Christian Metz, this is an exhibitionist cinema ... this is a cinema that displays its visibility, willing to rupture a self-enclosed fictional world for a chance to solicit the attention of the spectator" (230). The passage is from Gunning's essay titled "The Cinema of Attraction: Early Film, Its Spectator and the Avant-Garde" collected in *Film and Theory: An Anthology*.

that the aestheticization of China does carry a certain degree of positivity. Noting this aestheticization as "Primitivism," Chow explains that:

> ... in politicized modernity [the process] signifies not a longing for a past and a culture that can no longer be but the wishful thinking that, somehow, "China" is the first, the prime, the central. The two sides of primitivism go hand in hand: the aestheticizing of old China as "ancient" and "backward" cannot be understood without the images of modern self-strengthening and community building that continue to pervade nationalistic cultural productions with the insistence on the firstness and uniqueness of what is Chinese. [i]

Even though the visual representation of China as "backwards" and "primitive" hints at the perpetuation of orientalism in the ever-negotiating space between the "first-world" and the "third-world," Chow's optimism shows us that the "self-orientalizing" gesture could be appropriated as a strategic move[ii] to fortify the distinctiveness of a Chinese identity, which is useful and necessary for the nation's political, cultural and economic engagement with the rest of the world. Following Chow's logic, despite the fact that the film adaptation of *Balzac and the Little Chinese Seamstress* is first made under an ambiguous national category—a French production, and second it manipulates numerous pastoral images of China, aligning them to the audience's imagination of the old "China," the film succeeds beyond its literal meanings in triggering the reassessment of an important historical event—the Cultural Revolution. On the one hand, *Balzac and the Little Chinese Seamstress* represents a complicated identity that renders any national categorization impossible; alternative, it engages modern China in the production of global cultural facilitated by the Diaspora population. Henceforth, a particularism—China, is delineated through a discourse of universalism.

The significant value of the film adaptation of *Balzac and the Little Chinese Seamstress* is the introduction of the written text to a bigger audience. Surprisingly, Dai seems to be rather cautious with his film adaptation. The film does not differ much from the novel in terms of its plot and story. In order to attract a larger audience, Dai borrows visual tropes developed over time in film history that are generally familiar to the audience. In the scene when the Little Chinese Seamstress is first introduced, an added scene not found in the novel, Zhou Xun, the actress playing the Little Chinese Seamstress, is seen flirting with Luo (Chen Kun) and the narrator, Ma (Liu Ye). The scene resembles Ned

---

[i] From *Primitive Passions: Visuality, Sexuality, Ethnography and Contemporary Chinese Cinema*, published by Columbia University Press. The quote comes from Part I of the book titled "Visuality, Modernity and Primitive Passions." Pg. 36-7
[ii] Even though not specifically mentioned in this part of Rey Chow's essay, the concept echoes Postcolonial scholar Gayatri Spivak's notion of "Strategic Essentialism."

Faraday's (Herbert Marshall) first encounter with Helen (Marlene Dietrich), who is bathing in a pond with her fellow actresses in the Josef Von Sternberg's classic *Blonde Venus* (1932). Another example is at the end of the film, in which the film introduces a scene depicting the gradual flooding of a house with a sewing machine and the perfume the narrator has bought from France for the Little Chinese Seamstress. Water as the imagery of memory gradually fills up the house, which spatially symbolizes the narrator's past, encompassing the narrator's teenage love signified by the sewing machine. The perfume bottle seals off the memory for the narrator and concludes the film for the audience. The audience can almost immediately identify that as a film motif appropriated from James Cameron's blockbuster hit, *Titanic*. The prior scene foreshadows a possible romantic relationship between Luo and the Little Chinese Seamstress through the flirtatious encounter while the latter signifies the submerging and fading of the narrator's adolescent memories. In this sense, the film adaptation of *Balzac and the Little Chinese Seamstress* not only translates the film into Szechuan dialect but also into a technical language of film narrative.

As suggested earlier, the identity of the film *Balzac and the Little Chinese Seamstress* is much more complicated than that of the novel. Since the novel is categorized as a French novel because it was written in the French language, what identity does the film acquire with its use of Szechuan dialect as the language of the film? How does the use of the Szechuan dialect reshape the intended audience of the film?

The film *Balzac and the Little Chinese Seamstress* was released as a French production and represented France at the 2002 Academy Awards. The identity of the film significantly problematizes the representation of a text in relation to issues of nation and culture. Borrowing Thomas Elsaesser's analysis of the New German Cinema, Rey Chow explains:

> ... there are at least two types of translation at work in cinema. First, translation as inscription: a generation, a nation, and a culture are being translated or permuted into the medium of film; and second, translation as transformation of tradition and of being translated into one dominated by the image.[i]

Challenging Elsaesser's notion of national cinema, *Balzac and the Little Chinese Seamstress* seemingly retreats to the very basics of filmmaking, which to a great extent resists any form of national or cultural representation in image

---

[i] From *Primitive Passions: Visuality, Sexuality, Ethnography and Contemporary Chinese Cinema*, published by Columbia University Press. The quotes comes from the Part III titled "Film as Ethnography; or Translation Between Cultures in the Postcolonial World." Pg. 182

production. Any attempt to foster the translation of the novel into the film as inscription is troubled by the ambiguous visual representations. The "visually-and-thematically-Chinese" film cannot be "authentically" Chinese in any sense, cultural or national, because as a visual inscription, the opening credits, which are in the French language violently disrupt the film's "authenticity" as a Chinese film.   The establishing shot of the film provides a survey of the landscape of Phoenix Mountain as the content within the diegetic screen space. This aesthetic reproduction of conventional Chinese painting depicts a cultural and ethnic specificity that is enhanced by the Chinese folksong as the background music. This uniformity is visual and aural representation is however disrupted by the non-diegetic opening credits, which are exclusively in French. Similarly, the transformation of tradition within the cinematic frame cannot escape the contamination of the film's desire to inscribe a political agenda before the film concludes. The novel ends with a sense of closure marked by a structural documentation of a time in the past; in other words, a tradition is transformed through written language, in this case, the French language. The film, on the other hand concludes by depicting the narrator's return to China after seeing the news about Yangtze River flooding Phoenix Mountain due to the government's project to build the Three Gorges Dam. Upon the completion of the project, which began in 1994, much of the area where the film was shot will be flooded. Dai's lamentation and implicit disapproval of the nation's decision in the film disturbs the unity of the novel. The nationalistic stand in the film relays a message that the *bildungroman* was not designed to assume in the first place. On the level of the personal, it does embody a significant meaning. For Dai, the flooding of the area signifies that the memories of his teenage life will eventually be swept away with time and modernization. Thus, a contradiction evolves from the difference in representation between the film as a French production and its inclusion of a Chinese nationalistic claim in response to the governmental project. Nostalgia is safe only when it is contained within the very psychic space of the memory of the past. Dai's visual adaptation of the film intermingles the personal realm of memory with that of a public historical event.

If Dai had given up in writing "China" in the first place, should he still attempt to re-instill his political position in the film version of *Balzac and the Little Chinese Seamstress*? The political agenda at the level of cultural production is a strategic one that will probably satisfies audience that desires to see "China" on screen. Dai's inclusion of the extra plot engages the audience in his project in protecting "China" the original aesthetics from modernization and industrialization. In this sense, the political ending functions as the mediator between the audience and the director's desire. This gesture more directly imposes the imagery of the woman as the site for the ideology of nation building onto the Little Chinese Seamstress. In the novel, this level of representation is not suggested since the novel focuses mainly on the power of reading as a transforming force for individuals. The irony is that by adopting a different narrative medium the film version of *Balzac and the Little Chinese Seamstress* erases the significance of the theme of the novel which privileges the experience of reading.

The reliance on visual effects brings out the irony in the film adaptation of the novel. If there were a transformation for the audience, it was created through visual stimulations and not the act of reading as suggested in the novel. Any attempt to compare the creditability of the novel with that of the film is deemed insignificant. In discussing the medium-specific thesis, Noël Carroll stresses that each medium has its unique nature and there is always something a medium does best in comparison with other media.[i] In this sense, Dai Sijie's novel *Balzac and the Little Chinese Seamstress* and the film adaptation of the novel should be seen as two separate projects. The function of the novel is to engage its reader on a journey to self-enlightenment under the influence of literature. The film as a technical medium employs visual imagery to heighten the viewing pleasure of its audience and create a nostalgic atmosphere through beautiful scenery that satisfies both the director's lament for the past and the audience desire as a voyeur. By tracing the shift in focus in the narrative forms of *Balzac and the Little Chinese Seamstress*, we not only managed to delineate specific features of the two distinct textual representations, the comparison of the novel with the film also enables us to understand why and how each representation adopts a unique style to illuminate the meaning of the story and the purpose of the author or director.

---

[i] From Noel Carroll's essay titled "The Specificity of Media in the Arts" collected in *Film and Theory: An Anthology*. 54.

CHAPTER FOURTEEN

SEX, SCANDAL AND CORRUPTION IN *AN IDEAL HUSBAND*: HOW NEW LABOUR LOST ITS INNOCENCE IN THE POLITICAL *WILDE*RNESS

by Ann-Marie Cook

In his 1895 play, *An Ideal Husband*, Oscar Wilde served up a deliciously subversive satire of the Victorian political establishment and the society it represented. By exposing the political corruption beneath the façade of moral respectability, Wilde critiqued the hypocrisy inherent in moral idealism whilst advocating a worthy message of tolerance and forgiveness. These valuable lessons remained relevant to British culture during the late 1990s, when the production and release of Oliver Parker's adaptation of the play coincided with a series of scandals involving members of Parliament who received cash for asking questions in the House of Commons; MPs who had accepted gifts without disclosing them in the Registry of Members Interests; lobbyists who offered clients privileged access to information and influential government figures; and gay cabinet ministers who found themselves "outed" by the media. While any government would have been embarrassed by such events, Prime Minister Tony Blair's Labour government attracted particularly sharp criticism for its involvement in these scandals because it had presented itself to voters as an antidote to the political sleaze that had flourished under previous Conservative governments. The parallels between the scandal in the film and those that were being reported in the quality broadsheet press at the time were consistently highlighted in the production notes that circulated in press kits; in interviews with members of the production team; and in the general reviews of the film. Ironically, however, the changes that Parker's screenplay introduces to the plot and characterizations actually *downplay* the political and moral issues that were central to Wilde's version in order to concentrate on the love story, which transforms Lord Goring's character from a sexually ambiguous dandy into a heterosexual playboy who becomes the ideal husband.

Of course, it may be tempting to discount changes to plot and character as efforts to update the plot for modern audiences unaccustomed to the rigid "Victorian values" that Wilde and his audiences knew only too well. But, as

Raymond Williams avers in *The Long Revolution,* the selection and revision of texts from the past are informed by contemporary ideological concerns.

> In the analysis of contemporary culture, the existing state of the selective tradition is of vital importance, for it is often true that some change in this tradition—establishing new lines with the past, breaking or re-drawing existing lines—is a radical kind of *contemporary* change. We tend to underestimate the extent to which the cultural tradition is not only a selection but also an interpretation. We see most past work through our own experience .... The more actively all cultural work can be related, either to the whole organization within which it was expressed, or to the contemporary organization within which it is used, the more clearly we shall see its true values (65).

Williams' theory therefore invites the study of how *An Ideal Husband* re-creates the 1890s in a way that bares the imprints of a 1990s sensibility. Although the creative team openly acknowledged some of the correlations between Wilde's text and current events, Parker's adaptation actually engages much more extensively and critically with political discourses that were circulating in society at the time of the film's production and release. Drawing upon scholarship that assesses Wilde's authorship and the historical context of the late Victorian period itself, contemporary reviews and publicity material for the film, and coverage of political scandals in the quality broadsheet press, this paper will examine how Parker's adaptation *re-draws* the lines between past and present by reworking Wilde's play in ways that appeal to contemporary attitudes about sexuality and political scandal.

It's the "Gay Nineties" All Over Again

Two different film adaptations of *An Ideal Husband* went into production in England at roughly the same time during the month of June 1998, each offering a very different interpretation of the source material. One version, directed by Bill Cartlidge, jettisoned the period setting and highlighted the timeliness of Wilde's play by adopting the background of "present-day local government," and dealing with "such subjects as cash for questions" (Macnab 9; Stringer 15). Despite the creativity at the heart of this adaptation, however, the picture itself lacked cinematic qualities as a result of its meager budget and went virtually straight to video. The other version, written and directed by Oliver Parker, benefited from the involvement of Fragile Films, Icon Productions, Pathe Pictures, Miramax Films, and the Arts Council of England which invested the film with higher production values and attracted a cast of internationally recognized stars. With an estimated budget of $14,000,000 (Internet Movie Database), Parker's UK/US co-production had the resources to create a fairly lavish period piece that retained the play's late Victorian setting. The screenplay also retained "most of Wilde's dialogue," though it made some important changes to the basic storyline. While the film never hit the top of the popularity polls, it made a solid showing after its United Kingdom premiere on April 18, 1999 and recouped its production costs before it even opened in America (Internet Movie Database). Distribution deals with Miramax Films, Twentieth Century Fox Films, Pathe Pictures Ltd., and a variety of smaller firms in Europe and South America secured for the picture an international audience and guaranteed moderate box office profits. Despite the aesthetic and financial disparities between the two films, the existence of these concurrent adaptations begs the question of why Wilde's drawing room comedy was so appealing to filmmakers and audiences during this particular period.

Intriguingly, this was not the first time that interest in Oscar Wilde inspired two concurrent productions. *The Trials of Oscar Wilde* (Irving Allen and Ken Hughes, 1960) and *Oscar Wilde* (Gregory Ratoff, 1960) went into production within four days of each other, prompting critics such as Brian Prendreigh of *The Guardian* to observe that, the "production of two simultaneous biopics probably had as much to do with the growing, though still cautious, debate over homosexuality, as it did with interest in Wilde—Dirk Bogarde's film *Victim* followed soon after" (10). Just as the films that were made about Wilde in 1960 have been regarded as engagements with public debates about homosexuality, so too can the revival of *An Ideal Husband* be examined in relation to its own socio-political context. For Robin Stringer of *The Evening Standard*, the concurrent productions of *An Ideal Husband* reflected "the enduring topicality of Wilde's play which is about political sleaze" (15). Oliver Parker was keen to highlight the timeliness of the play's treatment of political scandal: the "recent 'cash for questions' scandals ... highlight how little 'society' life has changed in the past hundred years" (qtd. in Alberge 3). Actor Rupert Everett, who played Lord Goring in the film, echoed Parker's sentiments, suggesting that the film not only had definite analogies "with Bill Clinton and other contemporary political scandals," but also invited tolerance by showing that "lying at some point seems forgivable: everyone is a liar" (qtd. in Prendreigh 10.) Reviewers consistently took up the film in these terms. Dalya Alberge of *The Times* declared that "[i]n light of recent 'cash for questions' scandals, *An Ideal Husband*'s exploration of blackmail, honour and political principles has an obvious resonance, and highlights how little 'society' life has changed in the past one hundred years" (3). The *Evening Standard* critic Alexander Walker acknowledged the timeliness of Sir Robert Chiltern's behavior, suggesting that, "a leading light of government who fosters his career and sets himself up in comfort by doing shady deals with foreign plutocrats is still with us" (20). Tom Charity's review of the film for *Time Out* added that "Oscar Wilde's play still feels all too relevant in its witty dissection of public and private morality (Chiltern might suggest any one of half-a-dozen politicians whose hypocrisy has come to light over the last ten years)" (78). This sampling of reviews is indicative of the wider body of articles that promoted the film in terms of its relevance to contemporary society. But where these critics failed, in my opinion, was in leaving their assessments of the film at the stage of simply pointing to crashingly obvious corollaries between past and present instead of taking their observations to the next level by trying to analyze the political implications of the film's revision of Wilde's play. In light of the fact that the Wilde films of the 1960s were read in terms of their engagement with attitudes about sexuality, it seems rather odd that none of the critics raised this issue in their reviews of *An Ideal Husband*. By embellishing the romance theme beyond the way it is treated in Wilde's play, Parker's screenplay invests the film with a different sort of ideology that also taps into another aspect of contemporary society that film critics at the time overlooked: debates about sexuality and public life.

At the same time that Parker's film was being produced, debates over gay rights and sex scandals involving gay politicians highlighted the degree to which the moral repressiveness of Wilde's day was still a driving social force in contemporary Britain. Throughout the summer, the House of Lords flexed its political muscles by blocking the Labour government's efforts to repeal Section 28, the law that prohibits local authorities, such as teachers, libraries, and counselors, from promoting homosexuality, and equalize the age of consent for homosexuals and heterosexuals by making sixteen the legal age for both (Abrams 1; Schaefer 10; Waugh 6). By showing how an individual's private life impacts the rights and privileges granted them in society, these debates drove home the old feminist slogan of the 1960s that the personal is political. But the conflation between political issues and personal issues took on a whole new meaning during the autumn of 1998, when revelations about the sexual orientation of Labour cabinet ministers were treated as newsworthy events in both the quality broadsheets and tabloid media.

Unlike the charges being leveled at some Labour MPs for corruption and abuses of parliamentary privilege, the scandals involving Ron Davies, the Secretary for Wales, Nick Brown, the Minister for Agriculture, and Peter Mandelson, a former Secretary of State for Trade and Industry Trade (and one of Prime Minister Tony Blair's closest allies) centered around the homosexual relationships that these men carried on in their private lives. On October 27, 1998, Davies resigned from the cabinet after admitting that he'd been mugged whilst walking on Clapham Common, a notorious gay cruising spot in south London. Although the exact details surrounding the incident were surrounded in mystery, it nonetheless proved to be an embarrassment to Tony Blair's government and a devastating blow to Davies' career. Once favored to become

First Minister for Wales, he found himself relegated to the role of a mere backbencher and treated by many in his party as *persona non grata* following the scandal. The very next day after Davies' resignation, public attention shifted to Peter Mandelson after journalist Matthew Parris referred to the Mandelson's homosexuality during an interview on BBC's *Newsnight*. Unlike Davies, however, Mandelson fought back by demanding that his friend John Birt, the Director General of the BBC, issue a directive from the Corporation's Editorial Policy Unit to forbid further references to his private life and, later, by threatening to abolish the Press Complaints Commission when it refused to block the publication of a *Daily Express* story about his companion, Reinaldo de Silva (Cohen 27).

These actions prompted the *Observer* newspaper to criticize the minister for using his privileged position to seek a level of protection that New Labour was unwilling to grant the general public in the shape of a privacy law. Rather than allow the press to out him, Nick Brown went on the offensive and issued a public statement on November 8, 1998 acknowledging that he was involved in a committed relationship with his long-term partner. Despite the fact that Brown and Chris Smith, the Minister for Culture, were the only openly gay members of the Cabinet at the time, the front-page of the November 9th edition of *The Sun* was emblazoned with the headline: "Tell us the truth Tony: Are we being run by a gay mafia?". The editorial which followed warned that "The revelation that a fourth member of the Blair government is gay has set alarm bells ringing" and asserted that "the public has a right to know how many homosexuals occupy positions of high power ... the sexuality is not the problem. The worry is their membership of a closed world of men with a mutual self-interest" (Editorial, 1). Despite a lack of evidence that the sexual orientation was ever a factor in cabinet deliberations let along a basis for collusion among the four politicians targeted by the media, Trevor Kavanagh, *The Sun*'s editor-in-chief, nonetheless insisted that it was his paper's duty to enforce the public's right to know about the sexual orientation of government ministers ("Brown Bids to End 'Outing' Row"). The uproar that ensued prompted the political editor David Yelland to concede that his paper was "no longer in the business of destroying closet gays' lives by 'exposing' them as homosexuals" ("Sun Changes Mind Over Gays"). In the wake of the damage done to the careers and families of the four men outed in the media, this change in *The Sun*'s editorial policy came as too little too late and revealed a nasty truth: repressive attitudes about homosexuality did not die out with the Victorians.

Indeed, the parallels between the moral repressiveness of the 1890s and the 1990s were driven home at the public unveiling of Maggie Hambling's bronze statue entitled *A Conversation with Oscar Wilde*. Chris Smith used the occasion to deliver "a speech about how far society had come since the intolerant days of

Victoria's reign" since it could now honor a writer "whose name could not be mentioned in polite society for the best part of the 20th century" (qtd. in Sweet 21). The irony of the moment was not lost on Merlin Holland, Wilde's grandson, who "suggested to Channel 4 News later that same day, [that] some of the people schmoozing him at the post-unveiling drinks were the very types who sent his grandfather to Reading Gaol" (qtd. in Sweet 21). Others were more skeptical about how much progress had really been made in creating a more tolerant society in Britain. In an interview with Ed Stourton of BBC TV's *One O' Clock News*, Nigel Hawthorne, a prominent gay actor who had participated in the unveiling ceremony, attempted to discuss the broader cultural significance of the Wilde memorial by identifying parallels between Wilde's persecution and the present day treatment of Peter Mandelson. Stourton cut him off in accordance with the "BBC memo forbidding unnecessary reference to politicians' private lives" (Lister and Waugh 1). Hawthorne refused to be silenced, protesting that, "If you don't talk about individuals, then you miss the whole point of this. I think that it's purely that society picks on these individuals and turns them into martyrs very often, which is exactly what happened to Oscar Wilde" (qtd. in Lister and Waugh 1). *The Independent*'s coverage of the incident acknowledged that this incident "made an awkward footnote to the continuing history of a part of London that, a century on, we still don't know whether to celebrate or censure" (Sweet 21). The newspaper also published a scathing piece by Nigel Hawthorne condemning the BBC's censorship as clear evidence that contemporary society harbored the same sort of bigotry that existed during Wilde's day.

> The fact remains that what Peter Mandelson does is not my or anybody else's business. I do not know the man. I have never met him. But what, more importantly, I was not allowed by the BBC to infer, was that Mandelson's situation is not a million miles from Oscar Wilde's. Have we learnt nothing in the past 100 years? ... And to censor somebody because he has dared to draw attention to the parallel between the past and present and hint at the inherent dangers seems to me to be dangerously close to bigotry (4).

Given the point of Hawthorne's argument, it was obvious that it was not the sort of unnecessary reference to Mandelson's private which the BBC directive prohibited. But the fact that the policy was interpreted so broadly as to preclude *any* discussion of his sexuality revealed a shift in media discourses away from "outing" individuals to disavowing rhetoric that would require society to confront the taboo of homosexuality.

A year before *The Sun*'s gay witch-hunt and the controversy surrounding the unveiling of Hambling's monument, Merlin Holland acknowledged the lingering ambivalence that continued to plague his famous grandfather's legacy.

He shrewdly observed that "the British public are (sic) happy enough to read his children's stories to their children, or clap at revivals of The Importance of Being Earnest, but his private life you just didn't ask about" (qtd. in Moyes 11). But Hambling's statue draws upon these conflicted public sentiments in its representation of the playwright: the bronze head, which was responsible for producing works replete with wit and wisdom, is visible while the body, which symbolizes a 'deviant' mode of sexuality, is concealed within a granite sarcophagus. The metaphor of encasing, and thereby hiding, traces of transgressive sexuality seems to be rooted in the same homophobic sentiments that inspired the silencing of Nigel Hawthorne and others, who'd attempted to generate productive discussions about public attitudes about sexual orientation. Oliver's film engages with these discourses by transforming Wilde's critique of moral idealism into a romantic comedy whose narrative drive is the pursuit to form a heterosexual couple.

From the publicity surrounding it, to the changes it makes to Wilde's original script, Parker's film 'unqueer' Goring's dandy character by presenting him as a ladies' man whose connection to the three lead female characters is rooted in a romantic relationship. The casting of the gay actor Rupert Everett in the role of Lord Goring initially seemed to indicate that the film would adopt a rather sophisticated, tongue-in-cheek sense of humor about the sexual status of the dandy. The dandy's elitism and obsession with beauty and aesthetics rather than morality (which was a much more fashionable concern during Wilde's day), rendered him a foppish rebel who bucked the norms of Victorian masculinity. Although it should be acknowledged that dandyism was not synonymous with homosexuality, the two became inextricably intertwined in the case of Oscar Wilde. Wilde himself personified the dandy—so much so, in fact, that the "fleshly poet" Reginald Bunthorne of Gilbert and Sullivan's 1881 operetta *Patience* was rumored to have been based on Wilde (Bradley 269, 286). Wilde's work frequently featured a "flamboyant, self-absorbed 'dandy'—for 'dandy' read homosexual" that typically regarded as a projection of Wilde's own persona (Siegel). But, as *The Guardian* observed, "the Turkish bath shared with Jeremy Northam is a token gesture in what's otherwise a traditional, altogether unqueer Wilde" ("Oscar Bait" 9). Instead of playing upon the dandy's ambiguous sexuality and engaging with the queer subtext apparent in Wilde's work, Parker's revision of the source locates it firmly within heteronormative discourses in which the over-determination of heterosexual coupling pre-empts questions about Goring's sexual orientation.

Both the play and the film follow the same basic plot. Sir Robert Chiltern has built a reputation as an honorable politician and an ideal husband. Admired by his colleagues and worshipped by his wife, Gertrude, Robert seems to have it all until he becomes the target of a blackmail scheme concocted by Mrs.

Cheveley, the former paramour of his late mentor, Baron Arnheim. Mrs. Cheveley threatens to make public the contents of an incriminating letter that exposes Sir Robert as an opportunist who'd made his political fortune by obtaining access to a cabinet secret and selling it to the Baron unless he uses his political influence to promote Britain's support for a fraudulent Argentine Canal Scheme in which she has invested heavily. Although Lord Goring, a friend of Sir Robert's and former fiancé of Mrs. Cheveley, intervenes to prevent her from publicly exposing Sir Robert's secret, she takes her revenge by revealing to Gertrude the truth about the origins of her husband's wealth. After condemning him initially, Gertrude ultimately yields to Lord Goring's entreaties to forgive her husband and refrain from holding *anyone* to the standard of moral perfection. Despite having his own moral lapse forgiven, Sir Robert persists in "holier than thou" posturing by refusing on moral grounds to permit his sister Mabel to marry Goring: he had discovered Mrs. Cheveley in Lord Goring's room during a previous visit and jumped to the conclusion that she was his mistress. Gertrude saves the day, however, by explaining that Goring had been expecting a visit from her that night and had been genuinely shocked to discover Mrs. Cheveley instead. So that, in the end, what seems to be a happy ending is secured for both couples. Sir Robert not only escapes official punishment for trading on insider information, he finds himself promoted to a seat in the cabinet; and his reconciliation with Gertrude is paralleled by the promise of a union between Lord Goring and Mabel.

Publicity images used to promote the film in Britain and America implied that the film love story that revolved around Lord Goring. Although the color schemes and positioning of figures varied somewhat between the British quad and American one-sheet movie posters, both shared the romantic tagline "An Ideal Husband .... He just doesn't know it yet" and depicted Rupert Everett (Lord Goring) gazing roguishly at the viewer whilst being surrounded by actresses Cate Blanchett (Gertrude Chiltern), Julianne Moore, (Mrs. Cheveley), and Minnie Driver (Mabel Chiltern). Somewhat surprisingly, Jeremy Northam, who plays Sir Robert Chiltern—the eponymous ideal husband of Wilde's version—doesn't appear on the posters at all. Even the alternate one-sheet posters designed for the British market that *did* feature Northam still positioned Blanchett, Everett, and Driver more prominently in the frame. Despite the absence of the tagline featured in the other posters, the fact that the chief protagonist and antagonist of Wilde's play have been relegated to the background while the figures associated with the love story dominate the image suggests that British one-sheet was entirely consistent with the rest of the publicity material. All of these images graphically conveyed the extent to which Parker's screenplay had embellished the love story to the point that it literally and figuratively displaced the theme political scandal as the narrative's focal point.

The film lived up to expectations it had created for itself as a charming and witty love story by devoting considerable screen time to Lord Goring's relationships with women. Where the first act of the play begins at a political party hosted by the Chilterns, indicating the primacy of the political scandal theme, the film begins with a pair of sequences that emphasize the romance story line. This adaptation strategy is illustrated in three key sequences that depict scenes not found in the play: the prologue, the epilogue, and the negotiation scene between Goring and Cheveley. The prologue begins as Phipps (Peter Vaughan), the manservant, draws aside a curtain to admit light—as well as the voyeuristic gaze of viewers—into a bedroom filmed in shallow focus. Phipps stands in sharp focus in the foreground with his back diplomatically turned away from the bed, shown in softer focus in the depth of frame, while a pre-Raphaelite-looking woman with flowing red hair slips discretely out of bed and exists the frame. The camera moves with Phipps as he moves toward the bed to rouse his master, Lord Goring (Rupert Everett) , with a hangover-curing tonic. After Goring raises himself enough to groggily gulp down the drink, he falls back upon the bed, allowing his limp arm to dangle over an empty champagne bottle and ice bucket. Later, Goring sips his tea while Phipps reads from the newspaper that Sir Robert Chiltern and his wife Lady Gertrude Chiltern will host a party that will be the highlight of the social calendar. Phipp's recitation of the news article about the Chilterns is juxtaposed with the intercut images of Sir Robert emerging from the Commons surrounded by a crowd of MPs and crossing the lobby to greet Gertrude. In addition to serving as the means by which to introduce the characters, this cut-away also initiates the theme of the ideal politician by presenting the Chilterns along with the newspaper's praise that the "Couple represents what is best in English public life and is a noble contrast to the lax morality so common in foreign politicians."[i] As Phipps concludes the article, the sequence returns to Goring's bedroom, having economically constructed the industrious and respectable Sir Robert Chiltern as a foil to the lazy but lovable lothario Lord Goring. Furthermore, by inviting viewers to spy upon Goring in the privacy of his bedroom in this way, the film also establishes his status as a ladies' man.

The following sequence continues to play with the romance theme by departing from the play's settings to set the action against the backdrop of 'Rotten Row', the section of Hyde Park where aristocrats went to see and be seen. The exclusiveness of the locale is conveyed through an establishing shot that reveals crowds of men in top hats and morning suits strolling alongside

---

[i] All dialogue has been transcribed directly from the film unless otherwise noted.

women in elegant dresses with parasols in the foreground as the spires of the Houses of Parliament rise majestically in the background. Subtitles indicate that it is "1895 .... The London Season ... where people are either hunting for husbands ... or hiding from them." Historically, the Season lasted from mid-spring to early autumn when England's elite families migrated from their country estates to their London townhouses in order to attend sittings of Parliament—and arrange for the marriages of their children to suitable partners. As Daniel Poole notes, the daily routines of those who were in town for the Season revolved around social activities like paying calls to friends and acquaintances, visiting clubs (for men only), and riding in Hyde Park, where 'Rotten Row' served as a venue for eligible young men and women to see and be seen (Pool 50-54). While the fashionable riding habits, stately carriages, columns of Horse Guards trotting in formation, and serene atmosphere in the Hyde Park sequence may seem like little more than eye candy added purely for the sake of playing on viewers' desire for period spectacle, I would argue that the sequence actually sets the thematic tone for the rest of the film by framing the film within the context of the social season and foregrounding Lord Goring's romantic exploits in particular. The film pre-empts (and overcompensates for) any suggestion that Goring's preoccupation with fashion, accessories, and art is a sign of effeminacy by embellishing his romantic attachments with women and highlighting his playboy status. The liberties taken with the portrayal of Goring's relationship to Laura Cheveley and Miss Mabel serve as compelling evidence for the argument that the film is going out of its way to turn the play into a sentimental romance.

Goring's relationship with Mrs. Cheveley is more romantic and sentimental in the film than it is in the play. In Wilde's version, Goring persuades Mrs. Chevely to relinquish the letter incriminating Sir Robert only after threatening to turn her in for stealing a brooch-bracelet belonging to his cousin. By contrast, the film spares Lord Goring the unpleasant task of stooping to the ungentlemanly threat of blackmail, and instead allows him to triumph over her by maintaining a deep conviction that Robert would do the right thing by refusing to back the Argentine Canal scheme as she demanded. But that's not until after his attempts to seduce her fail. The two sit on a loveseat, gradually growing closer and closer to one another as Goring attempts to charm her into giving up the letter in her hand. The camera alternates between medium shots of Goring and Cheveley locked in an amorous kiss and close-ups of his hand moving first along the bodice of her dress toward the hand in which she holds the letter incriminating Sir Robert, then down the length of her arm toward her hand until the letter is almost in his own grasp. Between kisses, Goring tells her that if she crushes Robert, her power, as well as any feelings that Goring had for her, would die as well. Despite giving the impression that she would yield to his declarations of love, she abruptly pulls away and offers to give him Sir Robert's letter on the day he marries her. When Goring refuses, she modifies the proposal. According to the terms of the new deal, Mrs. Cheveley will give the letter back if Sir Robert stands by his principles and opposes the Argentine Canal scheme, but Goring will have to marry her if Sir Robert bows to her blackmail threat and supports the scheme. This use of Goring's highly sought after hand in marriage as a bargaining chip is a drastic change from the play that seems to water down the moral complexity of the story. Goring's willingness to resort to blackmail to save his friend illustrates brilliantly Wilde's basic message that absolutist moral ideals are sheer nonsense because good people can do bad things from time to time. But by (re)creating Goring as a character who never really gets his hands dirty in anything that is morally compromising, the film's zeal to create a foil to the moral hypocrisy of Sir Robert results in the elimination of a plot twist that communicates Wilde's subtle, yet powerful, critique of Victorian morality.

While the playboy image the film constructs for Goring may ward off questions about his sexuality, his character is ultimately transformed from a womanizer into a proper husband who ultimately preaches the principles of moral order. The marriage between Mabel and Goring does figure in Wilde's play, but the film opens up their relationship by making it part of the foreground action. With witty repartee and double-entendres crackling between them, the mutual attraction between the two is palpable; but Goring's previous failures with women inspire in him an emotional reserve that becomes the essential point of conflict in the love story. The suspense over whether he will overcome his shyness and tell Mabel how he feels before she gives in to the ever-persistent Tommy Trafford (who is himself transformed from a competent aide to Sir Robert in the play to a rather pathetic suitor for Mabel's hand in the film) drives the story forward as viewers await the resolution to the question of 'will he or won't he?' The play ends, just as it began, in the Chiltern mansion with the reconciliation between s and Robert and the promise of a union between Goring and Miss Mabel. Parker, however, adds as an epilogue a church scene that begins with an overhead establishing shot of a beautifully decorated chapel with Goring and Mabel standing at the altar, their backs toward the congregation. The sequence intersperses medium shots of the Chilterns and Tommy Trafford looking on from their seats in the pews with medium long shots of the happy couple standing before their guests. The camera then tracks with them as they make their way slowly back up the aisle followed by Goring's father, Lord Caversham (John Wood). Caversham warns his son "If you don't make her an ideal husband I'll cut you off with shilling." Mabel replies skeptically, "An ideal husband? Oh I don't think I should like that." "What do you want him to be then, my dear?" inquires Caversham. Mabel gazes thoughtfully at her husband

and declares, "I think he can be whatever he chooses." Caversham tells his son, "You don't deserve her, sir." Brandishing the famous Wildean wit like a sword, Goring retorts: "My dear Father, if we man married the women we deserve, we should have a very bad time of it." The trio pause, allowing Mabel and Goring turn and gaze into each other's eyes. Flanked by the young couple, Caversham chastises his son light-heartedly: "You're heartless sir, quite heartless." Goring leans in to give his bride a passionate kiss, but gets in the last word of the conversation with the slightly anti-climactic rejoinder: "Oh, I hope not, sir. I hope not". This epilogue shifts the focus away from the Chilterns (and the political corruption theme itself) by relegating the couple to the status of mere wedding guests who are shown only briefly in a sequence that is dominated by Goring and Mabel. Not only do the newlyweds receive more screen time, but they are also consistently depicted at the center of shots whose balanced composition convey a sense of order and stability. In this way, the sequence visually conveys the idea that Goring and Mabel have taken center stage as the torchbearers for the progressive, non-judgmental morality that Wilde endorsed. But perhaps even more importantly, by allowing Goring and Mabel, both literally and figuratively, to take center stage in the final sequence, the film's narrative structure brings the romantic love story full circle by confirming Goring's transformation from bachelor playboy to happily married husband. The fact that the film begins and ends with the love story implies that the issues of political corruption and moral idealism have been displaced in favor of a resolution that reconstitutes the heterosexual couple.

Julianne Pidduck is the only scholar to date who has addressed the film's treatment of sexuality. She notes that while *An Ideal Husband* does "not directly address homosexuality, queerness is manifested implicitly through intertextual codes of authorship and the ambiguously queer sensibilities of camp and theatricality" (149). The most obvious example of such intertextual coding, is the casting of openly gay actor Rupert Everett in the role of the dandy; and Pidduck claims that the conflation of Everett/Wilde/Goring invests the dandy with a sense of sexual ambiguity that serves to undercut his prominent role at the center of the love story (152). She argues that the film participates in a camp sensibility that parodies love and marriage by rendering absurd the rituals of courtship (153). Pidduck also observes that Wilde's appearance as a character in the film (following a performance of one of his own plays) "discreetly references the ambiguity of 'queer space', or the 'place of the homosexual', within the text, intertext and in the audience" without "interrupt[ing] the film's heterosexual narrative trajectory" (150). Despite these aspects of textual ambiguity, she concedes that the film functions as a "wryly performative but nonetheless resolutely heterosexual romantic comed[y] [that] contrasts starkly with [*Wilde's*] more difficult depiction of a contradictory 'queer' life" (153).

Obviously, the impact of Pidduck's analysis is that it problematizes the assertion that the film's emphasis on courtship, matrimony, and Lord Goring's status as London's most eligible bachelor serve to 'unqueer' the dandy.

However, it is important to distinguish between queer texts and queer readings of texts. As Alexander Doty observes, "the text or the performer's star image does not have to have obvious (so-called 'denotative') non-straight elements to be termed queer; it just needs to have gathered about it a number of non-straight cultural readings" (150). Along those lines, it is clear from Pidduck's discussion of the sexual orientation of Wilde and Everett and camp elements of the film that there are certainly non-straight elements in this text. However, Doty reminds us that "some queer critics contend that many popular culture texts that do contain visible gay, lesbian, bisexual, or otherwise non-straight characters and content … aren't necessarily queer texts as they work to oppress and eliminate queerness rather than to express it" (150). *An Ideal Husband* operates in precisely this way because the hetero-normative love story suppresses the queerness of the source text without ever being substantially undermined by the camp aesthetic Pidduck observes. This is not to say that Pidduck's arguments aren't compelling. But just as she claims that the intertextual coding of Goring's character generates a sense of sexual ambiguity, it is equally possible to read the narrative as a hetero-normative repackaging of Lord Goring as a dominant, straight-identifying leading man which ultimately suppresses references to the sexual orientation of Wilde and Everett. One could follow Pidduck in concluding that the depiction of love and marriage functions as a camp-inflected parody. But one could also just as easily conclude that the scenes featuring Goring's sexual liaisons and marriage to Miss Mabel contribute to the film's erasure of the sexual ambiguity that manifested itself more profoundly in Wilde's original version. Parker certainly did not have to make these sorts of changes to the source material in order to parody the rituals of courtship and marriage. In fact, there would be more reason to see this as a queer text if it were more faithful to the plot and characterizations of the original play because it leaves much of Goring's private life in more ambiguous terms. Moreover, by circulating promotional material that invited audiences to forge expectations about Goring as the romantic lead and equate the resolution of the narrative with his marriage, the filmmakers have arguably undercut any sense of parody—appealing instead to sentimentality. Ultimately, this is a fruitful debate to have because it comes down the way the critic chooses to interpret the text. But when this text is read in relation to the institutional political culture of the late 1990s, the erasure of overt references to the dandy's sexual ambiguity takes on very definite political implications that warrant consideration.

There is no evidence that the production team intended to unqueer the dandy or obfuscate the moral complexity of Wilde's play. Nonetheless, Parker's adaptation engages with late twentieth century British society's ambivalence about homosexuality and its political implications. There are, of course, obvious parallels between the scandals that jeopardized that careers of Ron Davies, Nick Brown, and Peter Mandelson and the one that ultimately destroyed Oscar Wilde himself. Moreover, the public's willingness to embrace Wilde's work whilst disavowing his sexuality seems to run in parallel with the conflicting desires to publicly name and shame gay politicians and simply avoid dealing with the sexuality issues altogether. Ultimately, the fact that *could* have exploited the queer possibilities of the text by retaining the sexual ambiguity of the dandy but chose not to do so represents a key example of how the adaptation filters Wilde's creative vision through the ideological biases circulating in British society during the final years of the twentieth century.

New Labour: "Purer than Pure" or Same Old Sleaze?

Despite the narrative emphasis on the love story, Parker's adaptation still addresses the themes of corruption and moral idealism in ways that engage with contemporary political discourses. Both the play and the film versions of *An Ideal Husband* treat politics as a world in which the relentless pursuit of money, and the extreme measures taken to cover up the unethical means by which it was accumulated, provide an environment in which scandals flourish. The letter that Robert Chiltern sold to Baron Arnheim was said to have been inspired by secret documents detailing the British government's plan to borrow £4,000,000 from the influential Rothschild family in 1875 in order to purchase controlling shares in the Suez Canal. Despite the initial secrecy that surrounded the transaction, Wilde's audiences would have known about it and recognized the play's reference to real world politics (Gagnier 130; Raby 154). Parker's adaptation, however, seems to draw knowingly upon more contemporary developments in British politics. New Labour ascended to power in the General Election of 1997 in the wake of general disenchantment with Prime Minister John Major's Conservative government. Although there were numerous reasons for Labour's landslide victory, the scandals involving Conservative MPs proved especially damaging to the Tory party re-election campaign. One high-profile case involved Harrods owner Mohammed Al-Fayed's claim that Conservative MP Neil Hamilton had accepted cash and dined at Ritz at Al-Fayed's expense in exchange for asking questions in the Commons on Al-Fayed's behalf ("Brown envelopes" 20). Although Hamilton was by no means the only politician charged with unethical conduct, he quickly became something of a poster child for Tory sleaze. Despite protesting his innocence, he lost his seat in a landslide to Martin Bell, a former journalist who ran as an independent candidate on an anti-sleaze platform. The Tories suffered another blow to their credibility when it was revealed that party had accepted large donations from foreign businessmen who were themselves at the center of allegations of corporate fraud and tax evasion (Boggan 7). The Parliamentary Commissioner for Standards, Sir Gordon Downey, issued a report that validated doubts about the ethics of the Tory government by identifying MPs who had committed offenses such as receiving cash from lobbyists, failing to declare donations and corporate interests, accepting cash for questions, and misleading the Parliamentary committees assigned the task of investigating the conduct of members (Wolmar 1). Although governments are always criticized when violations of professional ethics occur, the revelations about the unethical conduct by Conservative MPs were particularly embarrassing in light of the party's efforts to assert itself as the defender of moral and family values (White 9).

The transitional period from John Major to Tony Blair revealed that the temptation to engage in corrupt dealings would remain a constant fixture in political life—regardless of *which* party occupied the government benches. Labour sought to position itself as the guardian of political morality by pledging to rid Westminster of the sleaze that had undermined the institution during the years of Conservative rule. Despite insisting that all MPs must "register all agreements 'involving the provision of services in his or her capacity as a Member of Parliament' in an official Register of Members' Interests", the government attracted criticism for failing to reveal the names of its own party donors (Bevins 11; McElvoy, "Is Lord Neill's New Broom" 3). As a result, Tony Blair had to publicly apologize for accepting a £1 million donation from Bernie Ecclestone, the Formula One Racing chief in order to silence claims that the donation had led the government to reverse the policy that banned cigarette advertisements from Formula One motor-racing (Sweeney 22; Aaronovitch 9). Blair sought to consolidate his reputation for taking a hardline stance against sleaze by "suspend[ing] suspected wrongdoers" in Scotland's "corruption-prone local councils" (McElvoy, "Cash for Access Row" 3). Yet Blair's image as the golden boy of British politics would be tarnished by perceptions that he dealt harshly with the unethical conduct of his political opponents, but looked the other way in cases that involved his friends and allies. For instance, Blair supported Lord Simon, "the minister who was revealed to have undeclared off-shore holdings and defend[ed] Paymaster Geoffrey Robinson against allegations of financial impropriety" (McElvoy, "Cash for Access Row" 3). Robinson's financial support for Chancellor Gordon Brown and other key ministers during the 1997 campaign, as well as a personal loan he made to Peter Mandelson, became the subject of an investigation that raised serious questions about Labour's integrity (Hencke et al. 1). But instead of providing reassurance to the public that corruption would be eradicated, the government inquiry confirmed the doubts that had been circulating about its ability to tackle sleaze when

"Tony's cronies" were involved. Suspicions that the investigation into Robinson's conduct was little more than a public relations exercise were confirmed when it was revealed that Blair's involvement amounted to two telephone calls. When news leaked out that "Mr. Blair wanted to sack [Robinson] but agreed to step back at Mr. Brown's urging," many Labour MPs assumed that Gordon Brown had intervened on behalf of his benefactor and "express[ed] anger that the loan deal had weakened the government" (Hencke et al. 1). Although the scandal would eventually lead to the resignations of Peter Mandelson and Geoffrey Robinson in December 1998, the damage had already been done as a result of the government's initial failure to deal harshly with ministerial misconduct. If the public needed further evidence that Westminster was still defined by a political culture of sleaze, the "lobbygate" scandal removed all doubts. Derek Draper, a member of the lobbying firm GPC Market Access and an advisor to Mandelson, promised two undercover journalists posing as American clients that he could give them privileged access to Labour ministers and confidential information (Barnett and Palast 1; McElvoy, "Will Swagger" 3). Although Draper himself was not a member of the Labour government, his activities brought further discredit to a government that was already reeling from allegations of corruption. The damage done by all of these scandals to the government's legitimacy effectively signaled the fact that New Labour had reached the end of its post-election honeymoon period. Once the darling of the media, the government quickly became the target of increasing condemnation for its handling of political corruption.

Spin-doctors in Downing Street's Press Office attempted to rehabilitate the government's reputation by releasing statements designed to demonstrate that, despite some initial miscues, Blair was committed to eradicating sleaze. Journalists were briefed on the new regulations governing the conduct of lobbyists in order to demonstrate that New Labour—unlike the Tories—would act swiftly and decisively to tackle corruption (White, "Blair Warns" 7; White, "Labour's Big Guns" 9). In order to "stem the impression that the party is immobilised by factional feuds and sleaze," Blair called upon the government to relaunch itself as a source of social reform and political integrity (Wintour and McSmith 2). The Prime Minister declared that his government must "show itself 'purer than pure'" and take the severest action against anyone "guilty of impropriety" (Wintour and McSmith 2; Bell 21). But as Anne McElvoy's column for *The Independent* revealed, this strategy failed to impress critics who saw it as just another case of spin-doctoring rather than the *actual* transparency that the public demanded ("Labour Must" 3) Despite Blair's lofty moral rhetoric, few critics were convinced that any meaningful change would take place to remedy the climate of corruption that prevailed in Westminster and Whitehall. As a result, the Press Office waged an uphill battle as the broadsheet press continued to focus on the government's unethical conduct and hypocritical rhetoric.

For its part, the press consistently endorsed the public's right to expect, and indeed *demand*, from any government "the commitment to maximum transparency in the way that a ruling party conducts its own affairs" and a leader who was focused "on redressing national shortcomings, and not on the appointment of scapegoats" (McElvoy, "Labour Must" 3). However, instead of accepting the government's efforts to clean up corruption as a sign of their transparency and integrity, McElvoy observed that:

> [T]he 'cash for access' allegations ... exposed the fault line which runs through the middle of the Labour Party and which has, until now, been carefully papered over by the image-makers ... [and] revealed how dangerously fragile the acceptance of Mr. Blair's politics and style of government is inside his own party ("Draper Syndrome" 9).

Political commentator Andrew Marr's survey of the right-wing press revealed a particularly vicious trend on the Blair government:

> *The Times* runs a cartoon on 'The Lying King'. *The Mail* attacks [Blair] for the 'smell of decay', for sleaze, moral decline and hypocrisy. *The Telegraph* regularly reports on the New Labour Lie Machine; its columnists refer to Blair's 'repulsive political calculus' and applaud the 'sustained and violent attack' on the hypocrite Blair by William Hague (30).

Even *The Independent*, which had previously shown support for New Labour, asserted that the government's "arrogance ... compounds the impression that a weak flank is opening up—the one marked 'openness and transparency'" (McElvoy, "Will Swagger" 6). Rather than reassure the public that Blair would produce results, the paper asserted that the Prime Minister "surrounded himself with corrupt and cynical courtiers" and would "do anything for a vote" (McElvoy, "Will Swagger" 6). Pointing to the way in which Labour had "coordinated the most jeering, personalized and unfair attacks on the Major government," Andrew Marr argued that "New Labour ... helped fashion and knot [the] flail of scorpions for its own back ... [by reveling] so much in its cleverness at manipulating the media that it made attack-journalism necessary" (30). *Independent* columnist Geoffrey Wheatcroft went so far as to suggest that the Labour government was actually *sleazier* than the Conservatives because accepting cash for questions did not actually break the law, but making a false declaration on a mortgage application (as Mandelson had done) was illegal (25). New Labour's attempt to spin its identity as a "purer than pure" government had failed, leaving *The Independent* to declare that, "sleaze, for all the Prime Minister's promises to stamp it out, still hangs like a cloud over British politics"

(Blackhurst 18). After reviving the rhetoric of moral idealism to establish its superiority to the discredited Tories, the Blair government found itself 'hoist on its own petard'.

It seems only fitting that we should see a return to another time when the government's efforts to justify its behavior using the language of moral probity incurred accusations of hypocrisy: the Victorian era depicted in Oscar Wilde's *An Ideal Husband*. Indeed, the political scandal at the heart of the play involves all of the misdeeds New Labour was accused of perpetrating during their first year in office. The play involves the leaking of cabinet information. New Labour was accused of leaking documents and information before it was presented officially in the Commons. Sir Robert uses his access to government documents to provide Baron Arnheim with insider information and gains money necessary to establish his political career in return. Similarly, lobbyists like Derek Draper made a lucrative career out of promising clients privileged access to information about government policies just as MPs were compensated handsomely for advancing the interests of donors by asking questions in the Commons. Sir Robert is an easy target for blackmail because he kept secret the origins of his wealth. Likewise, ministers found themselves the subjects of inquiries because they too failed to disclose information about their personal and professional finances. Sir Robert is spared the humiliation of having his past indiscretions revealed publicly and given a promotion. Similarly, the Labour government was accused of attempting to cover up ministerial wrongdoing by initiating sham inquiries that lacked thoroughness and failed to punish those found guilty of improper conduct. Sir Robert's vulnerability to the blackmail threat hinges on the fact that he has cultivated a reputation for possessing moral character that is beyond reproach. In much the same way, New Labour promoted itself as the antidote to Conservative sleaze despite being involved in its fair share of dirty dealings. Finally, just as the press was vigilant in exposing the government's failures to live up to its promise to be "purer than pure", so too did Wilde's play and Parker's film expose the hypocrisy of Victorian politics and morality.

Oscar Wilde and the Victorian Obsession with the Moral Ideal

The themes Wilde explores in *An Ideal Husband* bear the indelible imprint of debates taking place at the end of the nineteenth century over whether men and women should be held to the same moral standards. As "Angels of the House", women were traditionally regarded as paragons of purity and moral virtue while men were granted freedom to have moral lapses without incurring substantial social stigma. But as the 'Woman Question' increasingly dominated public discourses throughout the 1890s, discussions of the role of women in society took up the issue of how to eliminate the moral double standard. One possibility was to allow women the same social liberties that men enjoyed. The other possibility, which was endorsed by feminists of the day, was to maintain the moral purity of women, but require men to live up to the same expectations that women had to fulfill as well. The idea of establishing higher standards for men was particularly well received by women's groups who were eager to achieve equal rights and privileges for men and women and put a stop to the husband's prerogative to abuse and cheat on his wife. As Sos Eltis points out, this debate over moral standards applied to the political realm as well because it was believed that the increasing involvement of women in public life might help to bring a greater level of ethics and morality to the field of public affairs (167). However, Kerry Powell argues that such measures sparked a crisis of masculinity by creating the impression that "the ideal husband [was] a womanly man" (101).

Wilde's play was therefore part of what Powell describes as "an energetic discussion—in journalism, in fiction, in the popular theatre—of a doomed scheme to make the sexes equal by enforcing upon men as well as women the most austere standard of virtue" (107).

> *An Ideal Husband* ... combats but imitates a type of late nineteenth century drama in which men are held to an impossible standard associated today almost entirely with Victorian demands made upon women. ... [I]t was an unlikely attempt to put an end to what Wilde once described as the insistence upon 'separate sorts of virtues and separate ideals of duty' in the sexes. Plays ... staged in   in 1889 ... assaulted the double standard of conduct by domesticating the ruthless male rather than altering the standard of purity by which women were judged. The "ideal husband," feminized in this way, elected to forgo the liberty given men to violate official morality in sex, business, and politics. In a half-dozen plays being staged in London when Wilde's was introduced in early 1895, this sanitized man is a central figure, and in most of them ... a revisionary masculinity is in some sense endorsed (Powell 8).

While this strand of late Victorian theater typically punished men for their private and public moral transgressions, Powell contends that "Wilde wished to pursue an opposite course, to encourage a new masculinism by shattering ethical constraints upon the male rather than multiplying and strengthening them" (107). Wilde's play was part of a larger cycle of plays that featured

> politicians whose drive for power was challenged by wife, daughter, or fiancée in the interest of higher or more homely values. Scarcely 'ideal,' the husband is portrayed—in one way or another—as a polluter of the domestic hearth. ... Frequently, such plays end with the guilty husband not only repenting, but atoning for his misdeed by "taking the Chiltern Hundreds"—official jargon for

resigning from Parliament. Released from the amoral, male preserve of politics, these sanitized men look forward to retirement in the country under the corrective surveillance of a woman's eye .... What Wilde resists in *An Ideal Husband* is thus not only a set of generic conventions, but the domestic authority of women (Powell 98).

Although *An Ideal Husband* adopts the settings and themes of these plays, even to the point of appearing to imitate their plots throughout the first three acts, Wilde deftly turns a clichéd plot into a drama of "bold individuation" by allowing the final act to finish "in upset of expectation, in paradox" (Powell 4). Where his dramatic brethren were forced to do penance for failing to live up to the moral ideal by ending their lives or at least resigning from their positions to live out the rest of their lives in the country where they can benefit from the moral guidance of their wives, Sir Robert bucks convention by refusing to genuinely acknowledge that he was guilty of wrongdoing.

[T]he easy tolerance of Sir Robert Chiltern toward his guilty past in *An Ideal Husband* is without parallel in these dramas of immaculate men. ... [H]e even refuses the hint supplied by his own name—that of taking ... the Chiltern Hundreds. He thinks of his decision years ago to accept Baron Arnheim's bribe as the mark of distinctive "strength and courage," not weakness ... (Powell 103).

Rather than simply grant Sir Robert the freedom *not* to be an ideal husband and politician, Wilde's play "turns the tables and unconverts the wife" in a manner that reflects a "demand for perfection in women ... to be relaxed ... rather than applied equally to men as some were urging in 1895" (Powell, 103). Thus, where other plays helped to further entrench the severe Victorian moral code by relentlessly punishing characters for transgressive behavior, *An Ideal Husband* undermined moral convention by criticizing "the late-Victorian demand for absolute purity in its political leaders—a public assumption of higher morality which meant that the politically ambitious must in private resort to hypocrisy and subterfuge in order to succeed" (Eltis 148).

Wilde's critique of the Victorian obsession with moral ideals takes the form of exposing the wrongdoing of those who are idealized most as well as the hypocrisy of those who put them on a moral pedestal in the first place.

Wilde treats all his variations on this character [the good woman] with a degree of irony by casting doubt on the self-righteous morality that underlies all their actions .... Lady Chiltern quickly sacrifices her motto that 'Circumstances should never alter principles' when circumstances offer ministerial office to her husband, though his corrupt past should, according to her principles, disqualify him from such a post (Kohl 218).

Eltis argues that "Sir Robert Chiltern is the vehicle for Wilde's implicit criticism of nineteenth-century politics. This ambitious and unscrupulous politician, whose entire career is based upon his reputation for upright character and unshakeable honesty, is not only rewarded with a seat in the Cabinet, but backed as a possible future leader for the country" (135). He is "genuinely corrupt and unscrupulous and his inclusion in government is an implicit criticism of that establishment" (Eltis 158). But in scrutinizing Sir Robert's character and finding it lacking, Wilde also shines the spotlight on the way in which the Establishment encourages, or at least fails to punish, an "end justifies the means" attitude. The play is not particularly concerned with punishing Robert for his sins, or even exploring the concept of moral guilt as much as it is concerned with exploring what Kohl regards as a central conflict "between the individual and society .... The subject-matter and the conflict in each of Wilde's comedies consists in the struggle of the insiders to maintain their position or of the outsiders to break in, and of the individual's need to fulfill himself independently of this pressure to conform" (208-209). By treating Robert's collusion with the Baron as the secret behind his success, Wilde undermined the moral credibility of the ruling elite as a whole by raising the suggestion that the Establishment is built upon lies and corruption. Wilde's treatment of the ruling class in his play echoes the words of the Victorian social reformer Beatrice Webb:

> [D]eep down in the unconscious herd instinct of the British governing class there *was* a test of fitness for membership of this most gigantic of all social clubs ... *the possession of some form of power over other people*. The most obvious form of power, and the most easily measurable, was the power of wealth .... The dominant impulse was neither the greed of riches nor the enjoyment of luxurious living, though both of these motives were present, but the desire for power (qtd. in Gagnier 126).

Wilde's critique deepens into a double indictment of a society which values money and power so highly that men like Sir Robert must act dishonorably to gain acceptance, but then claims the moral high ground by condemning those who follow the principle that the end justifies the means.

Wilde adds a final twist to the plot that exposes the moral poverty of British society by revealing the disparity between its proclamations of moral purity and its actual practice of embracing and promoting men like Sir Robert. By condemning moral idealism as a concept that is both impossible to achieve and selectively imposed on individuals, Wilde rejects unattainable idealism and calls for an alternative perspective that acknowledges human fallibility.

> The play's happy ending consists of the entry into the inner sanctum of the British government of a man who, without regrets, sold his political integrity for

personal gain .... The very fact that the audience accepted the play's ending so easily demonstrates Wilde's success in portraying British politics as a scene of compromise and hypocrisy (Eltis 135).

This exploration of Wilde's commentary on moral idealism and political corruption during the Victorian era reveals that he was responding to issues that once again plagued Britain in the 1990s. At a time when the press coverage of New Labour was increasingly critical, it seems appropriate that Wilde's critique should be revived—and updated to suit contemporary sensibilities.

From the 1890s to the 1990s: Constructing a Modern Ideal Husband

Though the film is certainly not faithful to the letter of Wilde's play, it does faithfully convey the playwright's plea to abandon the social obsession with the "ideal"—and to look askance at those who purport to be above reproach. Indeed, many of the changes introduced by Parker serve to adapt the text to the visual medium of cinema by expanding the duration of the narrative, introducing new settings, and using the device of the flashback to show Sir Robert's dealing with Baron Arnheim instead of relying on Sir Robert's verbal accounts as the play does. For example, where the play relies upon Lord Caversham to read a newspaper report about Sir Robert's opposition to the Argentine scheme, the film shows the actual parliamentary debate in which Sir Robert delivers an impassioned speech in the House of Commons. The scene becomes an opportunity to generate suspense and showcase Sir Robert's oratorical grandstanding as he gives the initial impression that he has succumbed to blackmail before finally rejecting the Argentine scheme and waxing idealistic about the need to act for higher purposes than self-interest. Refusing to yield to Mrs. Cheveley's efforts to blackmail him, Sir Robert self-righteously proclaims:

> Since I last addressed this House on the subject I have had the opportunity to investigate this scheme more thoroughly, and to grasp fully the ramifications of lending it our support. I have to inform the House that I was mistaken in my original perceptions, and that I have now taken a rather different view. I find that now I must agree with my Right Honorable friend that this is indeed an excellent scheme ... a genuine opportunity. An opportunity particularly if you happen to be a corrupt investor with nothing but self-interest at heart. For now it is my utter conviction that this scheme never should have had nor ever should have any chance of success. It is a fraud, an infamous fraud at that. Our involvement would be a political fraud of the worst possible kind. This great nation has long been a great commercial power. Now, it seems there exists a growing compulsion to use that power merely to beget more power, money merely to beget more money,

irrespective of the true cost to the nation's soul. And it is this sickness, a kind of moral blindness, commerce without conscience, which threatens to strike at the very soul of this nation. And the only remedy that I can see is to strike back and to strike now. As we stand at the end of this most eventful century, it seems that we do after all have a genuine opportunity, one honest chance to shed our sometimes imperfect past, to start again, to step unshackled into the next century and to look our future squarely and proudly in the face.

This speech offers yet another example of how Parker has re-scripted Wilde's play in a way that picks up on issues circulating in contemporary politics. Upon assuming the post of Foreign Secretary, Robin Cook pronounced "Our foreign policy must have an ethical dimension and must support the demands of other peoples for the democratic rights on which we insist for ourselves" (qtd. in Whitaker 21). However, Cook later denied that he had called for an "ethical foreign policy" and accused the press of misinterpreting him, thereby fueling accusations that Labour made promises it couldn't—or wouldn't—keep (Black 4). Regardless of whether it was trying to bring an "ethical dimension" to foreign policy or pursue an "ethical foreign policy," the government was criticized by the Select Committee on Foreign Affairs for failing to take a firm stand against human rights abuses committed by valued trading partners like China and allowing the sale of weapons to nations in Indonesia and Africa, which had been found guilty of human rights violations (Woolf 4). Thus, Sir Robert's call to strike back against the moral blindness that cuts straight to the nation's soul seemed entirely apposite at a time when real life politicians were still putting commercial interests ahead of moral principles and human rights.

In addition to engaging with the particular issues, concerns, and preoccupations of a 1990s audience, Parker's adaptation enhances Wilde's critique of the British Establishment by opening up this cultural milieu and exposing its numerous flaws. The film visually constructs the insulated world of London Society by using a variety of locations and extending the duration of the dramatic events that take place there. Instead of confining the action to twenty-four hours and containing it within the closed environs of the Chiltern's Grosvenor Square mansion and Lord Goring's Curzon Street townhouse, the film showcases such posh venues as Hyde Park, the Grosvenor Gallery, the House of Commons, a Women's Liberal Association meeting, Claridges Hotel, Goring's Club, a gentlemen's steam room, and a performance of *The Importance of Being Ernest* at the Haymarket Theatre. In each of these venues, the elite are shown to be hypocritical and disingenuous. Hyde Park is the setting for Gertrude's encounter with Lady Markby and Mrs. Cheveley, in which s's contempt is barely concealed beneath the veil of formal manners. At the Haymarket Theatre, the events on stage take a backseat to the drama unfolding in the audience. The sequence begins with a conversation between Sir Robert and Gertrude, in which he arouses her suspicions that something is amiss by telling her he has reason to re-think his opposition to the Argentine scheme. The camera cuts away from the Chilterns' private box and juxtaposes shots of the couple with a series of masking shots that feature the characters spying on one another when they are supposed to be watching the play. Lord Goring peers through his opera glasses in the direction of the box where Mrs. Cheveley and Lady Markby are sitting. Miss Mabel looks up from her opera glasses in the direction of Lord Goring's box, until he catches her gaze, at which point she quickly feigns disinterest and pretends to flirt with her date, Tommy Trafford. Mrs. Cheveley aims her opera glasses in the direction of the Chilterns' box to watch as Gertrude inquires whether Robert is telling her the truth and responds with relief at her husband's assurances that there is nothing in his past that she might not know. By creating the impression that viewers are looking through opera glasses themselves, the masking shot device highlights their status as voyeurs and suggests that the most interesting performances were the ones being given by the Chilterns, Mrs. Cheveley, and Mabel.   The historic Claridges Hotel is the site of Goring's assignation with Mrs. Cheveley, where she tells him of her plans for Robert. The House of Commons serves as a backdrop for Robert's speech expressing opposition to the Argentine scheme, but the idealistic rhetoric contained in the speech becomes ironic when spoken by someone whose own behavior is so at odds with those ideals. Moreover, the House becomes a theatrical space of its own as Lords Caversham and Goring Mabel,   Gertrude,   and Mrs. Cheveley watch the proceedings from the observation galleries that surround the main floor of Commons.

Of course, opening up the locations in this way also allows the film to pull out all the stops and provide a spectacular recreation of period detail. As a heritage film, *An Ideal Husband* belongs to a genre that has been criticized for allowing the elements of costume, setting, and décor to overshadow, and even undermine the themes of the narrative. However, the film's attention to period spectacle actually provides a basis for exploring Wilde's treatment of the Establishment (and its moral views) as a masquerade in which appearances are very much at odds with reality. The notion that class is a performance lies at the heart of Sir Robert's efforts to win a position in the Establishment. He correctly calculated that he would be admitted to the social circles of the elite, despite his humble beginnings, if he had the money to buy the right house, furnish it with the right things, marry the right wife, and actively cultivate the right image as a politician of unquestionable moral character. Thus, rather than serve as self-indulgent spectacle, the sequences which show off the elaborateness of the Chiltern mansion and convey the luxuriousness of the upper class lifestyle ironically comment on the trappings of wealth by framing it all as the product of ethically questionable dealings. As Reginia Gagnier observes, the "dramatic action [of the play] consists in the unmasking of the upper classes, showing their sham if not obliterating their power. The luxury of the Chilterns' home in Grosvenor Square was founded on the swindle with Baron Arnheim .... Chiltern ... was undeniably corrupt, although he attempted to couch it terms of a classical hero's fatal flaw" (129). In revealing the lavish interiors of the Chiltern mansion, a series of extreme long shots invites the viewer to see the luxury that was purchased at the expense of Sir Robert's personal integrity. Sos Eltis notes of the play that, "the richness of scenery, costume, and props demanded by the play visually emphasize the values which are paramount in this society" (32). This observation proves even more pertinent to the film. If one of the main reasons why this text was selected for adaptation was the similarity between the Victorian period and today, then it is necessary to visually locate viewers within that Victorian milieu through the use of costume, décor, and setting. Eltis' comments also lend further credence to the idea that the décor serves an expressive purpose by revealing the degree to which the Victorian Establishment judged the moral worthiness of individuals on the basis of their possessions and image rather than their actual character. Moreover, given the importance of spin-doctoring for the Labour government, the themes of theatricality and masquerade become metaphors for the cardinal rule of contemporary politics: image counts for much more than reality.

The film, like the play, engages with a masquerade motif that frames class identity as theatrical performance. Wilde moved in social circles dominated by the ruling class, yet his status as an outsider in this world enabled him to see through its façade of respectability and recognize their enduring hypocrisy. Peter Raby notes that *An Ideal Husband* treats Society as

> [a] fantastic masquerade, highlighting aspects of English public life which themselves inhabited the dimension of theatre: the smart dance, the country house party, the Chilterns' reception. At all of these there is a strong element of performance, and of audience, accentuated by the presence of almost silent 'extras', and a background of servants (157).

The theatricality of the space is suggested in several ways. First, the process by which guests dress and groom themselves for the party resembles the routine that an actor might follow in preparing for a stage performance. A montage sequence shows medium close-ups of Miss Mabel applying powder to her bosom, Sir Robert (shown from behind) putting on a starched white shirt, a servant's hands lacing up a corset, hands rolling white stockings up a shapely leg, Miss Mabel inspecting the diamond choker around her neck in the mirror, a servant's hands fixing the tie of Sir Robert's evening attire, a pearl and diamond necklace being placed around Mrs. Cheveley's neck, a finger applying lipstick, a servant's hands placing a flower-shaped hairpiece in Mrs. Cheveley's tight curls, Lord Goring affixing a flower in his buttonhole, and Miss Mabel placing a flower corsage on her own dress.

This notion of theatricality seems to have influenced Parker's depiction of the Chilterns' mansion as an elaborate stage upon which the Sir Robert, Gertrude, and their guests perform the roles of social and political respectability. Like the play, the film features a political party sequence in which all of the shots are organized around showcasing the splendor of the place and exclusiveness of the guest list. The sequence begins with a medium shot of a servant standing in front of a vase overflowing with flowers, announcing the names of guests as they arrive. The camera then pans to the left to reveal the enormity of the Chilterns' mansion. The décor reflects a Grecian influence with high ceilings, arched doorways, decorative friezes and wall engravings that suggest columns, and large statues that tower over the guests (including the statue of Achilles whose legendary hidden weakness makes him an appropriate symbol of Robert's own vulnerability). Palm plants and flower arrangements are in abundance throughout the house, complementing the elegance of a profusion of chandeliers, vases, and paintings. After revealing the splendor of the ground floor, the camera moves to a high angle long shot that allows viewers to look down on the guests from the elevated vantage point of the first floor balcony where Sir Robert, Gertrude, Lord Caversham, Tommy Trafford and Sir Edward (a newspaper editor) have gathered together to converse about Sir Robert's virtue as a politician. By depicting the space from both the ground floor and an elevated position, the camera reveals the immensity of the space and showcases all of the miscellaneous furnishings and objets d'art that fill the house. The house is therefore an essential element in Sir Robert's performance as the ideal politician. He is part of the *nouveau riche* and the ostentatiousness of his home reflects his need to show off wealth in order to establish his membership credentials in the ruling elite. By contrast, the real aristocrat, Lord Goring, who is under no such obligation to show off, lives in a home that is decorated with dark purple walls, flowers in simple urns, and a few tapestries and statues that suggest an Asian influence. Ironically, of course, house is rendered the ultimate façade after Mrs. Cheveleyreveals that Robert's wealth came from a dishonest act. And the fact that Mrs. Cheveley chooses the house as the setting for her performance as blackmailer adds even more drama to the situation.

The next component of the theatrical metaphor is a brand of dialogue which serves as a verbal mask to conceal the true intentions and thoughts of characters. Here, Wilde's genius for writing replete with paradoxes and witty epigrams brilliantly illustrates the extent to which polite conversation can be turned into a battlefield in which the prime casualty is moral hypocrisy. Raby contends that, "Wilde uncovers the relentless evasiveness of English speech, the attempts to make resounding definitions and statements of ideals within a world that is clearly no longer static and solid, attempts Wilde described as 'the vice of sincerity'" (158). Speech plays a particularly important role in *An Ideal Husband* because it belongs to the genre of the drawing room comedy, or comedy of manners, which relied upon dialogue rather than action in order to humorously imitate the behavior of the upper class and gently satirize their hypocrisy. It should be noted that conversation itself is a form of performance in which the role of actor and audience are constantly subject to renegotiation. As Mark Hallett points out

> [C]onversation was privileged as the primary means through which polite social and cultural status was displayed, and as something that bound together and refined the socially disparate, economically competitive and often newly monied elements of an increasingly commercialized and urbanized society .... [C]onversation was a highly developed form of private theatre, normally taking place among one's family, friends and social peers in the spaces of the home, club or assembly, and thus uninfected by the raucous representative signs of popular culture. It was a theatre, of course, in which participants moved continually between the roles of actor and audience ... (Hallett 54-55).

In shifting between the role of speaker and listener, the participants in a conversation in Wilde's play speak in ways that allow the character to avoid being "pinned to content or to any sort of commitment" (Kohl 227). Hence Lord Goring expresses himself through paradox, such as "I love talking about nothing, father. It is the only thing I know anything about", where the inherent contradiction of statements erases any real meaning from the words. Ironically, however, it is the statements that appear rest upon unambiguous moral absolutes that are shown to be the most bereft of meaning because Wilde frames this sort of rhetoric as the discourse of hypocrisy. When Mrs. Cheveley tells Sir Robert that the Argentine scheme is "a speculation ... a brilliant, daring speculation," he responds sanctimoniously, "Believe me, Mrs. Cheveley, it is a swindle. Let us call things by their proper names. It makes matters simpler." But later, when Robert tries to downplay the implications of his disclosure of the Cabinet secret, saying, "The affair to which you allude was no more than a speculation. The House of Commons had not yet passed the bill; it might have been rejected," Mrs. Cheveley savors the pleasure of using Robert's own words against him.

> It was a swindle, Sir Robert. Let us call things by their proper names. It makes everything simpler. And now I am going to sell you that letter, and the price I ask for it is your public support of the Argentine scheme. You made your own fortune out of one canal. You must help me and my friends to make our fortunes out of another!

A similar situation occurs when Gertrude attempts to adopt the moral high ground with Mrs. Cheveley, saying that "a person who has once been guilty of a dishonest and dishonourable action may be guilty of it a second time, and should be shunned." Mrs. Cheveley asks, "Would you apply that rule to every one?" When Gertrude answers," Yes, to every one, without exception," Mrs. Cheveley responds "Then I am sorry for you, Gertrude, very sorry for you." For in committing to the moral absolute by which she judges Mrs. Cheveley unworthy of crossing the threshold of the Chiltern home, Gertrude walks blindly into a trap which requires her either to judge her beloved husband by that absolute moral standard she has applied to others or become a hypocrite herself. Lord Goring ultimately liberates her from this unattractive dilemma by encouraging her to abandon the logic of absolute morality, to develop greater tolerance for imperfection, and support the personal growth it takes to overcome past mistakes. Counseling her that "it is not the perfect, but the imperfect who have need of love", Goring departs from the language of paradoxes to offer aphoristic words of wisdom that convey Wilde's own moral vision. Thus, film's use of language retains the element of artifice and revels in the dilution of its absolute meaning. In a modern world, where the question "How do you know a politician is lying?" elicits the answer "Their lips are moving," it is hardly surprising that the film should revive a theatrical masterpiece which exposes the language of lies.

As this investigation has demonstrated, the film's engagement with its political context goes well beyond the obvious correlations between its treatment of a fictional scandal and the real life controversies plaguing the Labour government. By conveying Wilde's critique of political idealism and moral hypocrisy at a time when media commentators were condemning New Labour in similar terms, the film functions as shrewd political commentary in its own right. Its rejection of hypocrisy translates into a critique of New Labour's efforts to present itself to the public as an antidote to Tory sleaze despite being embroiled in its own fair share of scandals. Moreover, it's treatment of the Victorian political Establishment as a masquerade in which moral respectability is merely a role to be performed comments critically on the Labour government's use of spin-doctors to create a public image of honesty and integrity in order to mask the dishonest and unethical conduct of its members. So, despite framing the love story as the central focus of plot development, the film nonetheless offers an insightful meditation on political corruption that lays bare New Labour's own hypocrisy.

Conclusion

As this study has demonstrated, Oliver Parker's adaptation of *An Ideal*

Husband revises the original play in ways that engaged with the contemporary discourses that were circulating in British society around the issues of homosexuality and political corruption. The film resolves the sexual ambiguity of the play's Wildean dandy by transforming Lord Goring into a raging playboy, thereby erasing references to the dandy's possible homosexuality at a time when many members of the public responded to the media's "outing" of gay politicians with an ambivalence best summarized by the catchphrase "don't ask, don't tell". Parker's film also underscores the idea that moral idealism is a prescription for hypocrisy and mobilizes a critique of New Labour's hypocrisy in several ways. The film showcases the hypocrisy of a politician whose actions resemble those of leading real-life leaders and whose speech to the House of Commons contains the lofty rhetoric typically heard in speeches made by Tony Blair and other members of the government. Moreover, by restructuring the events of the play in order to subordinate the 'ideal politician' plot to a love story in which the far-from-ideal Lord Goring emerges as the hero, the film seems to respond to the interests of modern audiences who have seen enough political scandals to know that there is no point in expecting politicians to be ideal anyway. By concluding with an epilogue that features Lord Goring's marriage to Mabel and her declaration that she does not want an *ideal* husband, the film leaves audiences with the optimistic sentiment that moral idealism can be rejected and that hypocrisy can be overcome after all. The film is nothing if not timely, for it distills the wit and wisdom of Oscar Wilde in a way that reminds audiences that it is sheer folly to expect perfect leaders. At the same time, it counters the moral rhetoric of the Labour government by revealing that those who cling most adamantly to claims of moral superiority are often the ones with the most to hide. And by simply articulating this message, Parker's adaptation of *An Ideal Husband* engaged with the critical media discourses that challenged the credibility of Tony Blair's government and mourned New Labour's lost innocence.

BIBLIOGRAPHY

Aaronovitch, David. "Moments that Made the Year." *The Independent*, 26 December, 1997, 9.

Abrams, Fran. "Ministers Move to End 'Anti-Gay' Law." *The Independent* 27 July 1998, 1.

Albee, Edward. "The Art of the Theater Iv." *Paris Review* 39 (1966): 92-127.

Alberge, Dalya. "British Film-Makers Do Double-Take on Wilde." *The Times* 25 May 1998, 3.

Alexander, Karen. "Daughters of the Dust," *Sight and Sound* 3:9 (1993): 20-22.

American Beauty. Dir. Sam Mendes. Perf. Kevin Spacey. DreamWorks Pictures, 1999.

Anthelme, Paul. *Nos deux consciences; pièce en cinq actes, en prose, de M. Paul Anthelme, représentée pour la première fois à la porte Saint-Martin le 15 novembre 1902*. Paris: L'Illustration, 1902.

Astruc, Alexandre. "The Birth of a new Avant-garde: la Caméra-Stylo." In *The New Wave*, edited by Peter Graham. London: Martin Secker & Warburg, 1968.

Bakhtin, M.M. *Problems of Dostoevsky's Poetics*. Minneapolis: University of Minnesota Press, 1984.

Barnett, Anthony and Gregory Palast. "New Labour Insiders Offer Secrets for Cash." *The Observer* 5 July 1998, sec: News: 1.

Barthes, Roland. "The Death of the Author" (1968). In *Theories of Authorship: a Reader*, edited by John Caughie. London and Boston: Routledge & Kegan Paul in association with the British Film Institute, 1981.

Bazin, André. *What is Cinema?* Trans. Hugh Gray. Berkeley and Los Angeles: University of California Press, 1967.

Bazin, André. *Qu'est-ce que le cinéma*. Paris: Éditions du Cerf, 1975.

Bell, Ian. "Anything Bill Can Do, President Blair seems to think he can do better and with impunity. Well, almost ...." *The Observer* 9 August 1998, 21.

Benjamin, Walter. "The Task of the Translator." *Illuminations: Essays and Reflections*. Tran. Hannah Arendt. New York: Schocken Books, 1969. 69-82.

Bennett, Tony and Janet Woollacott. *Bond and Beyond: The Political Career of a Popular Hero*. New York: Methuen, 1987.

Bergman, Ingmar. "Ingmar Bergman Discusses Film-Making." *Film and/as Literature*. Ed. John Harrington. New Jersey: Prentice-Hall, 1977. 224-228.

Bersani, Leo and Ulysse Dutoit (1993) *Arts of Impoverishment: Beckett, Rothko, Resnais*. Cambridge, MA: Cambridge University Press.

Bevins, Anthony. "MP's Interests: Downey's Rules Strike Terror into the Heart of the Commons." *The Independent* 21 November 1997, 11.

Bigsby, C. W. E. *Albee*. Writers and Critics. Edinburgh: Oliver and Boyd, 1969.

Black, Ian. "Cook Admits His Aims Fall Short of 'Ethical Policy.'" *The Guardian* 12 November 1998, 4.

Blackhurst, Chris. "The Good, the Great and the Fallen." *The Independent*, 21 December 1997, 18.

Blois, Marco de. Interview with Robert Lepage. "L'iconoclaste de Québec." *24 Images*, no. 80 (December-January 1995-1996): 14-17.

Blue Angel Films and Tyrone Productions (2001) *Beckett on Film*. London: Clarence Pictures.

Boggan, Steve. "Tory Scandal: History of Doubtful Donations." *The Independent* 20 January 1998, 7.

Booth, Wayne. *The Rhetoric of Fiction*. Chicago: University of Chicago Press, 1983.

Botta, Anna (1999) Detecting Identity in Time and Space: Modiano's *Rue des Boutiques Obscures* and Tabucchi's *Il Filo dell' Orizzonte*, in Patricia Merivale and Susan Elizabeth

Boyd, Brian. *Vladimir Nabokov: The American Years*. Princeton: Princeton UP, 1990.

Bradley, Ian. (ed.). *The Complete Annotated Gilbert and Sullivan* (Oxford: Oxford University Press, 1996).

Brater, Enoch (1987) *Beyond Minimalism: Beckett's Late Style in the Theater*. New York: Oxford University Press.

Brewster, Ben and Lea Jacobs (1997) *Theatre to Cinema: Stage Pictorialism and the Early Feature Film*. Oxford: Oxford University Press.

"Brown Bids to End 'Outing' Row." BBC News Online 9 November 1998. 2 August 2005 <*http://news.bbc.co.uk/ 1/low/uk_politics/211188.stm*>.

"Brown envelopes or no, Parliament cannot police itself." *The Independent*, 7 November 1997, 20.

Brustein, Robert. "Albee and the Medusa Head." *The New Republic* 147.18 (1962): 29-30.

Brouwer, Joel. "Repositioning: Center and Margin in Julie Dash's *Daughters of the Dust*," *African American Review* 29:1 (1995): 5-16.

Bruzzi, Stella. *Undressing Cinema. Clothing and Identity in the Movies*. Routledge: London & New York, 1997.

Burch, Noël (1986) Primitivism and the Avant-Gardes: A Dialectical Approach, in Philip Rosen (ed.), *Narrative, Apparatus, Ideology: A Film Theory Reader*. New York: Columbia University Press, pp. 483-507.

Burns, L. H. "Infertility as Boundary Ambiguity: One Theoretical Perspective." *Family Process* 26.3 (1987): 359-72.

Caron, André. Interview with Robert Lepage. "Dossier Robert Lepage: La première confession de Robert Lepage." *Séquences*, no. 180 (September-October 1995): 28-31.

Carroll, Noël. "The Specificity of Media in the Arts." *Film and Theory: An Anthology*. Eds. Robert Stam and Toby Miller. Massachusetts: Blackwell, 2000. 39-53.

Charity, Tom. "An Ideal Husband." *Time Out* 14-21 April 1999, 78.

Chatman, Seymour. "*Mrs. Dalloway's* Progeny: *The Hours* as Second-degree Narrative." In *A Companion to Narrative Theory*, ed. James Phelan and Peter J. Rabinowitz. Oxford: Basil Blackwell, 2005. 269-281.

Chen, Guidi and Chun Tao. *Zhongguo nongmin wenti diaocha* (An investigation of the problems of Chinese farmers). Beijing Renming Wenxue Chubanshe, 2004.

Chen, Hang and Ding Yilan. "*Nuan*: Xunzhao jiyi zhong huizhi buqu de guowang" (*Nuan*: Seeking for the inerasable past in the memory). Liu 100-04.

Chow, Rey. Primitive Passions: Visuality, Sexuality, Ethnography and Contemporary Chinese Cinema." New York: Columbia University Press: 1995.

Clandfield, Peter. "Bridgespotting : Lepage, Hitchcock, and Landmarks in Canadian Film." *Canadian Journal of Film Studies* 12, no. 1 (Spring 2003): 3-15.

Cohen, Nick. "Hold on a minute: Power, privacy and privilege." *The Observer* 6 December 1998, 27.

Cohen, Patricia. "The Nose Was the Final Straw." *The New York Times* 15 February, 2003. B9+11.

Conrad, Peter. *The Hitchcock Murders*. London: Faber and Faber, 2000.

Corliss, Richard. "Lolita: From Lyon to Lyne." Film Comment Sep/Oct 1998. Vol. 34, Iss. 5; 34-40

Craig, Cairns. "Rooms without a View," *Sight and Sound* 1:2 (1991): 10-13.

Critchley, Simon. *Ethics, Politics, Subjectivity: Essays on Derrida, Levinas and Contemporary French Thought*. London: Verso, 1999.

Cunningham, Michael. *The Hours*. New York: Farrar, Straus and Giroux, 1998.

——. Interview (with James Schiff). *The Missouri Review*. 26.2 (2003): 113-126.

Dai, Sijie. *Balzac and the Little Chinese Seamstress*. Trans. Ina Rilke. New York: Anchor Books, 2001.

Dai, Sijie and Nadine Perront adapt. *Balzac et la petite tailleuse*. By Dai Sijie. Dir. Dai Sijie. Les Films de la Saune, 1985.

Dash, Julie. *Daughters of the Dust. A Novel.* A Plume Book, 1999.

——. *Daughters of the Dust: The Making of an African American Woman's Film.* New York: The New Press, 1992.

Dawson, Kellie. "Rare and Unfamiliar Things: Vladimir Nabokov's 'Monsters.'" *Nabokov Studies* 9.1 (2005): 115-131.

Decherney, Peter. *Hollywood and the Cultural Elite: How the Movies Became American.* New York. Columbia University Press, 2005.

Dee, Jonathan. "The Reanimators: On the art of literary graverobbing." *Harper's Magazine* 298 (June 1999): 76-84.

de Lauretis, Teresa. *Technologies of Gender: essays on Theory, Film, and Fiction.* Bloomington: Indiana UP, 1987.

Derrida, Jacques. *Archive Fever: a Freudian Impression.* Translated from the French by Eric Prenowitz. Chicago: U of Chicago P, 1996.

——. *Of Grammatology.* Corrected Edition. Translated from the French by Gayatri Chakravorty Spivak. Baltimore, London: Johns Hopkins UP, 1998.

——. *Specters of Marx: the State of the Debt, the Work of Mourning, and the New International.* Translated from the French by Peggy Kamuf. New York: Routledge, 1994.

——. *Writing and Difference.* Translated from the French by Alan Bass. Chicago: U of Chicago P, 1978.

Doty, Alexander. "Queer Theory." in John Hill and Pamela Church Gibson (eds), *The Oxford Guide to Film Studies* (Oxford: Oxford University Press, 1998), 148-152.

Dundjerovic, Aleksandar. *The Cinema of Robert Lepage: The Poetics of Memory.* London: Wallflower Press, 2003.

Elsaesser, Thomas (1998) Louis Lumière—the Cinema's First Virtualist?, in Thomas Elsaesser and Kay Hoffmann (eds.), *Cinema Futures: Cain, Abel or Cable? The Screen Arts in the Digital Age.* Amsterdam: Amsterdam University Press, pp. 45-63

Eltis, Sos. *Revising Wilde: Society and Subversion in the Plays of Oscar Wilde* (Oxford: Clarendon Press, 1996).

Essif, Les (2001) *Empty Figure on an Empty Stage: The Theatre of Samuel Beckett and His Generation.* Bloomington, IN: Indiana University Press.

Esslin, Martin (1983) *Theatre of the Absurd.* 3rd ed. New York: Penguin.

Eternal Sunshine of the Spotless Mind. Michel Gondry. Focus Features, 2004.

Eugène Ionesco: Four Plays (The Bald Soprano. The Lesson. Jack or the Submission. The Chairs) (1958) Trans. Donald M. Allen. New York: Grove Press.

Foucault, Michel. *The History of Sexuality: An Introduction.* New York: Vintage Books (1990).

——. "What Is an Author?" in *Language, Counter-Memory, Practice: Selected Essays and Interviews by Michel Foucault,* edited by Donald F. Bouchard. Ithaca, NY: Cornell University Press, 1988.

Francke, Lizzie. "Daughters of the Dust," *Sight and Sound.* 3:9 (1993): 44

"Furusato Encore." *Amazon.co.jp.* 29 May 2005: <http://www.amazon.co.jp/exec/obidos/ASIN/B00009AV7C/249-2546891-6529907>.

Gagnier, Regina, *Idylls of the Marketplace: Oscar Wilde and the Victorian Public* (Stanford: Stanford University Press, 1986).

Gaut, Berys. "Film Authorship and Collaboration." In *Film Theory and Philosophy,* edited by Richard Allen and Murray Smith. Oxford and New York: Oxford UP, 2003.

Gelmis, Joseph. *The Film Director as Superstar.* London: Secker and Warburg, 1971.

Genette, Gérard. *Palimpsestes: la littérature au second degré.* Paris: Éditions du Seuil, 1982.

Goffman, Erving. *Stigma: Notes on the Management of Spoiled Identity.* Englewood Cliffs, NJ: Prentice-Hall, 1963.

Gunning, Tom. "The Cinema of Attraction: Early Film, Its Spectator, and the Avant-garde." *Film and Theory: An Anthology.* Eds. Robert Stam and Toby Miller. Massachusetts: Blackwell, 2000. 229-235.

Gunning, Tom (2004) Now You See It, Now You Don't: The Temporality of the Cinema of Attractions, in Lee Grieveson and Peter Krämer (eds.), *The Silent Cinema Reader.* London and New York: Routledge, pp. 41-51.

Hallett, Mark. *Hogarth* (London: Phaidon, 2000).

Hamon-Sirejols, C. and J. Gerstenkorn and A. Gardies. *Cinéma et théâtralité.* Lyon: Aléas, 1994.

Happiness. Dir. Todd Solondz. Trimark Home Video. 1998.

Harrington, John, ed. *Film and/as Literature.* New Jersey: Prentice-Hall, 1977.

Haskell, Molly. *From Reverence to Rape.* New York : Coward, McCann & Geoghegan, 1973.

Hawthorne, Nigel. "The Dangerous Bigotry of the BBC." *The Independent* 2 December 1998, 4.

Hayman, Ronald. *Edward Albee.* New York: Ungar, 1973.

Hencke, David et al. "Mandelson Wounded, Blair Furious, Questions for Brown." *The Guardian,* 23 December 1998, 1.

Henke, Suzette. "'The Prime Minister': A Key to *Mrs. Dalloway.*" In *Virginia Woolf: Centennial Essays,* ed. Elaine K. Ginsberg and Laura Moss Gottlieb.

——. "*Mrs. Dalloway*: The Communion of Saints." In *New Feminist Essays on Virginia Woolf.* Ed. Jane Marcus. Lincoln: University of Nebraska Press, 1981. 125-47.

Heritage Film," *Fires Were Started. British Cinema and Thatcherism*. Ed.
Lester Friedman. Minneapolis: U Minnesota P, 1993.

Higson, Andrew. "Re-presenting the National Past: Nostalgia and Pastiche in
the

Horkheimer, Max. "The Social Function of Philosophy." *Critical Theory:
Selected Essays*. Trans. Matthew J. O'Connell. New York: Continuum,
1972.

Hou, Liren and Xueguang Zhou. "Children of the Cultural Revolution: The
State and the Life Course in the People's Republic of China." *American
Sociological Review*. Vol 64:1(1999). 12-36.

Hunter, Stephen. "Gus Van Sant's *Psycho*. Review." *Rotten Tomatoes* website.
Zunpancic, Alenka. "A Perfect Place to Die : Theatre in Hitchcock's
Films." In *Everything You Always Wanted to Know about Lacan (But Were
Afraid to Ask Hitchcock)*, edited by Slavoj Zizek, 173-105. London and New
York: Verso, 1992.

Huo, Jianqi. *Nuan*. Beijing Jinhai Fangzhou Wenhua Fazhan Youxian Gongsi
(Beijing Aureate Ocean Ark Co. Ltd), 2003.

——. and Qiu Shi. "Cishi cidi" (This time, this place). Liu 77-80.

——. and Yi He. "Huo Jianqi, zhengchang ren" (Huo Jianqi, a normal person).
Liu 84-88.

I "Heart" Huckabees. David O. Russell. Fox Searchlight Pictures, 2004.

"International Furusato Parcels." 2005. 29 May 2005 *<https://www.postal-
jp.com/kaigai/index-e.html>*.

Internet Movie Database. 2005. Internet Movie Database Inc. 1 August 2005
<http://imdb.com/>.

Johnston, Sheila. "A Day in the Life." *Sight and Sound,* February 2003, 24-27.

Jonze, Spike, dir. *Adaptation*. Perf. Nicholas Cage, Meryl Streep, Chris Cooper.
(Columbia Tri-Star, 2003).

"Juurokuya Renka: Kami Furusato." *Game Spy PS2*. 29 May 2005
<http://ps2.gamespy.com/playstation-2/juurokuya-renka-kami-furusato/>.

Kalb, Jonathan (1989) *Beckett in Performance*. Cambridge: Cambridge
University Press.

Kaplan, E. A. "Melodrama/Subjectivity/Ideology: Western Melodrama Theories
and Their Relevance to Recent Chinese Cinema." *Melodrama and Asian
Cinema*. Ed. Wimal Dissanayake. Cambridge: Cambridge UP, 1993. 9-28.

Karlyn, Kathleen Rowe. "'Too Close For Comfort': *American Beauty* and the
Incest Motif." *Cinema Journal* 44, No. 1, Fall 2004.

Kaufman, Charlie and Donald Kaufman. *Adaptation: The Shooting Script*. New
York: Newmarket Press, 2002.

Keeling, Bret. "Continuing Woolf: Postmodern Homages to *Mrs. Dalloway*." In *Illuminations: New Readings of Virginia Woolf*. Ed. Carol Merli. New Delhi: Macmillan India Ltd., 2004, 143-56.

Kincaid, James R. *Erotic Innocence: The Culture of Child Molesting*. London: Duke University Press (1998).

Kohl, Norbert. *Oscar Wilde: The Works of a Conformist Rebel*. Trans. David Henry Wilson (Cambridge: Cambridge University Press, 1989).

Kroger, W. S., and S. C. Freed. "Psychosomatic Aspects of Sterility." *American Journal of Obstetrics and Gynecology* 59.4 (1950): 867-74.

Larue, Johanne. "Dossier Robert Lepage: Lepage /Hitchcock. Leçons d'histoire(s)." *Séquences*, no. 180 (September-October 1995): 28-31.

Lee, Hermione. *Virginia Woolf's Nose: Essays on Biography*. Princeton: Princeton NJ, 2005.

Lefebvre, Martin. "A Sense of Time and Place : the Chronotope in *I Confess* and *Le Confessionnal*." *Québec Studies*, no. 26 (1998-1999):88-98.

Leff, Leonard J. "Play into Film: Warner Brothers' 'Who's Afraid of Virginia Woolf?'" *Theatre Journal* 33 (1981): 453-66.

Leff, Leonard J., and Jerold Simmons. *The Dame in the Kimono: Hollywood, Censorship, and the Production Code from the 1920s to the 1960s*. New York: Grove Weidenfeld, 1990.

Lerner, Max. *America as a Civilization: Life and Thought in the United States Today*. New York: Simon and Schuster, 1957.

Levenbeck, Karen L. "The Hours" (Book Review). *Woolf Studies Annual* 6 (2000),198-206.

Lister, David and Paul Waugh. "A Fitting Testament to Oscar Wilde: A Monumental Row Over Gay Politics." *The Independent* 1 December 1998, 1.

Liu, Zhifu, ed. *Huo Jianqi dianying* Nuan (Collected articles on Huo Jianqi's film *Nuan*). Beijing: Zhongguo Mangwen Chubanshe, 2003.

Loiselle, André. *Stage-Bound: Feature Film Adaptations of Canadian and Québécois Drama*. Montreal: McGill University Press, 2003.

Lolita. Dir. Stanley Kubrick. Perf. James Mason, Peter Sellers, Shelly Winters, and Sue Lyon. Warner Brothers (1961).

Lolita. Dir. Adrian Lyne. Perf. Jeremy Irons, Melanie Griffith, Frank Langella, and Dominique Swain. Pathe (1997).

McElvoy, Anne. "Cash for Access Row: So Who Are Tony's Cronies?" *The Independent* 9 July 1998, 3.

——. "Draper Syndrome: Overpaid, Underage, in Power." *The Independent* 11 July 1998, 9.

——. "Is Lord Neill's New Broom Sweeping Too Close for Comfort?" *The Independent* 12 October 1998, 3.

——."Will Swagger and Testosterone Spin Labour Out of Control?" *The*

Independent 6 July 1998, 3.

Macnab, Geoffrey. "Wildes Apart." *The Observer* 12 July 1998, 9.

Madsen, Axel. "Who's Afraid of Alfred Hitchcock? An Interview of Sorts with Ernest Lehman." *Sight and Sound* 37.1 (1967/1968): 26-7.

Maltby, Richard. " 'To Prevent the Prevalent Type of Book': Censorship and Adaptation in Hollywood, 1924-1934." *Film Adaptation*. Ed. James Naremore. New Jersey: Rutgers University Press, 2000.

Manning, Erin. "The Haunted Home : Colour Spectrums in Robert Lepage's *Le Confessionnal*." *Canadian Journal of Film Studies* 7, no. 2 (Fall 1998): 49-65.

Marr, Andrew. "The Lying Game." *The Observer*, 24 October 1999, 30.

Marineau, Jean-Claude. "Hitchcock's Quebec Shoot." *Cinema Canada*, no. 116 (March 1985): 18-19.

Marshall, Bill. *Québec National Cinema*. Montreal: McGill-Queen's University Press, 2001.

May, Elaine Tyler. *Homeward Bound: American Families in the Cold War Era*. New York: Basic, 1988.

Mendenhall, Marie. "Through the Lens of Robert Lepage : Special Effects in Theater and Film." *Philological Papers* 47 (2001): 96-102.

Mo, Yan. "Baigou qiuqian jia" (*The white dog and the swing*). *Worlds of Modern Chinese Fiction*. Trans. and ed. Michael S. Duke. New York: M. E. Sharpe, 1991. 45-62.

—— and Ding Yilan. "Xiaoshuo shi wo erzi, dianying shi wo sunzi" (The short story is my son, the film is my grandson). Liu 81-83.

Morice, P., et al. "History of Infertility." *Human Reproduction* 1.5 (1995): 497-504.

Moyes, Jojo. "Britain Goes Wild for Wilde as New Film Makes a Winner Out of Oscar." *The Independent* 22 March 1997, sec. News: 11.

Mulvey, Laura. "Visual Pleasure and Narrative Cinema". *Film Theory and Criticism*. New York: Oxford University Press, 1992.

Murray, Rebecca and Fred Topel. "Writer Susan Orlean and Producer Edward Saxon Talk About 'Adaptation' and 'The Orchid Thief'". *http://romanticmovies.about.com/library/weekly/aaadaptationintc.htm*; (2002) accessed November 2004.

Muse, Zain. "Revolutionary Brilliance: The Afrofemcentric Aesthetic," *Arms Akimbo: Africana Women in Contemporary Literature*. Ed. Janice Lee Liddell and Yakini Belinda Kemp. UP Florida, 1999.

Nabokov, Vladimir. The Annotated Lolita. Ann. Alfred Appel, Jr. New York: Vintage Books,1991.

"*Nuan* mingnian yiyue quanxian zhaoyao riben" (Nuan will shine in Japan's nationwide theaters next January). *New Beijing Newspaper* (Xin jing bao) 3 November 2004: C54.

Olsen, Lance. *Lolita: A Janus Text*. New York: Twayne Publishers, 1995.

One Hour Photo. Dir. Mark Romanek. Fox Searchlight Pictures, 2002.

Oppenhein, Lois (2003) *The Painted Word: Samuel Beckett's Dialogue with Art*. Ann Arbor, MI: The University of Michigan Press.

Orlean, Susan. *The Orchid Thief*. New York: Ballantine Books, 2000.

———. *The Orchid Thief*. New York: Random House, 1998.

"Oscar Bait." *The Guardian* 16 April 1999, sec. 2: 9.

Perkins, V.F. "I Confess : Photographs of People Speaking." *Cineaction*, no. 52 (June 2000): 28-39.

Pickowicz, Paul G. "Melodramatic Representation and the 'May Fourth' Tradition of Chinese Cinema." *From May Fourth to June Fourth: Fiction and Film inTwentieth-Century China*. Ed. Ellen Widmer and David Der-wei Wang. Cambridge, Mass: Harvard UP, 1993. 295-326.

Pidduck, Julianne. *Contemporary Costume Film: Space, Place and the Past*. London: BFI Publishing, 2004.

Pohlman, E. "Childlessness, Intentional and Unintentional." *The Journal of Nervous and Mental Disease* 151.1 (1970): 2-12.

Pool, Daniel. *What Jane Austen Ate and Charles Dickens Knew* (New York: Touchstone, 1993).

Powell, Kerry Powell. *Oscar Wilde and the Theatre of the 1890s* (Cambridge: Cambridge University Press 1990).

Prendreigh, Brian. "And the world went Wilde." *The Guardian* 2 April 1999, sec. 2:10.

Pretty Baby. Dir. Louis Malle. Perf. Brooke Shields. Paramount, 1978.

The Professional. Dir. Luc Bresson. Columbia Pictures, 1994.

Psycho, DVD, directed by Alfred Hitchcock. (1960; Universal Home Entertainment, 2003).

Psycho, DVD, directed by Gus Van Sant. (1998; Universal Studios 1999).

Pudovkin, Vsevolod (1949) *Film Technique and Film Acting*. Trans. Ivor Montagu. New York: Lear Publishers.

Raby, Peter. "Wilde's Comedies of Society." In Raby (ed.), *The Cambridge Companion to Oscar Wilde* (Cambridge: Cambridge University Press, 1997), 143-160.

Reid, Panthea. *Art and Affection: A Life of Virginia Woolf*. New York: Oxford UP, 1996.

Richie, Donald. "*Spirited Away*." *International Herald Tribune* 10 August 2001: 8.

Robbe-Grillet, Alain (1965) *For a New Novel.* Trans. Richard Howard. New York: Grove Press.

Robertson, Jennifer. "It Takes a Village: Internationalization and Nostalgia in Postwar Japan." *Mirror of Modernity: Invented Traditions of Modern Japan.* Ed. Stephen Vlastos. Berkeley: U of California P, 1998. 110-29.

http://www.rottentomatoes.com/m/1084964-psycho/. (Accessed July 31, 2004).

Rosen, Marjorie. *Popcorn Venus: Women, Movies, and the American Dream.* New York: Coward, McCann & Geoghegan, 1973.

Rothman, William. *The Murderous Gaze.* Cambridge and Mass.:Harvard University Press. 1982.

Roudané, Matthew C. *Who's Afraid of Virginia Woolf? Necessary Fictions, Terrifying Realities.* Twayne's Masterwork Studies; No. 34. Boston: Twayne Publishers, 1990.

Rubenstein, Roberta. "To the Litehouse." *The Washington Post* 26 January, 2003. B3.

Russell, Catherine. "Insides and outsides: Cross-cultural criticism and Japanese film melodrama." *Melodrama and Asian Cinema.* Ed. Wimal Dissanayake. Cambridge: Cambridge UP, 1993. 143-54.

Santas, Constantine. "The Remake if *Psycho* (Gus Van Sant, 1998): Creativity or Cinematic Blasphemy?" *Senses of Cinema* 10 (2000): http://sensesofcinema.com/contents/00/10/psycho.html. (Accessed July 14, 2004).

Schaefer, Sarah. "Homosexual Reform: Lords Reject Lower Age of Gay Consent." *The Independent* 14 April 1999, 10.

Schatz, Thomas (1981) *Hollywood Genres: Formulas, Filmmaking and the Studio System.* New York: Random House.

Schneider, Stephen Jay. "A Tale of Two Psychos (Prelude to a Future Reassessment)." *Senses of Cinema* 10 (2000). 14 July 2004: http://www.sensesofcinema.com/contents/00/10/psychos.html.

Seligman, Daniel, and Lawrence A. Mayer. "The Future Population 'Mix'." *America in the Sixties: The Economy and the Society.* Ed. Editors of *Fortune.* New York: Harper, 1960. 1-22.

Shen, Jian. "Huo Jianqi he ta de *Nuan*" (Huo Jianqi and his *Nuan*). *Zhongguo dianying bao* (Chinese film newspaper) 45 (2003): 2.

Sheppard, Richard (2000) *Modernism-Dada-Postmodernism.* Evanston, Ill.: Northwestern University Press.

Siegel, Sandra F.. "Oscar Wilde: The Spectacle of Criticism." *Arts & Sciences Newsletter,*   17:2   (1996),   online, *http://www.arts.cornell.edu/newsletr/spring96/spring96.htm.*

Sinyard, Neil. *Filming Literature. The Art of Screen Adaptation.* London and Sydney: Croom Helm, 1986.

Sklar, Robert. *Movie-Made America: A Cultural History of American Movies.* New York: Vintage, 1994.

Sontag, Susan (1979) Film and Theatre, in Gerald Mast and Marshall Cohen (eds.), *Film Theory and Criticism..* New York: Oxford University Press, pp. 359-37.

Spengler, Birgit. "Michael Cunningham Rewriting Virginia Woolf: Pragmatist vs. Modernist Aesthetics."

Spivak, Gayatri. "Can the Subaltern Speak?," *Marxism and the Interpretation of Culture.* Ed. Cary Nelson and Larry Grossberg. Chicago: U of Illinois P, 1988.

Stam, Robert. "Beyond Fidelity : The Dialogics of Adaptation." In *Film Adaptation*, edited by James Naremore, 54-76. New Brunswick and New Jersey: Rutgers University Press, 2000.

Stam, Robert. *Literature Through Film: Realism, Magic and the Art of Adaptation.* Malden, MA, and Oxford: Blackwell Publishing, 2005.

———. *Reflexivity in Film and Literature : from Don Quixote to Jean-Luc Godard.* Ann Arbor, Mich.: UMI Research Press, 1985.

———. and Alessandra Raengo. *Literature and Film: A Guide to the Theory and Practice of Film Adaptation.* Malden, MA, and Oxford: Blackwell Publishing, 2005.

Stringer, Robin. "Film Rivals Go Wilde To Be First With an Ideal Husband." *The Evening Standard* 26 May 1998, 15.

Stroup, Atlee L. *Marriage and Family: A Developmental Approach.* New York: Appleton-Century-Crofts, 1966.

"Sun Changes Mind Over Gays". BBC News Online 12 November 1998. 2 August 2005 <*http://news.bbc.co.uk/1/hi/uk/212737.stm*>.

Sweeney (eds.), *Detecting Texts: The Metaphysical Detective Story from Poe to Postmodernism.* Philadelphia: University of Pennsylvania Press, pp. 218-230.

Sweeney, John. "How the New Labour Mafia Took Revenge on Martin Bell; Mob Smears Mr. Clean." *The Observer* 25 January 1998, 22.

Sweet, Matthew. "Resisting Everything Except Temptation". *The Independent* 27 July 1998, 21.

Telmissany, May. "La citation filmique comme anachronisme. " *Essays on Canadian Writing*, no. 76 (Spring 2002): 247-262.

"Tell us the truth Tony: Are we being run by a gay mafia?", Editorial. *The Sun* 9 November 1998, 1.

Thomas, Sue. "Virginia Woolf's Septimus Smith and Contemporary Perceptions of Shell Shock." *English Language Notes* 25.2 (1987): 49-57.

Thompson, Tommy. "Liz in a Film Shocker: Her Movie Shatters the Rules of Censorship." *Life* 10 June 1966: 87-91.

Tomas, Deborah. "Confession as Betrayal : Hitchcock's I Confess as Enigmatic Text." *CineAction*, no. 40 (May 1996): 32-37.

Truffault, Francois. *Hitchcock*. New York: Simon and Schuster, 1967.

Veevers, Jean E. *Childless by Choice*. Toronto: Butterworths, 1980.

Walker, Alexander Walker. "Wilde Would be Mad About These Boys ..." *The Evening Standard* 12 April 1999, 20.

Wang, Xuemei. "*Nuan* rang Huo Jianqi liang le xin" (The film *Nuan* makes Huo Jianqi's heart cold). *Jinling wanbao* (Jinling evening post) 18 April 2004. 24 June 2005. <*http://www.njnews.cn/i/ca448746.htm*>.

Wang, Yin. "Leishui dadong dongjing jie" (Tears won over the Tokyo Film Festival). *Nanfang zhoumo* (South weekend) 13 November 2003: C22.

——. "Xiangchuan Zhaozhi: ganxie zhongguo dianying" (Teruyuki Kagawa: Thanks for Chinese films). *Nanfang zhoumo* (South weekend) 13 November 2003: C22.

——. "Zhuan riben ren de yanlei qu" (To gain tears shed by the Japanese). *Nanfang zhoumo* (South weekend) 6 November 2003: C22.

Waugh, Paul. "Gay Sex Bill Will Survive Lords." *The Independent* 13 April 1999, 6.

Westoff, Charles F., et al. *Family Growth in Metropolitan America*. Princeton, NJ: Princeton UP, 1961.

Wheatcroft, Geoffrey. "What Decency? What Fair Play?" *The Independent* 24 January 1999, 25.

Whelpton, Pascal Kidder, et al. *Fertility and Family Planning in the United States*. Princeton, NJ: Princeton UP, 1966.

Whitaker, Raymond. "Flat earth." *The Independent* 15 November 1998, 21

White, Michael. "Labour's Big Guns Avoid Major Error." *The Guardian* 12 January 1999, 9.

——. "Blair Warns 'We must be pure'." *The Guardian* 8 July 1998 1.

Williams, Linda. "Melodrama Revised." *Refiguring American Film Genres: History and Theory*. Ed. Nick Browne. Berkeley: U of California P, 1998. 42-88.

Wintour, Patrick and Andy McSmith. "Blair Plans 'Harsh' Relaunch." *The Observer* 10 January 1999, 2.

Wollen, Peter. *Signs and Meanings in the Cinema*. Bloomington: Indiana University Press, 1972.

Wollen, Tana. "Over our shoulders: nostalgic screen fictions for the 1980s," *Enterprise and Heritage. Crosscurrents of National Culture*. Ed. John Corner and Sylvia Harvey. London & New York: Routledge, 1991.

Wolmar, Christian. "The Sleaze Report: The End of a Grubby Affair." *The Independent* 4 July 1997, 1.

Woolf, Maria. "Government Putting Trade Ahead of Human Rights." *The*

Independent 20 December 1998, 4.

Woolf, Virginia. *The Diary of Virginia Woolf.* Ed. Anne Olivier Bell and Andrew McNeilllie. 5 vols. New York: Harcourt Brace, 1977-84. Cited in the text as *D* 1-5+page number.

——. *"The Hours": The British Museum Manuscript of* Mrs. Dalloway. Transcribed and Ed. Helen M. Wussow. New York: Pace UP 1996.

——. *The Letters of Virginia Woolf.* Ed. Nigel Nicolson and Joanne Trautmann. 6 vols. New York: Harcourt Brace, 1975-80. Cited in the text as *L* 1-6+page number.

——. *Moments of Being.* Ed. Jeanne Schulkind. New York: Harcourt Brace, 1976; 2nd Ed. 1985. Cited in the text as *MOB*.

——. *Mrs. Dalloway.* 1925; rpt. New York: Harcourt Brace, 1990. Abbreviated *MD*.

——. "The Prime Minister." In Jacob's Room Holograph Notebook, Part III. New York: Henry W. and Albert A. Berg Collection, The New York Public Library, Astor, Lenox and Tilden Foundations. 132-51, 155-67.

——. "A Sketch of the Past." In *Moments of Being*, ed. Schulkind.

Xiao, Hong. *Shengsi Chang* (Field of life and death). Trans. Howard Goldblatt and Ellen Yeung. Bloomington: Indiana UP, 1979.

Yardley, Jim. "Farmers Being Moved Aside by China's Real Estate Boom." *New York Times* 8 December 2004: A1.

Young, Tory. *Michael Cunningham's* The Hours: *A Reader's Guide.* New York: Continuum, 2003.

Zhang, Yingjin. "Zhongguo dalu dianying guancha" (Observations made on Mainland Chinese films). *2000 Taiwan dianyingwenhua ditu* (2000 Mapping Taiwan films in 2000). Taipei: Yuanliu Chubanshe, 2001. 253-62.

——. and Zhiwei Xiao. *Encyclopedia of Chinese Film.* London: Routeledge, 1998.

Zhong, Xueping. *Masculinity Besieged? : Issues of Modernity and Male Subjectivity in Chinese Literature of the Late Twentieth Century.* Durham: Duke UP, 2000.

Zizek, Slavoj. *Everything You Always Wanted to Know About Lacan ... But Were Afraid To Ask Hitchcock.* New York: Verso, 1992.

LADIES AND GENTLEMEN, THE STARS OF THE SHOW: OUR LIST OF CONTRIBUTORS

Sylvie Bissonnette is a graduate student in Film Studies at the Université de Montréal, writing a Master's thesis on the film adaptations made by Robert Lepage of his own plays. She is also a member of the Groupe de recherche sur l'avènement et la formation des institutions cinématographique et scénique (GRAFICS), a research group dedicated to silent cinema. Sylvie contributes to the film periodical "Nouvelles «vues» sur le cinéma québécois". She discovered the wonderful world of adaptation through the television series "Les rois maudits" (Claude Barma, 1972). After having watched over and over again this series, until she knew all the historical details about this incredible medieval saga, she avidly read nonstop the seven books written by Maurice Druon.

Ann-Marie Cook teaches film and English literature at University of the Pacific in California. As an avid Anglo-phile, she regularly indulges her passion for British literary adaptations and braves the often inhospitable English weather to carry out her research on this sumptuous body of films. Ann-Marie's other publications include chapters on the silent film star Florence Turner, the adaptation of Alan Moore's graphic novel From Hell, and the critique of Christian rhetoric in Rolf de Heer's Australian cult classic, Bad Boy Bubby. She is currently working on a book that examines how British heritage films of the late 1990s and 2000s engage critically with the policies and ideologies promoted by New Labour.

Kellie Dawson is currently teaching American Literature at the University of Southern California and Popular Culture at California State University, Northridge. In addition to the essay that appears here, Kellie's thoughts on the subject of *Lolita* can be read in *Nabokov Studies* and *American Sexuality*. As if that weren't enough, she's also working on a book exploring the various ways *Lolita* has affected American culture. She has been known to sometimes read a book or view a film without a pencil and notebook in hand.Suzette Henke

Shannon Donaldson-McHugh is a PhD candidate at McMaster University in English and Cultural Studies. She has published articles on topics varying from Middle English literature to theories of film adaptation. [Her dissertation Genre Trouble?: Jeanette Winterson's Sexual/Textual Politics of the Performative? investigates how contemporary subversions of generic codes function as performative speech acts that further problematize hegemonic definitions of gender, sexuality, subjectivity, and conventional narrative form.] A version of this chapter appears in the April 2006 issue of the 'Journal of Popular Culture.' Incidentally, she always showers with the curtain pulled back.

Suzette Henke joined the University of Louisville in 1991 as Thruston B. Morton, Sr. Professor of Literary Studies. She is author of Joyce's Moraculous Sindbook: A Study of "Ulysses" and James Joyce and the Politics of Desire (Routledge, 1990). Professor Henke has published widely in the field of modern literature, with particular attention to such figures as Virginia Woolf, Dorothy Richardson, Doris Lessing, Anais Nin, and Samuel Beckett. More recent work has included contemporary writers like Dorothy Allison, Maya Angelou, Maxine Hong Kingston, Audre Lorde and Alice Walker, as well as postcolonial authors such as Sally Morgan, Keri Hulme, and Janet Frame (after a Fulbright year in Australia). In the field of film studies, Suzette has published essays on Jane Campion's biopic of Frame's autobiography, Angel At My Table, and on James Joyce and film. Her book Shattered Subjects: Trauma And Testimony in Women's Life-Writing was brought out by Palgrave/St. Martin's Press in 2000.

Erin Hill-Parks is an independent scholar and editor who received her graduate degree from Georgetown University in Communication, Culture & Technology with a focus in film theory. She has worked in almost all aspects of film–from serving popcorn at a movie theater to working at a film production company in London. She has written for nation publications such as *The Journal of Film and History* and presented at several national and international conferences on issues of identity and memory, the cultural impact of modern war films, and the tension between humanity and technology in science fiction films.

Rebecca Housel is a professor of writing and literature at Rochester Institute of Technology. Her love of film and the hero has developed over a lifetime of reading comics, watching bad (and sometimes good) movies, playing video games, and being a perpetual supporter of all things popular culture. In her next life, Rebecca plans on taking Hollywood by storm as the first handicapped, sex-kitten actress/comedian/screen-writer/director under the name, *Raven Red.* Rebecca has published chapters in the *Popular Culture and Philosophy Series* on poker (2006), Monty Python (2006), and X-Men (2005). She also writes book reviews and articles for the *Journal of Popular Culture, Journal of American Culture,* and national publications like *Redbook.* Rebecca's first love is narrative and published a series of middle-grade novels, the *High Seas Series* (2001) and has also recently published creative non-fiction with *Quiet Mountain Essays* (2005) and *Brevity* (2006). Rebecca completed a forthcoming illness narrative anthology for the University of New South Wales (2008). She hopes Hollywood begins to take notice ... soon.

Don Moore is a PhD candidate at McMaster University in the department of English and Cultural Studies where he specializes in Critical and Cultural Theory. He has published articles on Critical Theory, Canadian adaptations of Shakespeare, ethics, politics, 9/11, and globalization, in such journals as *Politics and Culture,* the *Journal of Popular Culture,* and the celebrated, PREA award-winning *Canadian Shakespeares* website. Don's thesis interrogates the Bush administration's post-9/11 ethical rhetoric as a dubious remodeling of Humanity and human rights, and as a symptom of late-globalization, or what Antonio Negri and Michael Hardt have dubbed "Empire." Don's interest in film adaptation stems from his earlier graduate work on deconstructive approaches to adaptations of Shakespeare, but his love for movies—both the originals and the remakes—began much earlier when, as a young boy, he and his dad spent some glorious hours together at the movie theatre watching classics like *Clash of the Titans* and Roger Moore as *007.*

Alina Patriche graduated in 1990 from the University of Bucharest with a B.A. in Comparative Literature. She completed her M.A. in British literature from University of Illinois at Urbana-Champaign 1998 and graduated with a PhD in film studies from the same university in 2003. Since 1997, Patriche has taught Composition, Literature and Film in the English department of the University of Illinois and Media Literacy in the Communication department at Carthage College. Her main research interests include identity construction and film genre, heritage films, contemporary British cinema and visual literacy.

Jody W. Pennington is Associate Professor in Media and Culture Studies at the Department of English, University of Aarhus, Denmark, where he teaches Media and Cultural Studies as well as American Studies. Educated at Georgia Southwestern College and the University of Aarhus, he has published articles and presented papers on various aspects of film and popular music, as well as American constitutional law. He is currently writing a history of sex in American film Praeger.

Cecilia Sayad is completing her PhD dissertation in the department of Cinema Studies at New York University, where she also teaches as an adjunct. In Brazil, she worked as a film journalist and critic for daily newspaper *Folha de S. Paulo* and published articles in *Jornal do Brasil* and *Tropico.* At the turn of the century, she decided to leave the masses of newspaper readers for the Ivory Tower of Academia, and moved to the U.S. to get a Masters and work towards a doctorate. After watching Spike Jonze's *Adaptation* eight times in the theaters, she decided to write an essay so as to redeem a guilty pleasure through academic productivity. Her interests include film authorship, national cinemas (she taught Latin American cinema at Vassar), and narrative theory. She is currently working on a book on Charlie Kaufman to be published in Brazil.

Lars Söderlund is a graduate student and instructor at the University of South Carolina. He believes that the current wave of feature films by music video directors (Michel Gondry, Spike Jonze, David Fincher, McG) is a worthwhile topic of study, and he hopes to continue investigating this trend. He also wishes to eventually meet Charles Kaufman and, to fly.

E. K. Tan is a PhD Candidate in the Program of Comparative and World Literature at the University of Illinois at Urbana-Champaign. His areas of interest include Diaspora Studies, Postcolonial Studies, Psychoanalysis, and Film Theory. He is presently working on his dissertation project on the works of Southeast Asian Chinese diaspora writers and filmmakers. Since college, he has spent most of his leisure time going to movies and theater performances. Film adaptations fascinate him because they provide him with different ways to understand the textual significance of the adapted works and the autonomous lives of the adaptations.

Karen R. Tolchin is assistant professor of English at Florida Gulf Coast University in Fort Myers, Florida, where she teaches courses on writing, literature, and film, and tries to come to terms with her mediocre ability as a tennis player. She is a newly minted member of the Executive Board of the Southern Humanities Council. Her writings include the history of American literature for *The New York Times Guide to Essential Knowledge: A Desk Reference for the Curious Mind* (St. Martin's 2004). Previous forays into film scholarship include an essay on Karyn Kusama's *Girlfight* (University of Texas Press 2006). Her 2006 presentation at the PCA/ACA bore the title "Special Literary Effects: Tracing their Proliferation in Film Adaptations from *The Year of Living Dangerously* (1982) to *In the Bedroom* (2001)." Professor Tolchin is currently at work on a collective of creative non-fiction essays titled *Escape of the Edible Woman, and Other Essays on Lust, Longing, and Literature.*

Temenuga Trifonova teaches film and screenwriting at the University of New Brunswick, Canada. Day in and day out she aspires to fidelity and adaptability but increasingly finds that such aspirations reduce her to being jejune and unfaithful to herself, something she finds difficult to adapt to. Her recent and forthcoming publications examine contemporary European cinema, science fiction film and philosophy, yakuza films, realism and film theory. She is currently completing two manuscripts: The Image in French Philosophy; Realism and Theatricality in Cinema.

Hui Xiao is a Ph.D. candidate in the Department of East Asian Languages and Cultures at the University of Illinois, Urbana-Champaign. Her special areas of interest are modern Chinese literature, film studies and popular culture. Her obsessions with both literature and films have lead to the production of several papers and dissertation chapters on film adaptation. She has published articles in *Orientations: Transcultural Perspectives on Asia*, *Concentric: Literary and Cultural Studies* , *Asian Cinema*, *China Society Periodical*(Zhongguo shehui daokan), *Frontiers* (Tianya*)*, *Globalization and Chineseness: Postcolonial Readings of Contemporary Culture* (Hong Kong University Press, 2006, forthcoming), the proceedings of the Biennial Conference of the Association of Chinese and Comparative Literature, forthcoming, and the proceedings of the Fourth International Conference on Chinese Language Pedagogy, 2004.

INDEX